THE FEMALE AVENGER, WOMEN'S ANGER AND RAPE-REVENGE FILM AND TELEVISION

THE FEMALE AVENGER, WOMEN'S ANGER AND RAPE-REVENGE FILM AND TELEVISION

Margrethe Bruun Vaage

EDINBURGH
University Press

Edinburgh University Press is one of the leading university presses in the UK. We publish academic books and journals in our selected subject areas across the humanities and social sciences, combining cutting-edge scholarship with high editorial and production values to produce academic works of lasting importance. For more information visit our website: edinburghuniversitypress.com

© Margrethe Bruun Vaage, 2024, 2025

Grateful acknowledgement is made to the sources listed in the List of Illustrations for permission to reproduce material previously published elsewhere. Every effort has been made to trace the copyright holders, but if any have been inadvertently overlooked, the publisher will be pleased to make the necessary arrangements at the first opportunity.

Edinburgh University Press Ltd
13 Infirmary Street
Edinburgh EH1 1LT

First published in hardback by Edinburgh University Press 2024

Typeset in 10/12.5 pt Sabon by
Cheshire Typesetting Ltd, Cuddington, Cheshire

A CIP record for this book is available from the British Library

ISBN 978 1 3995 3209 9 (hardback)
ISBN 978 1 3995 3210 5 (paperback)
ISBN 978 1 3995 3211 2 (webready PDF)
ISBN 978 1 3995 3212 9 (epub)

The right of Margrethe Bruun Vaage to be identified as the author of this work has been asserted in accordance with the Copyright, Designs and Patents Act 1988, and the Copyright and Related Rights Regulations 2003 (SI No. 2498).

CONTENTS

List of Figures	vii
Acknowledgements	ix
Introduction: The Controversy of the Rape-Revenge Film	1
1. The Affective Structure of the Rape-Revenge Film	15
The rape-revenge film in feminist film theory: what about the female spectator?	15
Turning to cognitive film theory	23
Going full on *Girl with the Dragon Tattoo* in *Orange Is the New Black*	25
Outlining the affective structure of the rape-revenge film	28
2. On Punishment, Fiction and Femininity	33
Punishment in fiction	34
Blending realism and the fantastic: Lisbeth Salander of the Millennium trilogy	36
Lisbeth Salander as a fictional relief	41
The transformation of the rape-avenger	44
The transformation as fantasy space and inversion of conventional femininity	46

3. On Revenge: Rape-Revenge Storylines and the Evolutionary Origin
    of Payback   59
   An introduction to revenge   60
   Revenge in the rape-revenge film   65
   Honour and revenge   70
   A function for revenge fantasies   78

4. On Anger: A Philosophical Exploration of Women's Anger and its
    Functions   80
   Feminists on women's anger   81
   The functions of anger   84
   Anger eliminativists: on sadness and unconditional forgiveness as
      alternative responses   89
   Unconditional forgiveness in *Twilight Portrait* and *Women Talking*   95
   Rape-revenge film as a place of rage   101

5. Race and the Rape-Revenge Film   105
   The Black rape-avenger   106
   Silencing the Black woman's experience of rape   113
   The Nightingale as post-colonial rape-revenge film   117
   Critique of conventions: *I May Destroy You*   122

6. Containing the Threat of the Female Avenger On-Screen   128
   Gender trouble: *Blue Steel*   129
   The action heroine explained and contained   135
   Explanatory devices and containment strategies in the rape-revenge
      film: *Promising Young Woman*   139

7. Emotions in Contemporary Film Theory and Rape-Revenge Film
    as Exploitative   149
   The didactic argument against revenge stories   150
   The realist argument against rape-revenge film   155
   The exploitation argument against explicit portrayal of rape   157
   The ethics of making us watch   162
   The explicit rape sequence and argumentative context: *Irreversible*
      and *Holiday*   171

Conclusion: The Rape-Revenge Convention in Complex Contexts   182

Bibliography   189
Index   200

FIGURES

1.1	'This is my gift to you to help you work through that rage and anger', says Boo to Pennsatucky (*Orange Is the New Black*, 2015).	27
2.1	'He was a pig who hated women', says Lisbeth the avenger (*The Girl with the Dragon Tattoo*, 2009)	38
2.2	Jen before the transformation into an avenger (*Revenge*, 2017).	48
2.3	Jen after the transformation into an avenger (*Revenge*, 2017).	48
2.4	Thana before her transformation (*Ms. 45*, 1981).	52
2.5	Thana after her transformation (*Ms. 45*, 1981).	52
3.1	Thelma and Louise in the desert landscape of the Western (*Thelma and Louise*, 1991).	67
4.1	Marina forgives the rapist Andrei unconditionally and shows him love (*Twilight Portrait*, 2011).	96
4.2	Greta apologises to her daughter Mariche for asking her repeatedly to forgive her violent and abusive husband (*Women Talking*, 2022).	100
5.1	Foxy Brown makes her escape from the farm (*Foxy Brown*, 1974).	117
5.2	Lowanna is a minor character who is raped, and quickly killed (*The Nightingale*, 2018).	121
5.3	Arabella's imagined revenge on the man who raped her (*I May Destroy You*, 2020).	125

6.1	Megan takes aim to shoot and kill her rapist and tormentor confidently and unhesitatingly (*Blue Steel*, 1990).	135
6.2	Cassie watching a recording of the rape of her best friend (*Promising Young Woman*, 2020).	147
7.1	Luke finds Noelle's accusation of rape ludicrous (*M.F.A.*, 2017).	167
7.2	Alex is terrified when a stranger turns his anger towards her in an underpass (*Irreversible*, 2002).	175
7.3	Michael carefully removes his wristwatch before raping his girlfriend Sascha (*Holiday*, 2018).	178
8.1	Jackie is drawn to Clyde but also disgusted by him (*Red Road*, 2006).	186

ACKNOWLEDGEMENTS

I want to thank Tamar Jeffers McDonald and Dan Flory for reading drafts of Chapter 2 and 3, respectively, and the participants at various conferences and workshops where I presented material from this project. This includes the annual conferences of the Society for the Cognitive Study of the Moving Images (SCSMI), which was online in 2020 and in Valencia in Spain in 2022. I also presented this project at a research seminar at the Centre for the Study of Conflict, Emotion and Social Justice in Bournemouth in 2023, and want to thank Catalin Brylla for inviting me. Thank you to the organisers of the Cognitive Futures in the Arts and Humanities for inviting me to give a keynote on the topic in 2018, and to Brett Mills for inviting me to give a research seminar talk at the University of East Anglia the same year. The comments, questions and suggestions on all occasions have been most appreciated.

Many colleagues in various countries have been supportive of the work, such as Cynthia Freeland, whose encouragement was important to me, as has been Rikke Schubart's enthusiasm for the project. Both Cynthia and Rikke are of course central to the SCSMI, and I want to thank this entire, vibrant community of cognitive scholars for their continued support, and to Todd Berliner for offering several good suggestions.

I want to express my heartfelt gratitude to colleagues at the University of Kent, and to various student cohorts over the years, first in the module entitled 'Transgressive Women', and then in the module 'Film, Politics and Identity', both of which I have convened for several years, and also the students present in various guest appearances I have made on other modules, such as 'Psychology of the Arts' and 'Film Studies: Innovation and Writing'. Frances Kamm taught with me on 'Transgressive Women', and I thank her for our many discussions. I have explored many of the questions I pose in this book with students first, and I have found the students amazingly brave and dedicated in exploring these thorny topics, which has surely demanded a lot of them. I have benefited greatly from our discussions, both in terms of theoretical insights, and also in terms of films and television series to look at – more than once students have drawn my attention to a film or series that has become a central case study. I have been very lucky to have such courageous, perceptive and reflective students. It is tempting to list some individual students here, but out of fear of forgetting someone, I will not, and thank all students collectively. Thank you also so much to Michael Clark, who helped me with the figures.

I also want to thank the anonymous reviewers of draft versions of this book manuscript, whose reports were both encouraging and very helpful, with insightful suggestions and observations that I believe enabled me to really improve the manuscript. I greatly appreciate their thoughtful feedback and generosity. And not least of all, I want to thank the three editors I have worked with at Edinburgh University Press; Gillian Leslie, Sam Johnson and Kelly O'Brien, who have been fantastic: you made me feel appreciated and supported. It was heartening to me that the female avenger was instantly welcomed.

Parts of Chapter 2 have previously been published as the first half of the article 'On Punishment and Why We Enjoy It in Fiction: Lisbeth Salander of the Millennium Trilogy and Eli in *Let the Right One In* as Scandinavian Avengers' in the journal *Poetics Today* 40(3), 2019: 543–57. I thank Duke University Press for permission to re-use this material here, and also the guest editor of that issue, Nancy Easterlin, for all her thoughtful feedback.

Finally, I want to thank family, friends and other supporters; the only one of whom I will single out here being my mum, Toril: let us celebrate the strength of women.

INTRODUCTION: THE CONTROVERSY OF THE RAPE-REVENGE FILM

This is a book about a contested figure, namely the female rape survivor turned avenger in rape-revenge film. I examine her contentious nature through the lens of film theory, arguing that it is caused by a little-understood emotion in the film-viewing experience: vindictive anger. At the very core of the controversy around the rape-revenge film stands a woman who is raped and who turns angry and violent: this is a revenge fantasy.

The rape-revenge film is defined by its two-part structure: the rape of the female protagonist, often depicted graphically, is followed by her revenge, typically very violent and portrayed in vivid detail too, as she tracks down her rapists to punish them. Though there are older predecessors, such as Ingmar Bergman's *The Virgin Spring* (1960) where a father takes revenge on his daughter's rapist and murderer, it became popularised as a subtype of exploitation film in the 1970s with a female avenger.[1] One of the most notorious examples is *I Spit on Your Grave* (Meir Zarchi, 1978). Rape-revenge storylines were integrated into mainstream American film culture in the 1980s and 1990s, and are now found in both commercial film and art film in many different national contexts (Clover 1992; Heller-Nicholas 2021; Henry 2014; Read 2000; Schubart 2007). Alexandra Heller-Nicholas points to a recent spike of rape-revenge films including *The Girl with the Dragon Tattoo* (Niels Arden Oplev, 2009), *Kill Bill: Volume 1* (Quentin Tarantino, 2003) and *Kill Bill:*

---

[1] For a survey of early beginnings of a rape-revenge film see Heller-Nicholas (2011: 14ff).

Volume 2 (Quentin Tarantino, 2004), *Irreversible* (Gaspar Noé, 2002) and *Dogville* (Lars von Trier, 2003) as well as television series with rape-revenge features such as *Dexter* (James Manos Jr, 2006–13) and *The Shield* (Shawn Ryan, 2002–8), and argues that 'to suggest that rape-revenge film can be generically, historically or regionally defined ignores the broad range of movies that fall under the rape-revenge heading' (Heller-Nicholas 2011: 155).

Rape-revenge films are sometimes discussed as a subtype of the horror genre, and sometimes as a narrative structure running across various genres. As I discuss both films and television series where rape-revenge storylines are found mixed in with various genres and storytelling modes, I will simply refer to the rape-revenge convention, aligning my discussion closer to Jacinda Read's approach to rape-revenge as a narrative structure in this sense (Read 2000). But I hold, as do Carol Clover and Barbara Creed, that affectively the convention is rooted, at least partly, in horror film (Clover 1992; Creed 1993). I will also explore other relevant genre contexts, such as action film and Western film.

Of particular interest to me are rape-revenge films made recently by women filmmakers, such as *Baise-moi* (Virginie Despentes and Coralie Trin Thi, 2000), *Holiday* (Isabella Eklöf, 2018), *M.F.A* (Natalia Leite, 2017), *Monster* (Patty Jenkins, 2003) *Promising Young Woman* (Emerald Fennell, 2020), *Revenge* (Coralie Fargeat, 2017), *The Nightingale* (Jennifer Kent, 2018), *Stella Does Tricks* (Coky Giedroyc, 1996), *Twilight Portrait* (Angelina Nikonova, 2011) and *Violation* (Dusty Mancinelli and Madeleine Sims-Fewer, 2020), as well as *Orange Is the New Black* (Jenji Kohan, 2013–19) and *I May Destroy You* (Michaela Coel, 2020), television series where rape-revenge storylines are included in complex contexts. It is also interesting to note here how the rare women filmmaker in Hollywood explored the topic, such as in the drama *Outrage* (Ida Lupino, 1950), which explores the trauma of rape for the female protagonist Ann Walter. Another early example is the inclusion of an explicit sequence in which the main character Megan Turner is raped in the thriller *Blue Steel* (Kathryn Bigelow, 1990). Yet another early predecessor of a revenge story made by a woman filmmaker is Chantal Akerman's *Jeanne Dielman, 23 Quai de Commerce, 1080 Bruxelles* (1975).[2] All of these films can be seen as feeding into, and leading up to, the contemporary trend of women making rape-revenge films.

Indeed, although a current cycle of woman-made rape-revenge films is rightly often explored as part of a cultural and political movement of focus on and resistance to male violence against women, Alexandra Heller-Nicholas carefully outlines how women filmmakers have explored rape-revenge storylines long before the #MeToo movement (Heller-Nicholas 2021: 152ff). Her outline includes early films such as *Bad Girls Go to Hell* (Doris Wishman, 1965) and

---

[2] See McHugh (2021) for a discussion.

The Velvet Vampire (Stephanie Rothman, 1971), and a film such as *I Was a Teenage Serial Killer* (Sarah Jacobson, 1992), rarely considered a rape-revenge film but a film that does encompass 'the desire for revenge for male atrocities that include, but are not limited to, rape' (ibid. 157). She also demonstrates how woman-made rape-revenge film is found in many cultural contexts, from the Indian *Bulbbul* (Anvita Dutt, 2020) and the Koran film *An Old Lady* (Lim Seon-ae, 2019), *Marlina the Murderer in Four Acts* (Mouly Surya, 2017) from Indonesia, and the episode *Culture Shock* (Gigi Saul Guerrero, 2019) by a Mexican filmmaker. Her exploration of woman-directed rape-revenge film offers a comprehensive mapping and an important contextualisation of the films that I will concentrate on in this book.

As Creed observes in her recent book, in the new millennium 'more women have turned to the rape-revenge film to explore the relationship between the oppression of women, male violence, and rape culture' (Creed 2022: 51). She discusses *Revenge, The Nightingale* and *Promising Young Woman* as exemplary cases of Feminist New Wave Cinema, and she sees these filmmakers as redefining the rape-revenge genre in what she labels as rape-revolt film. Although my focus is predominantly also on this contemporary context of women filmmaking, I include in my study some much-discussed older rape-revenge films made by men as well, because they are central to the rape-revenge convention. Thus, I also want to explore the continuity in the rape-revenge convention to a greater extent than Creed does, and argue that these Feminist New Wave filmmakers draw out a political potential for critique in this type of film. This latter assumption is shared by several feminist film theorists writing about the rape-revenge film, such as Read and also Claire Henry, who regards the rape-revenge film as

> a *cultural key* that can help to reveal and interrogate the meanings of rape and the political, ethical, and affective responses to it [...]. The contemporary genre provides insight into these issues and a cultural forum for the complexities of rape politics to be worked though. (Henry 2014: 3, emphasis original)

The present study adds to the examination of the affective responses to rape in rape-revenge films, and how this response can be harnessed to work through complex questions about rape.

The rape-revenge story is a persistent feature of film culture. Equally persistent is the controversy triggered by these stories, often deemed misogynistic and harmful by critics. Two good sources mapping the outraged reception of early rape-revenge films are found in David Maguire's analysis of *I Spit on Your Grave* (Maguire 2018) and Heller-Nicholas's discussion of *Ms. 45* (Abel Ferrara, 1981) (Heller-Nicholas 2017). Kathleen McHugh discusses the enraged response to *The Nightingale* as another case in point, serving to illustrate that rape-revenge films continue to be controversial (McHugh 2021: 14ff). As argued by Read, rape-revenge stories can be seen as ongoing negotiations in popular culture of rape, the feminine and feminism (Read 2000). She sees the cycle of rape-revenge film emerging in the 1970s as a historically specific response to second-wave feminism. In line with this reasoning, it may not be a coincidence that there is an increasing number of works with rape-revenge storylines co-occurring with the #MeToo movement, yet at a time where, in the UK for example, the victims' commissioner for England and Wales, Dame Vera Baird, has argued that the low level of rape prosecutions equals a 'decriminalisation of rape' (Baird quoted in Saddique 2020).

Although it is the portrayal of rape in rape-revenge film that is often explicitly claimed as unacceptable by critics, a central argument in this book is that the portrayal of the protagonist's response to rape might just as well explain the controversy of this type of film. The rape survivor turns violent and takes revenge on her rapists, and first and foremost, these are films about anger – and they trigger anger in the spectator as well. Indeed, the potential value of these films is the anger they explore and elicit.[3] The female avenger steps out of conventional femininity, leaving her old self behind and emerging as its dark shadow – this is a revenge fantasy in which the woman who was raped becomes an embodiment of outlaw emotions and behaviours for women, such as rage and violent aggression. The female avenger is pure vindictive anger.

A woman's vindictiveness is controversial, also among feminists: the point has been made that the #MeToo movement was fuelled by a desire for revenge, and that it was problematic for this reason, mirroring in its punitiveness the original abuse in a way that might inadvertently fuel the far-right.[4] Mapping the complexities of this movement and its manifestation in the public sphere is beyond the reach of this project, but inasmuch as there was vengefulness in the #MeToo movement, at least for some women, Read's point about film as popular culture working through this feminist dilemma is clarifying. Contemporary rape-revenge films would channel this very problematic. It is therefore important to analyse carefully what revenge is and what kind of response watching revenge stirs up.

---

[3] I use the notions emotion and affect somewhat interchangeably in this book, as they are closely related. See Carl Plantinga's discussion of the two: he defines emotion as an intentional mental state based on the construal or appraisal of any given situation, accompanied by physiological arousal (Plantinga 2009: 54), whereas affects are felt bodily states that may not include higher cognitive processing to the same degree (ibid. 57).

[4] Katherine Parker-Hay sums up this problematic elegantly in her book review of Alison Phipps's *Me, Not You* and Jennifer Cooke's *Contemporary Feminist Life-Writing: The New Audacity* (Parker-Hay 2023).

Henry's study of the rape-revenge film is in many ways the starting point for my exploration, and we share many assumptions, including the focus on revenge and the idea that 'the genre persists because it is really about an unresolved (and more obvious) question: how to *define* and *respond to* rape' (Henry 2014: 10, emphasis original). Henry makes several important observations that I want to expand on. Most notably, she sees the pleasures offered by watching revenge as central to the rape-revenge film, and notes that anger is part of this response. Building on these observations, in this book I explore in depth the emotions triggered by watching a rape survivor take revenge, a central part of the affective nature of watching rape-revenge film that is yet to be explored properly.

Within a framework of cognitive film theory, at the intersection between film theory, cognitive psychology and analytic philosophy, I expand the fertile mapping of emotional engagement with fiction in this field by narrowing in on anger, an underexplored emotion in this context.[5] I map the core emotional response to watching a woman take revenge on the man who raped her, which I argue is vindictive anger, and devise an interdisciplinary framework for assessing the potential function of this emotional response. I analyse the female avenger using a film theoretical framework spanning from the exploration of the female spectator of horror in psychoanalytic film theory, to contemporary film theory about rape-revenge film and also women in action film, and bring this back to my base in cognitive film theory to propose that the crux of the question is the value of anger. I turn to moral and evolutionary psychology and the philosophy of emotion to explore the psychological underpinnings of the desire to punish and take revenge on wrongdoers, and then to philosophy to examine the function of anger in general and for women in particular. As such, this book bridges the research on rape, anger, punishment and revenge in film theory, psychology and philosophy.

My use of evolutionary psychology might be different from what many expect from this research tradition, especially the popularised versions thereof used to justify essentialist gender roles, and thus warrants a brief note here. It is beyond the scope of the present study to explore the groundbreaking work of feminist researchers in psychology, biology and philosophy who examine evolutionary theory to show how it has consistently been shaped by patriarchal ideology, such as Cordelia Fine (2017), Lucy Cooke (2022) and Griet Vandermassen's important work (2005, 2011). They offer feminist rereadings of evolutionary psychology, and show how feminism can be compatible with

---

[5] One exception here is Julian Hanich's phenomenological exploration of anger, but his focus is broadly on feelings of, and expressions of, anger among the audience in the cinema (Hanich 2018: 248ff).

evolutionary psychology. I hope my analysis in Chapters 2 and 3 can also serve to illustrate how evolutionary theory can be used within a feminist framework.

The central premise in this book is that understanding the emotions stirred up by this type of story is crucial in order to understand its recurring, contentious presence in popular culture. I offer a cultural and political analysis grounded in the psychological and philosophical study of the emotions. My main contribution to the literature on the rape-revenge film is to truly hone in on, and drill into, the anger response these films tend to stir up. A second main contribution of this book is to extend the interdisciplinary reach of cognitive film theory by creating a dialogue with feminist film theory and feminist philosophy in an exploration of women's anger, thus also demonstrating how the study of an emotion such as anger can be deeply political. Some contemporary women directors have arguably used the rape-revenge convention to draw out these political implications.[6] Thus, I will also extend the literature on rape-revenge film by focusing on a recent trend of films made by women. However, I do not offer a broad corpus analysis of rape-revenge film, but draw on the existing literature on this type of film to discuss some central features of the genre.[7]

It might be helpful to start with one example of the controversy stirred up by rape-revenge film in the reception of the French art film *Baise-moi*. This is a story about two women, Manu and Nadine, who go on a road trip where they rob and kill men, occasionally also having sex with some of them first. Manu and another friend are raped in the beginning of the film, and the graphic portrayal of this gang rape includes hard-core porn close-up inserts, which were censored in some countries, including the UK. Leila Wimmer sums up the vitriolic response to this film from (mainly male) French film critics: the film was described as 'formless, chaotic, uncontrolled'; 'not even vile, just worthless, a trash version of *Thelma and Louise*'; 'a film made of hatred and revenge'; 'gratuitous violence [...] essentially primitive'; 'the worst populist impluses [...] adding nothing'; 'disgusting and fascist'; and finally, 'neither film nor cinema'.[8] However, in stark contrast to this critical reception, film theorist

---

[6] However, as Heller-Nicholas is right to point out, having a woman filmmaker at the helm is in no way a guarantee that a rape-revenge film is progressive. She discusses several problematic cases of porn films made by women where rape is glamorised (Heller-Nicholas 2021: 154–5).

[7] See, for example, Heller-Nicholas's impressive corpus analysis of rape-revenge films (Heller-Nicholas 2011, 2021). It should be noted here that Heller-Nicholas emphasises the wide variety of treatments of rape and revenge in rape-revenge film. I will narrow in on what can be said to be the most well-known, and most-discussed, features of this type of film, and explore in depth its affective structure. I do not discuss all variations of the rape-revenge film, such as films exploring rape of men for example, but point to Heller-Nicholas, and also Henry (2014) for broader, comprehensive overviews.

[8] Reviews cited in Wimmer (2011: 135–6).

Scott MacKenzie sees the film as an interstitial form of cinema by 'infusing the film with a political point of view that destablizes both art-house audiences and the consumers of more typical pornographic product' (MacKenzie 2002: 316).⁹ In other words, he praises the film as politically provoking. There is a tension between the critical reception of the rape-revenge film, in which there may be wholesale dismissal of it and where viewers and critics are commonly outraged, and a more nuanced approach in film theory where the rape-revenge film may be seen as a place of resistance – where some kind of political, progressive potential may be found in its extreme violence.¹⁰

The French film critics were clearly deeply provoked by something in *Baise-moi*, and I want to suggest that it is these women's aggression towards men that was perceived as unacceptable – indeed, that this is what made these critics see *Baise-moi* as not even worthy of the label film. As one of the film's directors, Virginie Despentes, who also wrote the novel the film is an adaptation of, puts it: 'A lot of people don't want to see two North African women who have been raped taking up arms and shooting European men' (Despentes quoted in Wimmer 2011: 139). Despentes is a filmmaker, novelist, activist and rape survivor who explores her own experience of gang rape as a young woman in her book *King Kong Theory* (Despentes 2020). In light of all the violence against women commonly found in films, one should be careful to dismiss this rape survivor's voice as culturally unacceptable. Wimmer concludes her analysis of the critical reception of *Baise-moi* with the observation that 'what is at stake in the debates around *Baise-moi* is the notion of women responding to violence, which was perceived as extremely disturbing to reviewers' (Wimmer 2011: 136). Indeed, I think this observation can be applied to rape-revenge film generally.

The gendered nature of film critique is of course also relevant here. The critics that vehemently dismissed *Baise-moi* were mostly male, as were the critics that were outraged by *I Spit on Your Grave*, as discussed by Clover (1992: 114ff). Read makes a related point in her analysis of Robert Ebert's much-cited diatribe against *I Spit on Your Grave*: although he claims to be critical of the film because of the way the woman protagonist is portrayed as being in danger and is victimised, Read shows how he actually seems more angered by the way men are represented as being in danger and being 'implicated in (and punished

---

⁹ See also Loreck (2016: 54–74).

¹⁰ One such exploration is found in Clover's discussion of rape-revenge film in her classical study of the horror film (Clover 1992: 114ff). Related discussions of the alleged misogyny in the extreme violence of exploitation film, and its relationship to feminism, is found in Cook (1976) and Modleski (2007). A helpful contextualisation of these discussions of the progressive potential in many B-films is also found in Klinger (1984). For a discussion of the shocked response to *Baise-moi*, and the high degree of cineliteracy in the film, often overlooked by critics, see also Williams (2001b).

for) male violence against women' (Read 2000: 34). In Read's analysis, this film is not primarily about female victimisation, but rather very much about a woman's refusal of such a passive position.

Of particular interest and importance to me is to examine how the female spectator is invited to engage with these scenarios and what it might mean for women to watch such films. Stories about rape are difficult to watch for many, if not most, women, as the fear of rape is probably familiar, as women move around in the world. I explore how these filmmakers explore the topic of rape for a general viewership with the assumption that the films do elicit the fear of rape, which is real, but then move away from realism and explore the anger response to rape in a realm of fantasy. Exploring the full effects of the trauma of rape through realism in film would be a different project. For some women who have experienced sexual violence themselves, rape-revenge films might of course be too triggering and traumatic to watch. However, I caution against the assumption that rape-revenge films are not watched by any rape survivors.[11] For example, the writer and rape survivor B. J. Colangelo speaks about her experience of *I Spit on Your Grave* as life-transforming, making her realise that 'it's okay to be angry. It's okay to move on with your life. You don't have to become this shell of a human that they show on *Law and Order: SVU*' (Colangelo quoted in Abley 2021, n.p.).

Revenge fantasies are described in several first-person accounts of rape, typically as part of a slow formation of rage that is described as healing. Following a rape and attempted murder while on holiday, philosopher Susan J. Brison describes how she was shocked to discover that most of the women in her rape survivor support group were unable to feel angry at all, and how she herself conjured up a 'justified, healing rage' directed at the rapist only when she started taking up self-defence classes (Brison 2002: 14). In her book about the experience of rape, essayist and author Nancy Venable Raine also discusses how at first she did not allow herself to feel hatred towards the rapist, turning the anger inward in self-blame instead, but at some point did experience vengeful fantasies of hurting him badly as pleasurable and empowering, as part of a rage forming (Raine 1999: 84, 158, 241–2, 256–7). Anthropologist Catherine Winkler also questions her initial lack of anger in the seven-year ordeal to bring the man who raped her in her own home to justice (Winkler 2002: 113). She suggests that anger might be important to deal with the pain of rape trauma, and described how she would engage in detailed and very violent revenge fantasies in order to be able to fall asleep. She watched films about rape, and describes her response to watching a rape-revenge film:

---

[11] See also Henry (2014: 170) for a discussion.

> My reaction startled me. As [the avenging protagonist] shot the rapist again and again, I yelled: 'Don't stop shooting until there is nothing left of him.' My body arched as if I had the gun in my hands, and I acted out that scene. In my mind, the rifle kept firing until there was nothing left of the rapist […]. (Winkler 2002: 117–18)

Winkler is describing a strong case of immersive participation in this revenge sequence. Raine simply notes that watching rape sequences in film is not triggering for her, in that they 'do not come close to the horror of the real thing' (Raine 1999: 206). Some rape survivors who have carefully explored their own experience of rape in their writing thus point to revenge fantasies as part of the healing process, and one also discusses rape-revenge films. However, as Colangelo points out, there is not one correct response for rape survivors to this type of film: for some these films will be triggering and offensive.

I do not actively discuss rape survivors' response to rape-revenge film in this book, as the trauma of rape in real life is not my field of expertise. Rather, the female rape-avenger is taken as a case study in a philosophical exploration of the function of revenge fantasies, and its emotional core of vindictive anger, for the female spectator generally. I want to suggest that the reason some female filmmakers explore this convention is because it is all about an emotion that is difficult for women, and used to label women as difficult, namely anger, and this is the potential political value of this type of story.

Women's anger is a topic consistently neglected in feminist film and media theory. A commentary and criticism section of the journal *Feminist Media Studies* published in 2019 takes as its starting point the notable neglect of this emotion in feminist media theory. Jilly Boyce Kay writes in her introduction to the section that 'a search for "anger" or "angry" in the titles of articles published in the entire archive of *Feminist Media Studies* returns only four results', and '"anger" seems never to have been used as a keyword for an article in the entire history of the journal' (Kay 2019: 592). She points out that women's anger has been perceived as 'deviant, monstrous or otherwise taboo' (ibid. 591), and 'cast as unreasonable, hysterical, as the opposite of reason' (ibid. 595). However, women's anger is becoming more visible in the public sphere, such as through the #MeToo movement, and 'anger that is feminist […] infuses the contemporary zeitgeist', as observed by McHugh (McHugh 2021: 10). Yet, as argued by Shani Orgad and Rosalind Gill, women's anger is still outlawed, as women are taught to favour positive affects and shy away from negative feelings, for example in the extensive market for self-help books (Orgad and Gill 2019: 598). They analyse the response to Uma Thurman's carefully controlled display of anger when talking about her own experiences in the film industry in response to the #MeToo movement: Thurman restrains herself, and these authors argue that this is because of a tendency to denounce female rage as immature. Thurman, and many women with her, struggle to communicate their anger, and if displaying anger, tend to experience that everyone's focus becomes her anger rather than the causes of her anger, as Orgad and Gill point out.

A feminist exploration of anger must also be intersectional, as the anger of women of colour has been pathologised even more so and used to exclude them from the public sphere.[12] Attention to the difference between a White woman's anger and the anger of a woman of colour brings a necessary intersectional awareness at several stages in my discussion: as I will explore in Chapter 4, anger was recognised as important in anti-racist feminism first, in particular with the writings of African American Audre Lorde, and this is the starting point for the philosophical exploration of the value of anger. Furthermore, the trend of violent action heroines in film, intertwined with the rise of the rape-avenger, started with Black women in Blaxploitation film, as will be explored in Chapter 5.[13] However, the Black woman's experience has systematically been left out of rape-revenge film in which the White woman came to dominate. This racial problematic thus surfaces at various points in this study.

So let us turn our attention to women's anger, keeping in mind also the heterogeneity of this group. Is anger basically corrosive, a counterproductive response that the rape-revenge film simplistically and ruthlessly exploits with negative effects, or can watching portrayals of revenge in response to sexual violence on-screen serve a function for the individual and in society? I will explore both rape-revenge films with violent revenge as well as so-called revisionist rape-revenge films in which the protagonist's revenge is somehow thwarted or discarded. Revisionist rape-revenge films are sometimes praised as morally preferable to classic manifestations of the convention because they are seen as distancing the spectator from the primitive moral urge to see wrongdoers punished, making her reflect on morally difficult questions instead in what Henry discusses as ethical spectatorship (Henry 2013). This is in line with a strong current in contemporary film theory that has been labelled estrangement theory by Carl Plantinga, in which distanced reflection is per definition always more praiseworthy and productive, and emotional engagement is seen as somehow ideologically suspect and to be avoided (Plantinga 2018). Plantinga argues that this tradition overlooks how central emotional engagement is to film viewing, and that emotional engagement can sometimes

[12] See, for example, Cooper (2018), Orgad and Gill (2019: 597) and Kay and Banet-Weiser (2019: 605) for discussions.

[13] A note on style: I capitalise both Black and White in discussions of race to emphasise that 'both are historically created racial identities', as called for by Kwame Anthony Appiah (Appiah 2020).

be at the core of a film's potential for learning, growth and reflection. This is a central assumption in this book as well. I am in agreement with Plantinga's critique of the dominant strain of estrangement theory in film studies, but I negotiate his scepticism of revenge scenarios in film. I discuss this in the very last chapter in this book.

Perhaps surprisingly, when taking the typical outrage in critical reception over the rape-revenge film into consideration, in feminist film theory in the 1990s its political potential is explored, and this is where I begin my analysis. Chapter 1, 'The affective structure of the rape-revenge film', starts with psychoanalytic feminist film theory in the 1980s and 90s, which I argue is on the right track when suggesting, albeit briefly, that the potential pleasures for the female spectator of horror film are found in anger and empowerment. However, women finding pleasure in watching violent women on-screen appeared inexplicable in the rigid dichotomy of active male vs passive female offered by this theoretical framework. I argue that by including a wider and more updated array of psychological theories supported by empirical research on the human mind, the cognitive film theorist can continue the investigation of the female spectator as an interdisciplinary dialogue with contemporary psychology and philosophy. I turn to the storyline about the rape of Pennsatucky in *Orange Is the New Black* in order to start exploring the function of rape-revenge stories, and outline the affective structure of the rape-revenge film – fear and horror followed by vindictive anger. Rape evokes a strong desire for punishment and revenge. I suggest that the potential value of the rape-revenge film lies in the exploration of the strong emotions triggered by watching the revenge sequences, with the convention's most radical potential thus being its affective structure.

In Chapter 2, 'On punishment, fiction and femininity', I first explore the spectator's response to punishment. I propose an explanation for why spectators enjoy excessive punishment when watching fiction, and suggest that we allow ourselves to enjoy punishment more readily when the character who punishes is clearly fictional. In *The Girl with the Dragon Tattoo* fantastic and clearly fictional elements seep into a work otherwise characterised more by realism, and allow the spectator to fully enjoy the main character Lisbeth Salander's revenge. This facilitates an affective, intuitive path to moral judgement, through which her revenge might be perceived as enjoyable, running counter to the more reflective, considered view that taking the law into one's own hands is wrong.

I explore how the protagonist of the rape-revenge film typically transforms after the rape, becoming more fantastical and/or clearly fictional, as she emerges as violent avenger. This moves the remainder of the film to a realm of fantasy and facilitates enjoyment of her revenge. Furthermore, her change resonates with the trope of the transformation found in other genres, such as in action film, but I focus in particular on the complex ways it often also inverts the transformation of the female protagonists in romantic comedies and melodramas. The transformed rape-avenger not only facilitates enjoyment of her revenge, but also opens up a fantasy space where the conventional delineation between the feminine and masculine is negotiated, which is what allows her to turn violently punitive.

Chapter 3, 'On revenge: rape-revenge storylines and the evolutionary origin of payback', explores the central role revenge takes up in many works of fiction, and yet how it is seen as the very antithesis of justice. In order to understand the link between revenge and justice, it is important to understand what its functions have been evolutionarily and historically. In psychology, the desire for revenge is seen as tied to self-respect, easing the victim's feeling of powerlessness. Revenge served as a regulator in societies without central justice. Rape-revenge film takes us right back to these retributive practices. The law is typically unavailable, unable or unwilling to help the rape survivor, and she reverts to revenge as an ancient route to power equalisation. The rape-avenger's vengeance in the rape-revenge film typically mirrors the pain and horror of the rape.

I turn to philosophy to examine how revenge is tied to concepts of honour. Honour and revenge norms are gendered: for women, honour has traditionally been tied to chastity as measured in shamefulness, an emotion that can still be evoked by rape in contemporary society. In *The Searchers* (John Ford, 1956) a rape survivor is portrayed as a source of shame for the male head of the family. In contrast, in the rape-revenge film it is the rapist who is dishonourable, and the rape survivor is not shameful. The female avenger steps out of the limited role traditionally assigned to her and into what has been, and still is, a male domain. This is another way the female avenger is an inversion of conventional femininity.

Chapter 4 is entitled 'On anger: a philosophical exploration of women's anger and its functions'. Rape-revenge stories are prone to trigger anger, and this chapter explores this emotion and its potential function for the female spectator. I forge connections between cognitive film theory and feminism through exploration of the philosophical study of women's anger. Anger is seen as an important emotion in feminist and anti-racist activism: it is a refusal to accept injustices. The curtailing of women's anger is tied to a tendency to socialise girls into a feeling of vulnerability, fear and helplessness, and anger is not easily accessible to women. Women's anger is hard to handle, an outlaw emotion. In a world that is systematically unjust and oppressive, anger may be needed.

In philosophy of emotion and moral philosophy, anger is controversial. Anger can be seen as a drive to maintain one's self, and as an emotion with important functions, among them to communicate that one has been wronged.

I defend this as the value of anger, and argue that sadness and forgiveness cannot fulfil the same functions. I illustrate this point through a discussion of the revisionist rape-revenge film *Twilight Portrait*, where the rape survivor forgives the rapist unconditionally, and also of forgiveness in *Women Talking* (Sarah Polley, 2022). I suggest that the rape-revenge film can be a burdened viewing experience: the rape-revenge story takes the female spectator to a place of rage that a subservient female self has been taught never to go.

In Chapter 5, 'Race and the rape-revenge film', I turn to questions of ethnicity and race, and how racist stereotypes were at work when the action heroines and rape-avengers first appeared on-screen in Blaxploitation film. Yet when female action heroes were integrated into mainstream film in high-budget action films, the trend became near all White. In the rape-revenge film too, the rape survivor is typically White, and when a Black woman is raped, such as in the Blaxploitation film *Foxy Brown* (Jack Hill, 1974), her trauma is not emphasised. Conventional femininity is not class-less or race-less, and in the rape-revenge film the rape survivor is typically middle-class and White. Women of colour are systematically displaced in rape stories in the media, and not given a voice.

I analyse how both class and race play into the portrayals of victimhood and revenge in *The Nightingale*, a post-colonial rape-revenge film, where the focus is on the White Irish woman Clare's experience of rape and revenge. The Indigenous Australian woman Lowanna is also raped, but as a minor character who is quickly killed her trauma is not given a central role. I then discuss how *I May Destroy You* explores rape story and rape-revenge conventions with its Black British protagonist rape survivor Arabella. *I May Destroy You* actively examines and critiques notions of victimhood, consent and the response to rape, revising tendencies in rape stories in film and television, and putting an intersectional focus on race firmly into the picture.

In Chapter 6, 'Containing the threat of the female avenger on-screen', I engage with the literature in film theory on the female action hero, who tended to stir up 'gender trouble' in that she transgresses conventional femininity. I turn to *Blue Steel* and its oscillation between the feminine and the masculine. I sum up the explanatory devices and containment strategies that are in use in the portrayal of action heroines in order to make them appear less threatening and more acceptable culturally, and explore how these strategies are at work in portrayals of the rape-avenger. I turn to a recent rape-revenge film that was made, distributed and celebrated in the mainstream, namely *Promising Young Woman*, to discuss to what extent these techniques are still at work, or whether a female avenger is now perceived as less threatening. In line with my analysis of women's anger and aggression as the core of the controversy of the rape-revenge film, it is notable how much the protagonist Cassie's anger and aggression are tuned down in this film. Indeed, breaking with rape-revenge conventions, *Promising Young Woman* displays little violence at all. This nudges Cassie closer to conventional femininity.

The final chapter, 'Emotions in contemporary film theory and rape-revenge film as exploitative', addresses some arguments against rape-revenge conventions. The wholesale rejection of the rape-revenge film often dismisses it as exploitative: the graphic violence is seen as excessive and gratuitous, serving no legitimate function. Both the rape and the revenge sequences in rape-revenge film are subject to this critique. In this chapter I examine three arguments against the rape-revenge film, all of which basically question why portray rape and revenge in such gruesome detail. I argue that revenge stories can be productive for ethical reflection, and that explicit portrayal of rape can also be defended if harnessed by a feminist argumentative context. I turn to a comparison between the explicit rape sequences in *Irreversible* and *Holiday* to illustrate how there is arguably such an argumentative context in the latter but not the former.

In the conclusion I sum up what characterises the rape-revenge films made by women that I have focused on, the function that the rape-revenge film can have for reflection on rape and the response to rape, and conclude that the main contribution in this book is to explain the rape-avenger's contentious place in popular culture, and, by extension, in our moral minds.

1. THE AFFECTIVE STRUCTURE OF THE RAPE-REVENGE FILM

Linda Williams asked in 1984 what happens when the woman looks at horror (Williams 1984), but later admitted that her essay failed to address 'the *pleasures*, however, problematic, women viewers may take in this genre', or in other words, 'the feminine pleasures of fear' (Williams 2001a, n.p., emphasis original). Although there was a call for further analysis of the female spectator of horror in feminist film theory, the effort ran into difficulties due in large part to the shortcomings of the psychoanalytic framework within which they worked, as pointed out at the time as well. By turning to current research in philosophy and psychology, I will continue what psychoanalytically informed feminist film theorists started by exploring the potential pleasures the female avenger can offer the female spectator; in short, the pleasures of watching the culturally taboo emotion that is female rage. In this chapter I examine the early discussions of rape-revenge film and take these as my starting point when outlining the affective structure of watching rape-revenge film for the female spectator.

THE RAPE-REVENGE FILM IN FEMINIST FILM THEORY: WHAT ABOUT THE FEMALE SPECTATOR?

In one of the first, and by now classical, discussions of rape-revenge film, feminist film theorist Carol Clover discusses these films as a subtype of horror. In contrast to the critical reception of films such as *I Spit On Your Grave*

(Meir Zarchi, 1978) and *Ms. 45* (Abel Ferrara, 1981), she points to what is new in the rape-revenge film, compared to the way rape had traditionally been depicted in American film. In what she labels old-style rape films, such as *Straw Dogs* (Sam Peckinpah, 1971), she observes that rape is portrayed highly problematically as a male act of revenge on a woman who is asking for it, and the spectator may be invited to identify with the rapist, for example, through point-of-view shots. What is new in rape-revenge films is that rape takes centre stage, and it is portrayed as a heinous crime that deserves full-scale revenge, argues Clover. She goes on to point out that in the rape-revenge film, rape and revenge constitute sufficient drama for a feature film, and that the victim should be the avenger (Clover 1992: 138ff). In short, there is a change from 'a more or less justifiable male-centered event to an unjustifiable female-centered one' in the emerging cycle of rape-revenge films (ibid. 140). This is the progressive potential in Clover's analysis: not only do rape-revenge films have 'female heroes and male villains, they repeatedly and explicitly articulate feminist politics. So trenchant is the critique of masculine attitudes and behaviour in such films [...] that, were they made by women, they would be derided as male-bashing' (ibid. 151).

Clover suggests that when features of the rape-revenge film appear in mainstream film culture, such as in *The Accused* (Jonathan Kaplan, 1988), the film may lose 'sight of what the lower forms of the rape drama unfailingly keep at center stage: the raped woman herself' (ibid. 148).[1] The significant difference this focus on the rape survivor makes is also emphasised in later studies. Sarah Projansky, for example, argues that whereas in some (early) rape-revenge films a man takes revenge (a father or husband), only rape-revenge films where the woman herself takes revenge can be understood as feminist narratives (Projansky 2001: 60).

Nevertheless, Clover's focus is on what has been seen as the horror film's main audience, namely the male spectator. The question driving her exploration of the horror film is why the protagonist in horror and slasher film is predominantly female – a character she names the Final Girl – when the filmmaker and the intended audience are male. This is where the female-centred nature of the rape-revenge film is arguably explained away: Clover holds that 'these films are predicated on cross-gender identification of the most extreme, corporeal sort' (ibid. 154). The Final Girl is used to explore the victim experience for the male viewer, as the victim's suffering is so 'messy and unwholesome' that it must be run through a woman (ibid. 18). This is an opportunity for male

---

[1] The notion 'mainstream' is typically used about big studio productions, in contrast to independent and/or low-budget filmmaking. See Clover (1992: 5) for an illustration of the way she uses the notion, and Lane (2000: 29–40) for a careful discussion of mainstream vs independent film.

viewers to experience forbidden desires and anxieties, and at the same time keep them at a safe distance, as the character one identifies with is only a girl. The male viewer is masochistically identifying with the Final Girl's suffering, Clover argues, and 'females figure in it only insofar as they "read" some aspect of male experience' (ibid. 53).

Clover's focus, then, is on the masochistic male spectator. She acknowledges the female spectator only briefly in an offhand remark: 'while it may be that the audience for slasher films is mainly male, this does not mean that there are not also many female viewers who actively like such films' (ibid. 54). This focus on the male experience is mirrored in other early accounts of rape-revenge film, such as in Peter Lehman's, who writes of the female protagonist in rape-revenge that the film 'enlists her in the service of the male desire for an eroticized form of revenge [...] such eroticized deaths are male fantasies which are unlikely to be of "interest" to women' (Lehman 1993: 111). There is enjoyment of revenge in Lehman's theory, but only for male spectators.

This aspect of the early theories about rape-revenge film has been criticised in later accounts. Jacinda Read, for example, argues that femininity is 'repressed or disavowed' in Clover's analysis in two ways: in her focus on the male spectator's identification, and her denigration of mainstream rape-revenge films, seen as 'too feminine too be feminist' (Read 2000: 8–9). Read argues that Clover fails to account for the rape-revenge film as a site of ongoing negotiations about feminism.

A related view on articulations of the feminine as oppressed is found in Tania Modleski's discussion of the feminist potential in Alfred Hitchcock's films. She holds that Hitchcock's female protagonists are often portrayed as trapped within an oppressive structure, and his films can be seen as a critique of this structure. Furthermore, she suggests that 'insofar as Hitchcock films repeatedly reveal the way women are oppressed in patriarchy, they allow the female spectator to feel an anger' (Modleski 2016: 4). Anger is crucial to theorising the female spectator, according to Modleski,

> even if that anger remains unconscious or is quickly suppressed. In my opinion, feminist film theory has yet to explore and work through this anger, which for women continues to be, as it has been historically, the most unacceptable of all emotions. (Ibid. 24)

This is why it can be pleasurable to have one's anger triggered by a film such as *Blackmail* (Alfred Hitchcock, 1929) in which an attempted rape makes the female protagonist kill her attacker in self-defence: 'one can find pleasure in acknowledging and working through one's anger, especially when that anger has long been denied or repressed' (ibid. 25). This makes sense for rape-revenge films more generally, although Modleski does not make that connection.

And Modleski does not explore this anger further. Her account does, however, open up a more complicated picture of rape-revenge films than the mere positioning of the male spectator as masochistic, and she firmly emphasises the female spectator as taking up a much more active position.

This latter view is also evident in Barbara Creed's discussion of the horror film, and the portrayal of the monstrous-feminine specifically. Creed criticises Freudian theory for misunderstanding why the woman represents a threat in patriarchal society: Freud saw her as suffering from penis envy, and as such defined by the lack of a penis, and as frightening for the male child because she is seemingly castrated. Creed argues that what Freud overlooks is that the woman can also be perceived as frightening for the little boy because she poses the threat of castration. In line with Clover, she includes rape-revenge films in her exploration of horror. She demonstrates how the main character in *I Spit on Your Grave* is an example of the *femme castratice* – part of the rape survivor's revenge is indeed to castrate one of the rapists. Creed points to the presence of castrating women in myths, religion and art, and argues that this active, threatening woman is the repressed in Freudian theory. Notably, Creed disagrees with Clover's view that the Final Girl is a pseudo-man, and ends her book by discussing, albeit again briefly, the appeal of the horror film to the female spectator, and suggests that even though these horror films may be misogynistic due to their problematic portrayal of the monstrous-feminine, female spectator may nevertheless 'feel empowerment from identifying with the castrating heroine of the rape-revenge film when the latter takes revenge on the male rapist' (Creed 1993: 155). Indeed, in Creed's theory the horror film is all about our deepest fears:

> the unconscious fears and desires of both the human subject (pain, bodily attack, disintegration, death) and the gendered subject (male fears of woman's reproductive role and of castration and woman's fears of phallic aggressivity and rape). No doubt if women made horror films, the latter area would be explored more fully. (Ibid., 156)

What is at stake here for Creed is the fact that in Freudian theory the woman is by her very nature passive, defined by lack and absence (ibid. 7, 152ff). This view is articulated clearly in Laura Mulvey's classical discussion of the portrayal of women in film (Mulvey 1975), in which the male spectator is seen as identifying with the active male character on-screen, whereas the female character is typically portrayed as passive, as someone to be looked at. Furthermore, the camera's gaze is seen as wedded to the male character's, thus enforcing his objectifying gaze on the female characters: this is how Hollywood film is structured to accommodate the male gaze. In feminist film theory, this rigid dichotomy between the active male and the passive female was influential but also controversial. In Miriam Hansen's words, Mulvey's masculinisation of the spectator position 'has been criticized frequently for the difficulty of conceptualizing a female spectator other than in terms of absence', and attempts have been made to 'rescue female spectatorship from its "locus of impossibility"' (Hansen 1986: 7). As we have seen, attempts to break down the active male vs passive female dichotomy have been mounted by arguing that the male is sometimes passive and masochistic (Clover) or that the female is sometimes active (Modleski and Creed).

Yet discussions of female sadism are hard to come by. One exception is Jeffrey A. Brown's discussion of American action films with female action heroines. He argues that 'the symbolic function of the dominatrix is at the root of all the images of tough women that populate action films' (Brown 2011: 59). Powerful, sadistic female characters, such as the main character Sydney Bristow in the television series *Alias* (J. J. Abrams, 2001–6), are both feared and desired; Brown argues that overly fetishised images exploit and contain male fear of female sexuality. The female action heroine is fetishised active. However, in Brown's discussion the focus is again on how this active woman on-screen is exploited to contain male fear, thus stipulating a male spectator and having less to say in his analysis about the female spectator watching the female dominatrix-like figure. It seems that Carol Siegler is right when she argues that although male masochism is problematic for feminism, female sadism is even more so. She suggests that female sadism 'constitutes a category crisis [a]s it does in popular culture generally, which avoids representation of sadistic desires in women as anything other than grotesquely unnatural and evil' (Siegler 2007: 66).

Indeed, Creed points out that the 'feminine imagination is seen as essentially non-violent, peaceful, unaggressive [...] women by definition are "pure" creatures' (Creed 1993: 156). This might explain further why it has been difficult to find clear-cut articulations and explorations of the pleasures of horror, violence and revenge for the female spectator in film theory until recently: women are supposed to be morally pure and not aggressive. Kirsten Marthe Lentz points to a similar dilemma in her discussion of the popular pleasures of female revenge in the action film: it may be even more pleasurable for the female spectator to see a female rather than a male character seek revenge for what is unjust, but in contrast to action films with a male protagonist, the female action heroine's violence is 'often problematized by a pervasive ideology which insists upon "woman's" special relationship to moral purity' (Lentz 1993: 378).

Isabel Cristina Pinedo makes a related point about the taboo against women wielding violence. She holds that horror films with violent women construct a subject position that is pleasurable for female viewers, and she counters the objection that some women report no pleasure from watching such films because the films are too frightening, by suggesting that 'more than the reported fear of victimization is at stake in this terror, that what motivates the avoidance of this violent genre is not only fear of being victimized but also fear of being violently aggressive' (Pinedo 1997: 85).

Rescuing the female spectator from her locus of impossibility, as Hansen put it, led some to reject the theoretical construct discussed as 'the spectator' in film theory, a textually constructed position teased out through careful close analysis of the film backed up by psychological theories of the human mind. Film theorists turned instead to empirical investigations of actual audiences in order to map how female viewers engage in film.[2] For example, one study by Tiina Vares of women watching *Thelma and Louise* (Ridley Scott, 1991) included women in a peace group, and women in a martial arts group, amongst others, and she writes that whereas some enjoyed the violence on-screen, many women did not, or felt conflicted: 'pleasures were muted, contradictory, resisted, and critiqued' (Vares 2001: 229). Notably, she concludes that '"pleasures", and lack thereof, in action heroines cannot be "read" off film texts' (ibid. 240). One could thus say that the focus on the female spectator watching transgressive female characters on-screen turned out to be so problematic for film theory that it changed its methodology: in Hansen's words, 'the difficulty of conceptualizing a female spectator has led feminists to recast the problem of identification in terms of instability, mobility, multiplicity' (Hansen 1986: 16).

Another qualitative study of women watching violence is found in Annette Hill's study of a controversial trend of extreme, brutally violent movies in the 1990s, such as *Pulp Fiction* (Quentin Tarantino, 1994), *Reservoir Dogs* (Quentin Tarantino, 1992) and *Man Bites Dog* (Rémy Belvaux, André Bonzel and Benoît Poelvoorde, 1992). Hill's starting point is her own enjoyment of violent films, and frustration with the conventional head-shaking response she would often be met with when speaking about this to other women. Indeed, Hill's respondents were typically highly aware that watching violence on-screen was a 'masculine domain' (Hill 2001: 140).[3] These women would sometimes choose to watch violent films exactly because of this, in order to push personal and cultural boundaries: they were aware that 'society expected women to be repulsed by, rather than attracted to, violent cinema' (ibid. 146). Yet many of the respondents enjoyed watching these violent films, partly because they were different from regular Hollywood fare and thus unpredictable, but also because the women enjoyed challenging their fears in a safe context.

What is suggested by Hill's discussion is that testing boundaries and challenging oneself is perceived as empowering by these women. One respondent,

---

[2] See, for example, Stacey (1993). For an exploration of audience reception of rape-revenge more generally, and not tied to the focus on female spectators specifically, see also Baker (2011).

[3] See also Heller-Nicholas (2017: 110ff) for a discussion.

Alison, makes some observations that are worth dwelling on. Alison had personal experience of violence in real life from a knife attack. She therefore shied away from violent scenes with knives in particular, but interestingly, she also explained how she sometimes watched violence and enjoyed it as a fantasy in which the tables are turned and she gets to be the aggressor rather than the victim. From her description it sounds like it is this violent rage that made her need to control her exposure to violent films, in line with Pinedo's point about women's fear of being violent. This is how Alison puts it:

> If there is a knife involved I just – I get quite angry and it has definitely affected me as a person as well because I sort – it sort of brings out – I have a lot of violence in me actually. For me – I know this is a very important thing to say but for me I kind of will it to happen again so that I can act it out – although I wasn't violently attacked, there was no violence at all apart from a knife. I didn't – in that respect I keep thinking I wish I could have fought back and so if I see things like a rape scene I think – wouldn't it be great if she could just do something violent, do this and do fucking that. (Quoted in Hill 2001: 142)

Alison thus uses some violent films as a fantasy 'to relive her attack in such a way that she is no longer the victim', as Hill points out (ibid.).

For women, viewing violence – and in particular, viewing women who are violent on-screen – may be prone to stir up a difficult mix of emotions, from empowerment to fear to anger and aggression, the latter two of which will probably be perceived as something one should self-censor. Women watching violent women on-screen thus poke at a cultural taboo. This is perhaps one reason why it has been difficult to find in-depth explorations in film theory of the potentially pleasurable nature of watching the female character's violent revenge for the female spectator of rape-revenge film.

One interesting case is Claire Henry's recent discussion of revisionist rape-revenge films (Henry 2014). Revisionist rape-revenge films are ambiguous and self-reflexive, and call for reflection on the ethical, affective and political consequences of revenge. When it comes to the question of gender, Henry maintains the assumption that we are aligned with and form an allegiance with the female protagonists, but she wants to 'avoid assumptions about the gender of the ideal spectator [...]. The assumption of male spectatorship – indeed, the assumption that spectatorship is primarily gendered spectatorship – has become outdated' (Henry 2014: 12). So female spectators are implicitly included, but it is interesting to note that discussions of the female spectator of rape-revenge films specifically are hard to come by. However, one can also question whether the inclusion of the female spectator influences Henry's views on the experience of watching rape-revenge films. Although stating in her introductory remarks that 'watching graphic acts of revenge is a key generic pleasure of rape-revenge' (ibid. 6), in her discussion of *I Spit on Your Grave*, she argues that although there is empathic sharing of the victim's experience of rape, the spectator is made to engage in a more distanced way during her revenge:

> the rape-avenger's transformation becomes the moment we are cut loose and stand outside this identification. Even though we often celebrate and enjoy the revenge sequences, when this separation is successful it creates a space to simultaneously reflect on the protagonist's response to rape in terms of the political and ethical questions it raises. (Ibid. 49)

Although I agree with Henry in seeing the potential for political and ethical reflection in revenge sequences, one is left to wonder whether including female spectators in the analysis of violent revenge downplays the pleasure of female revenge. If we think of Henry's ideal spectator as female only, it is in line with the psychoanalytic, Mulveyian paradigm to postulate that she identifies with the victim's suffering (woman as passive), but falls out of identification when the victim turns violent avenger (woman as active).

Furthermore, in the introduction and conclusion to her book she postulates that traditionally, rape-revenge film offered the pleasure of revenge, but in her analysis of one of the most classic early examples little is said about this pleasure. What is left unexplained is how and why we celebrate the revenge if we do not identify with the avenger – what kind of pleasure does revenge then offer? Although reflecting on the political and ethical questions raised by revenge is most certainly valuable, it is hardly affectively pleasurable. It is this pleasure that I will concentrate on in this book, and I will return to Henry's account in the last chapter.

Creed picks up on her own exploration of the monstrous-feminine in horror film from 1993 in her recent book, and describes a trend she labels as Feminist New Wave Cinema (Creed 2022).[4] She observes that although female characters took on monstrous features in horror films that initially were made by male directors to cater to male viewers' 'imbedded fears of female sexuality', 'feminist viewers often found her empowering': indeed, 'since then her oppositional stance as represented by feminist directors has transformed into one of revolt' (ibid. 4). In Feminist New Wave films, the monstrous-feminine is emancipatory, as the protagonist is made to face her worst nightmares, to face male violence and emerge changed (ibid. 14). In doing so she serves to 'upend and undermine patriarchal myths about woman

---

[4] Creed points to other recent publications on women and horror published since 2016, including Peirse (2020) and Pisters (2020) that I discuss briefly in the introduction. See Creed (2022: 19 n.1).

as weak and ineffective' (ibid. 5). The female protagonist of Feminist New Wave horror films invites a feminist gaze and takes the spectator on a journey that may lead to transformation.

Turning to cognitive film theory

In the present study I turn to cognitive film theory to continue the exploration of the feminine pleasures of anger in feminist film theory. This might seem paradoxical, as the links between feminist film theory and cognitive film theory are few. One notable exception is Cynthia Freeland, who also discusses why the reliance on psychoanalytic theory in feminist film theory is restrictive (Freeland 1996). Indeed, she writes that psychoanalytic approaches have 'acquired a predominance within feminist film theory that is completely disproportionate to its status within contemporary feminist theorizing in general', and points out that there is a wide range of theoretical bases to be found between American, French and Third World feminists, for example, but where none of which are typically psychoanalytic (ibid. 201). What cognitive film theory does offer is a tradition for careful exploration of the spectator's affective responses by turning to psychology and philosophy, and this is the perspective that I suggest can add an important perspective to the literature on rape-revenge film.

Cognitive film theory started as a rebellion against the dominance of politicised psychoanalytic film theory, typically discussed as Screen Theory or Grand Theory,[5] and as a cognitive film theorist I concur with some of this critique. However, *pace* some of my fellow cognitivists, I nonetheless hold that the psychoanalytic film theorists did not get the methodological approach entirely wrong.

It is worth noting briefly what cognitive film theory is before moving on. Ted Nannicelli and Paul Taberham point to four characteristic features: in addition to being committed to 'inter-theoretical criticism and debate', and a 'focus on the mental activity of viewers', a cognitive film theorist is dedicated 'to the highest standards of reasoning and evidence (…) including, but not limited to, empirical data from the natural sciences', and as such he or she would accept 'a naturalistic perspective, broadly construed' (Nannicelli and Taberham 2014: 4).[6] Nevertheless, to reiterate a point made by Nannicelli and Taberham, many cognitive film theorists, such as myself, do employ the

---

[5] See, for example, Bordwell (1996) and Carroll (1996) for discussions, and Nannicelli and Taberham (2014) for a good, recent introduction to cognitive film theory.

[6] Cognitive film theory has been criticised for this naturalism, or, its alleged scientism: according to film theorist D. N. Rodowick, for example, cognitive theory is engaged in 'a de facto epistemological dismissal of the humanities' (Rodowick 2007: 98).

methods and explanations of the humanities. My approach is to be 'marshalling evidence to advance an argument rather than actually empirically testing a hypothesis', the latter of which is what the researcher in the natural sciences would do (Nannicelli and Taberham 2014: 16). The 'evidence', or backing, I am marshalling is taken from various fields, drawing on research in cognitive psychology to some extent but mostly exploring literature on the emotions in philosophy. My analysis will also be supported by analysis of films and television series. As a cognitive film theorist, I can thus in some ways be said to build on and expand the study of the spectator in psychoanalytic film theory, and as such my approach is in line with traditional methodologies in the humanities. The contested part is predominantly which psychological theory we as film theorists should rely on in order to find intersubjective regularities.

Another methodological feature shared by the psychoanalytic and cognitive film theorist is that both explore the spectator's response as something universal, almost sounding as if it is given by the film, teased out through close analysis. Arguably, the response discussed by the film theorist should be seen as akin to claims about statistical tendencies. What I will claim about 'the spectator' in this book is thus to be taken as my argument about the most probable response to any given feature of a film based on close analysis of the film backed up by theories and empirical studies, i.e. to the best of our knowledge of the human mind this is what the spectator's response will *tend* to be like. This cognitive approach can shed light on spectator experiences that we might not readily admit to having: it may be particularly well suited when exploring topics that are taboo and riddled by controversy, and emotions that are poorly understood. And the spectator response I am dealing with in this book is not, as has been stressed already, culturally condoned. Although Hill's study did present us with complex, nuanced reflections, it might be difficult for women in general to speak freely about their own fears, pleasures and desires in relation to on-screen violence, and this is why it is helpful to turn to a methodological approach suited to reveal what might be at work intuitively and affectively, beyond and before what any given spectator is reflectively aware of and perhaps even able to articulate. However, I will turn to what contemporary psychology says about intuitive processes rather than relying on the Freudian unconscious.

The psychoanalytic theorist explores a spectator position invited by a film through explorations of theory about human psychology mapped onto film in close analysis, and I too see this theoretical construct as fertile. Psychoanalytic theory was merely too restricted in its dependence on psychoanalytic theories alone, seen by many cognitive film theorists as dogmatic and fundamentally

I will not discuss this at length here, as others have refuted this claim convincingly (Turvey 2007; Nannicelli and Taberham 2014).

flawed because it was not informed by empirical science.[7] By including a wider and more updated array of psychological theories supported by research on the human mind, the cognitive film theorist can continue the investigation of the female spectator in an interdisciplinary dialogue with psychology and philosophy. I will do so by drawing on literature on the emotions in cognitive psychology and philosophy, an interdisciplinary endeavour that is well established in cognitive film theory. This analysis will explain why revenge sequences stir up such strong emotions, first and foremost among them vindictive anger, and how this emotion has important functions. A cognitive study of this emotion can thus explain the observation, articulated by several early theorists as demonstrated in this chapter, that engaging with a female avenger on-screen might be empowering for women. The cognitive approach in this book is evident in the entire trajectory of the study, where in the following two chapters I will dwell on and carefully examine the psychological effects of watching punishment and revenge, narrowing in on what kind of emotions and affects this stirs up. This brings me to the emotion of anger in Chapter 4, its psychological functions and effects, all of which will also be explored in depth through relevant research in psychology and philosophy of emotion before returning to film theory in Chapter 5.

My study of vindictive anger aims to bring out an untapped feminist, political potential in cognitive film theory. I will demonstrate how the female avenger challenges gender expectations on multiple levels, drawing on feminist theory. Vares's point about women feeling conflicted when watching violent women on-screen is spot on – but we need to understand why. This is what I set out to explain in this book. In this chapter I have argued that early psychoanalytic feminist film theoretical accounts of horror and the spectator were basically right about the potential pleasures of the rape-revenge film for the female spectator in terms of anger and empowerment. Cognitive film theory offers a way to return the film theorist's focus to affective responses, a focus that is arguably needed in order to explain the full force of the rape-revenge story.

GOING FULL ON *GIRL WITH THE DRAGON TATTOO* IN *ORANGE IS THE NEW BLACK*

At this stage it might be helpful to look at one example from *Orange Is the New Black* that fits Henry's category of revisionist rape-revenge; an ambiguous and self-reflexive exploration of rape and revenge in a storyline in season

---

[7] See Andrews (2012), who makes a similar point in his analysis of the literature on rape-revenge film.

three about the rape of Pennsatucky and its aftermath.⁸ Tiffany 'Pennsatucky' Doggett is one of the many inmates the spectator gets to know in this television series, a young woman from a poor, rural background. She is raped by the prison guard Charlie Coates, with whom she had been exploring an emerging friendship, but she does not define this as rape until her friend Carrie 'Boo' Black, another inmate, makes her realise that boundaries were crossed and it is not her fault. Boo explicitly references rape-revenge films as part of her efforts to raise Pennsatucky's awareness and help her cope with this trauma. The law is quickly dismissed as unavailable – the guard will be believed, not the female inmate, Boo observes, and she adds that women are seen as deserving everything that happens to them. She then declares that they are going to take revenge, or more specifically, to 'go full on *Girl with the Dragon Tattoo*' on him. This is a reference to the first instalment of the Millennium trilogy, effectively a rape-revenge story in which Lisbeth Salander takes revenge on her legal guardian Niels Bjurman, after he brutally rapes her, by raping him back. I analyse this story about Salander in the next chapter. Pennsatucky and Boo carefully plan how they are going to tranquilise Coates and pull him down to the basement where they will rape him, as Salander rapes Bjurman. However, when they stand there behind this sleeping man, who is undressed and bent over a table, they are unable to go through with it. The revenge is not sweet at all. 'But this is my gift to you', says Boo, 'to help you work through that rage and anger' (Figure 1.1). Pennsatucky mournfully remarks that she just feels sad. The creators emphasise – perhaps rightly, according to some research on the feelings triggered by revenge – that although we might think that revenge will make us feel better, it may not.⁹ This is a revisionist rape-revenge scenario in that it invites reflection on the feelings that might actually be invoked by taking revenge.

However, the rape-revenge pattern is used in this episode of *Orange Is the New Black* in a way that could also be said to emphasise its potential: it is used as part of Boo's efforts to make Pennsatucky realise that the act was indeed a rape, a heinous crime. Through thinking about revenge Pennsatucky is encouraged to see the rape as unacceptable, and not something that was her fault.

⁸ Season 3, episodes 10–12. The series' roots in exploitation film, or more specifically the women-in-prison film, is interesting to note here, where rape-revenge plotlines often play a role. For a historical overview of the women-in-prison genre, see, for example, Walters (2001), and for a discussion of how *Orange Is the New Black* subverts women-in-prison genre conventions, see for example Schwan (2016).

⁹ The issue is contested in empirical psychology: some studies show that although people expect revenge to feel satisfying, it only makes them feel worse, see, for example, Carlsmith, Wilson and Gilbert (2008), whereas other studies found both negative and favourable reactions, see, for example, Eadeh, Peak and Lambert (2017).

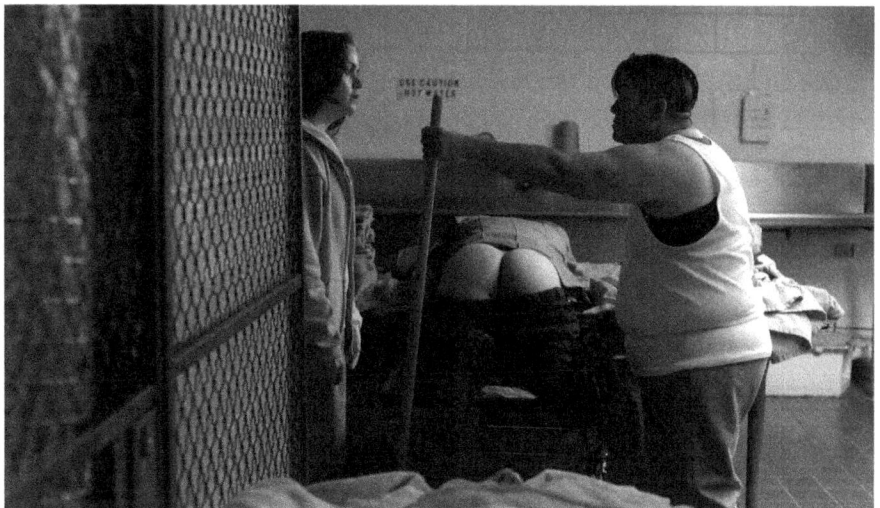

Figure 1.1 'This is my gift to you to help you work through that rage and anger', says Boo to Pennsatucky (*Orange Is the New Black*, 2015).

Although *Orange Is the New Black* ends up problematising revenge, which is aborted, in the process of setting this up Pennsatucky goes through a significant change of attitude, and the rape-revenge convention plays a central role. Pennsatucky changes from being confused and ambivalent about the event, feeling shameful and blaming herself, to feeling anger towards the perpetrator and blaming him.

Expanding on Clover's emphasis on what is new in the rape-revenge film, one feature that has been overlooked is that there is no misattribution of blame in rape-revenge films: no self-blaming, shameful victim, but mere outward-directed anger felt towards the rapist(s). In this sense, what is striking about the classic rape-revenge films is perhaps also what is absent – the victim's shame and self-blaming. In portrayals of rape more closely wedded to realism, and in real life, rape survivors are often blamed, and do often painfully blame themselves. This aspect of the rape-revenge film might be key to the potential pleasures it offers the female spectator. In terms of the female character's experience of rape and its aftermath, and the spectator's vicarious feelings through empathic engagement, this might indeed be perceived as a seismic shift, standing in stark opposition to the shameful rape victim who is blamed for her own misfortune. When circling in on the anger that Modleski saw as central to women's experience under patriarchy, and as the repressed in feminist film theory, this affective shift might be what the rape-revenge film specifically can offer – be angry with and blame the rapist. This is the way the rape-revenge convention is used in this storyline in *Orange Is the New Black*.

OUTLINING THE AFFECTIVE STRUCTURE OF THE RAPE-REVENGE FILM

Although I will focus on the revenge sequences, what initiates the avenger's violence is rape – so a few words at the onset here about rape are needed. Watching rape is typically a disturbing experience. Portrayals of rape elicit not only feelings of anger, but also disgust (Vaage 2015 and 2016: 120ff). The strong negative emotions triggered by rape are often used narratively to enhance antipathy and strong dislike of the villain. In the antihero series on television, for example, the antihero is often a murderer but only the proper villain is a rapist. In the morally murky antihero series, rape can thus be used to make the antihero morally preferable, as compared to a rapist villain. Rape is also typically used as justification for vigilante revenge. My research suggests that rape triggers extremely strong emotional reactions – perhaps more so than most other violations and crimes, and even more so than murder.

This could perhaps explain why Arthur A. Raney found in one empirical study that rape eliminated the effect of different social-justice beliefs among respondents. Attitudes towards justice predicted viewers' enjoyment of punishment when showed sequences from the film *Rob Roy*, which included physical violation and the ensuing revenge: the more viewers supported harsh punishment, the more they enjoyed Rob Roy's violent revenge on the offenders. However, including the depiction of the rape of Rob Roy's wife eliminated any variance. 'All viewers thought that the act was deplorable', Raney writes (Raney 2002: 319). Watching rape eliminates differences between respondents' principled views on punishment and makes them all want to see the offenders punished.

Rape thus has a strong polarising effect morally, and it triggers a strong desire for punishment, or what Nico Frijda discusses as wrath, an immensely powerful urge. In Frijda's analysis, rape is an offence that represents one of the deepest injuries to personhood (Frijda 1994: 282). His analysis backs up the point that rape evokes a strong desire for punishment and revenge. Frijda also observes that vengeful fantasies are remarkable for their degree of violence and persistence, and I will argue that the rape-revenge film is a revenge fantasy.

The important point here is that this affective structure – the horror of watching rape, and vindictive anger and the desire for punishment – is stripped to the bone in the rape-revenge film. To the best of our knowledge of the human mind, depiction of revenge in response to rape probably evokes strong feelings of disgust, righteous anger and wrath. What I am going to suggest is that the rape-revenge film faces the female spectator with something she fears, and that after this, when watching a fictional representation of vengeful rage in response to rape, the spectator might experience vicariously some of the gains of revenge, as discussed by Frijda and others, to which I return in Chapter 3: her revenge is typically both excessively painful and humiliating for the rapist, mirroring the initial violation of self-worth and self-identity, firmly emphasising the magnitude of the rape and its consequences, as well as rape as sexualised torture, and finally the correct attribution of blame. Frijda discusses revenge as a power equaliser, enabling the avenger to regain a sense of self-respect and empowerment by literally reclaiming the gains someone else has enjoyed by disempowering a victim. Of course, in real life, the rape survivor, and others witnessing or hearing about rape, cannot and should not seek violent retribution – even when, as we know, most rapes either pass unreported or, if reported, unpunished in our legal systems. No wonder, as pointed out by Clover, the rape-revenge film is about 'a nervous relationship to third-party dispute settlement, at least as far as rape is concerned' (Clover 1992: 123).

Let me now end this chapter with an outline of the affective structure of the rape-revenge film that I will continue to explore throughout this book. I argue that rape-revenge stories invite a very particular kind of response: first a mix of strong emotions in watching rape, including dreading watching it, fearing it, feeling reluctant to watch it perhaps, most likely followed by feelings of utter horror and disgust as one is watching the rape unfold – or knowing that it is unfolding if it is not portrayed explicitly. Some spectators might not be able to or want to watch this at all, and may turn away or turn off to protect themselves. This first response is probably for many closely tied to a real-life fear of rape, and this is an important difference brushed over by Carol when discussing the rape-revenge film as horror: it is true that watching rape is horrific, and tends to stir up emotions that are similar to those evoked by monsters in horror film, but there is a very real aspect to this fear that distinguishes the response to rape-revenge film. Empathising with the protagonist as she is raped will be viscerally painful and deeply disturbing. For some it might be downright traumatising. There is good reason to think that this is among the most difficult type of material to watch in fiction film for many spectators.

Then comes the response that I am honing in on in this book, namely anger, which is explored in the revenge sequences. The spectator might find herself swept up in a sort of wave of bloodlust, cheering on the avenger's brutal revenge through gritted teeth, quite possibly beside herself and against her better judgement. Again, empathising with the protagonist when she is taking revenge can be fraught with difficulties, as accessing one's own aggression can be difficult for many women, culturally unacceptable as the feeling is. Some spectators might be more resistant to this violent and vindictive urge, but I will argue that it is a powerful urge, difficult to resist completely and probably prone to stir up some kind of enjoyment, which in turn might make some feel conflicted about their own response.

It would not be surprising to find many spectators left feeling disturbed, conflicted and angry after watching a rape-revenge film. I am going to suggest that in order to allow the spectator to explore all of these feelings, the rape-revenge film takes a distinct turn away from realism: the revenge sequences turn to an imaginary space to explore the protagonist's response to rape. These films stir up a real fear of rape and then a response to it that is off limits in real life, stepping out of realism and into a clearly imaginary sphere when taking violent revenge. I want to argue that this tension between reality and the imaginary is central to the rape-revenge film and its affective structure.

One notable theory about the female spectator in cognitive film theory is Rikke Schubart's exploration of how a fictional context can offer the spectator a safe(er) context for exploring difficult and dangerous experiences. Schubart discusses horror in film and television fiction as potentially adaptive because it offers the spectator the opportunity to engage challenging emotions in 'painful and potentially traumatizing scenarios' (Schubart 2018: 1). She argues that due to this function, horror can be beneficial especially for women. Horror offers the opportunity to engage what one fears the most, and by doing so perhaps learning to master fear. She compares watching horror to play fighting, and argues that 'horror is a mental form of play fighting and a dark stage [...] especially appealing to women because it can challenge society's gender stereotype and re-author negative gender scripts' (ibid. 4). Indeed, she postulates that 'if women watch less horror and play fight less than men, it is not because women are less active, more empathic, or less aggressive. It is due to the gender stereotype' (ibid. 9). Horror thus offers women the opportunity to do self-work by facing what they fear. Schubart does not discuss the rape-revenge film specifically, but one can again speculate that when engaging with this type of horrific film, the spectator is invited to feel anger and disgust in relation to rape, and rather than seeing the victim blame herself and feel shameful, see a powerful survivor direct her anger where it belongs.

The moral clarity of rape-revenge film stands in stark contrast to the often muddled responses to rape in real life. One explanation for the victim-blaming in real life is that rape poses a fundamental threat to our sense of justice and fairness, and so much so that we tend to blame the victim, as predicted by the Just World Theory.[10] A tendency to want to cling to the belief that the world is essentially just is often discussed as one of the fundamental attributional errors humans make – the Just World Bias. According to this heuristic, there is a tendency to blame the victim in order to reassure oneself that everyone gets their just deserts, and that bad things will not happen to good people. Responses to rape victims is one prominent case study in this line of research.[11] In her autobiography *Know My Name* Chanel Miller describes the shock and pain of reading all the comments online suggesting she was at fault when being

---

[10] See, for example, Lerner and Miller (1978) and Lerner and Simmons (1966).
[11] See, for example, Carli (1999) for one empirical study. See also Vaage (2016: 144ff) for a discussion.

raped on the Stanford campus in 2016 (Miller 2020). These comments are a contemporary example of the widespread tendency to blame the victim. Miller also mentions how her district attorney told her that 'women aren't preferred on juries of rape cases because they're likely to resist empathizing with the victim, insisting *there must be something wrong with her because that would never happen to me*' (Miller 2020: 152, emphasis original). The latter biased reasoning is explained by the Just World Theory. The undiluted horror of the rape experience can be explored more safely within the confines of a fictional context. Perhaps this can explain why there is so much victim-blaming in real life, whereas rape usually fulfils a clearly vilifying function in fiction.

One can thus argue that the potential value of the rape-revenge film lies in the feelings stirred up by the revenge sequences, and that the genre's most radical potential is indeed its affective structure. Women are not supposed to feel rage, and are made to feel shameful and guilty if assaulted, and internalise the blame. Miller again offers a helpful example of this dynamic. When preparing for trial, she is warned by her district attorney not to get angry as she might then sound defensive (ibid. 149). All those online comments to her ongoing, much publicised rape case in the media keep reminding her that many people do blame her. In the cross-examination of her and her sister, Miller discusses how the defence attorney kept trying to poke at any feeling of guilt until he 'found it, hooked into it, injected it, grew it until the guilt was all-consuming. Until we became so inundated by self-blame, so blinded by the pain, we lost the ability to see' (ibid. 186). Miller describes the pain from experiencing this as clarifying, and also a growing anger, all of which gives her strength. As she puts it, '[r]age had arrived to burn the timidness away' (ibid. 222).

The rape-revenge film offers the opportunity to see a woman who has undergone extreme victimisation and humiliation step up and step out of the self-deprecating role assigned to her. She is not feeling guilty or shameful. She is not blaming herself. She typically immediately directs her anger at the guilty party and has her revenge, which in its bodily gruesomeness articulates clearly how painful the initial violation was. Perhaps this is a case where the pure, undiluted affective structure can be more progressive than distancing techniques and questioning of revenge. Indeed, Clover argues that a film such as *I Spit on Your Grave* 'closes all the intellectual doors and windows and leaves us staring at the lex talionis [law of retaliation] unadorned' (Clover 1992: 151). In Clover's analysis, films such as *The Accused* are potentially less powerful because they offer an intellectual exit door when turning to the law for a resolution, an escape from the affective horror of rape as it is experienced by the protagonist. The same could be said of the revisionist rape-revenge film that is often praised to a higher degree in critical reception, perhaps exactly because of the intellectual exit door it provides. The intellectualising efforts of revisionist rape-revenge film may make the film theorist miss out on the full affective force of these films. I will return to these discussions of revisionist rape-revenge film in the final chapter in this book.

Before this, however, I will explore carefully the affective response I have only sketched here: what exactly does it feel like to be staring at the *lex talionis* in dramatic form? This is the topic for the following chapters. In the next chapter I start with punishment, and how enjoyment of punishment is facilitated in fiction.

2. ON PUNISHMENT, FICTION AND FEMININITY

I start narrowing in on the affective force of revenge by exploring punishment. In order to do so, I will take a Scandinavian avenger as a case study. Scandinavian countries are renowned for their humane penal systems. Punishment is downplayed in legal reasoning in favour of rehabilitation: the aim of Scandinavian prisons is to rehabilitate the offenders and successfully reintegrate them into society.[1] In commercial Scandinavian fiction, however, punishment can be quite harsh: in the first film adaptation of Stieg Larsson's Millennium trilogy, Lisbeth Salander takes revenge on her rapist by raping him back. This is an eye-for-an-eye morality far removed from the official consensus of Scandinavian society. The aim of this analysis is not to argue that Scandinavians secretly root for harder punishment in real life. Rather, my starting point is an observation made by Arthur A. Raney (Raney 2005: 151): when we engage with fiction, we as spectators expect over-punishment. I propose that the spectator enjoys excessive punishment more easily when watching fiction.

In order to explore how this is so, I will first look at the rape-avenger Lisbeth Salander in the Swedish film adaptation of Stieg Larsson's trilogy, *The Girl with the Dragon Tattoo* (Niels Arden Oplev, 2009), *The Girl Who Played with Fire* (Daniel Alfredson, 2009) and *The Girl Who Kicked the Hornet's Nest* (Daniel

---

[1] 'Prison is not for punishment in Sweden: we get people into better shape', says the director-general of the Swedish prison and probation service in one interview (James 2014).

Alfredson, 2009). I argue that making the avenger a clearly fictional character facilitates enjoyment of punishment, because the spectator arguably enjoys overpunishment more readily when the character carrying it out is fictional. In the latter half of the chapter I will broaden this analysis and explore how the rape-avenger tends to transform after the rape in ways that could be said to facilitate enjoyment of her revenge, using a few classical rape-revenge films and some contemporary ones made by women directors as examples. The transformed rape-avenger not only facilitates enjoyment of her revenge, but also opens up a fantasy space where the conventional delineation between the feminine and masculine is negotiated, which is what allows her to turn violently punitive.

Punishment in fiction

Perhaps surprisingly, considering that punishment in some form or another features prominently in most commercial fiction, there is not a lot of research on the topic. However, William Flesch offers a relevant explanation for the human interest in narrative, arguing that the punishment of wrongdoers is critical (Flesch 2007). In evolutionary psychology, the dominant view is that human morality evolved in order to facilitate collaboration. Our species developed moral emotions and intuitions to ensure the value of cooperation. One of these moral emotions is righteous anger in response to wrongdoing, which is accompanied by the desire to see the wrongdoer punished and by a feeling of pleasure when witnessing the punishment. Indeed, humans are *altruistic* or *prosocial punishers* who desire to see wrongdoers punished even if no harm has been done to them personally (see, for example, Greene 2013: 57–59, 61, 74).

According to Flesch, the tendency to monitor the behaviour of others to track their display – or lack – of cooperation is essentially what draws us to fiction:

> Human sociality, or the cooperative or altruistic dispositions of most humans, combines these features: we monitor others, tallying the history of their cooperative behaviour; we monitor how others respond or fail to respond to what *they* discover about the history of the cooperative behaviour of their fellows; we are moved to punish defectors, even if they do not harm us, and to reward altruists, even if their altruism doesn't benefit us; and we are moved to approve of others who do punish defectors and reward altruism. Much human emotional life consists in and commits us to these responses to the behaviour of others, and to these emotions, which impel and guarantee that behaviour (Flesch 2007: 127–28).

Thus, our interest in narratives stems from our tendency to want to monitor others, because it is intrinsically interesting to keep track of altruism or its absence, according to Flesch. The gratification of seeing wrongdoers punished is given a central role in this theory, and a critic might reasonably object that this explanation for our interest in all kinds of narratives is flawed, as surely there are stories without punishment. Nevertheless, Flesch's observations may explain our enjoyment of stories with wrongdoing, at least in part. Indeed, in commercial entertainment, there is typically a villain who is punished at the end.

Additionally, much empirical research on a model known as Affective Disposition Theory (ADT) supports the idea that people enjoy stories where wrongdoers are punished and dislike stories where wrongdoers get away with perceived injustices (cf. Raney 2002, 2011; Raney and Bryant 2002; Zillmann 2000; Zillmann and Bryant 1975; Zillmann and Cantor 1977). Yet Raney found one puzzling effect when investigating enjoyment of the so-called justice sequence, defined as 'a series of events that portray the committing of a crime and the ultimate consequences experienced by the offender' (Raney and Bryant 2002: 404). In line with ADT, viewers are expected to enjoy stories where offenders are punished proportionately to the crime they committed, but Raney actually found that

> respondents in the study who enjoyed the drama the most were those who thought that the crime portrayed actually warranted less punishment. Conversely, those who enjoyed the drama the least reported that the villain deserved a greater punishment [. . .]. In other words, viewers of crime dramas might tend to expect and demand (for the sake of enjoyment) a punishment that is greater than what is morally acceptable in reality; only such over-punishment will lead to enjoyment (Raney 2005: 151).

So viewers' enjoyment of justice sequences is not representative of what we would endorse in real life. We want punishment in fiction to be more severe, and we enjoy the story less if it is not.

Why is that so? In his study of violence in film, Henry Bacon points out that punishment used to be a public ritual where the crowd played a central role. Although he warns that 'it is difficult to establish a causal relationship between the decreasing of opportunities to observe real violence in public and the increase of representations of violence in fiction', he suggests that '*representations of executions seem to have the same double function as public executions*: to moralistically impress the people of the mighty arm of law and to give the spectators an experience to be remembered' (Bacon 2015: 19, my emphasis). He ties this to what he labels 'the revenge instinct': we 'might not approve of revenge in real life, but we may nevertheless find it profoundly satisfying when in a story those who have been wronged and humiliated succeed in beating their tormentors – or if someone altruistically punishes them' (ibid. 19). He suggests that punishment in fiction serves as an emotional substitute for public executions of wrongdoers, since modern social systems led to more humane punishment: whereas criminals are punished behind closed doors – or, in Scandinavia, for very good reasons reformed instead – commercial fiction caters to moral emotions, such as righteous anger, and thus offers violent punishment for consumers to enjoy.

However, in spite of Bacon's conclusion that witnessing punishment is intended to impress the onlooker of the power of the law, vigilante avengers are one of the most clear-cut examples of activation of the revenge instinct in fiction, as he also observes. Bacon argues that this is 'one of the most typical narrative patterns in American action films of the past few decades: the ability of the regular law enforcement is seriously flawed and a lonely hero, a vigilante, is needed to punish the baddies' (ibid. 42). He ties this to the characteristically American resentment of government control and points out that 'for one reason or another, law enforcement is not available or is exasperatingly inefficient' (ibid. 42). One thing to keep in mind is the excessive violence of the vigilante's retribution compared to the punishment that would be meted out by law enforcement, even in the United States. One explanation for the absence of the law in the vigilante narrative may be that it offers the spectator the pleasures of an especially violent punishment.

This suggests an intriguing link between punishment in fiction and in real life – indeed, that fiction has perhaps taken over the function public punishment once had.[2] This retributive feature of human nature is not new, as the discourse on media violence sometimes seems to imply, a point to which I will return in the following chapter. What is new is that punishment in real life has increasingly turned less corporeal and violent, which many of us of course believe is a good thing. It is better to explore the revenge instinct in fiction.

Bacon sees the vigilante avenger as typically American because 'it is difficult to think of another film culture which would have produced even in proportional terms so many films in this theme', yet he also recognises that 'the appeal is universal' (ibid. 43). I think he is right to point to the vigilante's cross-cultural appeal. Although it might be that it is in American film culture that the vigilante has proliferated most prominently, in the transnational exchange of tropes, cycles, genres and narrative patterns among film cultures, the avenger is also found on the other side of the Atlantic Ocean, in Scandinavia.

Blending realism and the fantastic: Lisbeth Salander of the Millennium trilogy

Scandinavian crime fiction and film culture are traditionally by and large dominated by realism. Steven Peacock ties Swedish crime fiction to the 'fractured

---

[2] The role played by social media in terms of public punishment is an intriguing, huge question that is beyond the scope of my project.

dream of the welfare state' and maintains that the 'Swedishness' of Swedish crime fiction is to be found in its verisimilitude and realism (Peacock 2014: 3, 16). Quoting Peter Cowie, he links this to the national film culture, which from the 1960s was dominated by realist aesthetics: 'Fantasy took second place to a jarring grainy realism that sought to use film if not quite as agit-prop then certainly as an essay form, a vehicle for comment on injustice and corruption' (Cowie quoted in Peacock 2014: 42). Paula Arvas and Andrew Nestingen point out that Scandinavian crime fiction often criticises social behaviour, national institutions and gender politics, and is gloomy, pensive and pessimistic. They argue that 'combined in the Scandinavian crime novel [these factors] form a unique constellation' (Arvas and Nestingen 2011: 2). This gloomy mood is probably what made British critics label Scandinavian crime series Nordic Noir (see, for example, Agger 2016). One central topic in Swedish crime fiction is the character who suffers injustice and inequality at the hands of corrupt representatives of the welfare state.

Whereas the Millennium trilogy (both the novels and the film adaptations) is characterised by realism in many ways, it also goes beyond realism in its portrayal of Lisbeth in particular. Lisbeth embodies the failings of the Swedish welfare state in that she has been subjected to years of abuse by its officials (for example, she is subject to false imprisonment both in a psychiatric ward as a child and in prison as an adult, declared incapable of managing her own affairs, and raped by her legally appointed guardian). Lisbeth is a victim: disempowered, humiliated and insignificant in the view of the corrupt powers that be. However, she is also so much more than this. Lisbeth's story intriguingly draws on international film culture.

Rikke Schubart maps the female action hero in popular cinema and singles out five female archetypes. One of these is the rape-avenger (Schubart 2007).[3] The first instalment of the Millennium trilogy is effectively a rape-revenge story. Lisbeth is raped twice by her legal guardian Nils Bjurman and takes revenge on him not by killing him but by brutally raping him back and then tattooing 'I'm a sadist pig and a rapist' on his stomach. The spectator later learns that this is not the first time Lisbeth has taken the law into her own hands; as a twelve-year-old child she threw gasoline on her violent father and set him ablaze to prevent him from physically and sexually abusing her mother. Lisbeth is avenging both her own rape and that of her mother. Although Bjurman is not killed (by Lisbeth), she does kill another serial rapist and murderer, Martin Vanger. Lisbeth could save him but instead watches him burn to death. She

---

[3] There are rape-revenge films to be found in a Scandinavian context before this too, such as *Thriller: A Cruel Picture* (Bo Arne Vibenius, 1973), and, as mentioned already, Ingmar Bergman's *The Virgin Spring* (1960), where a father avenges the rape and death of his daughter, is also discussed as an early rape-revenge film.

Figure 2.1 'He was a pig who hated women', says Lisbeth the avenger (*The Girl with the Dragon Tattoo*, 2009).

is scolded for this by her partner, the journalist Michael Blomkvist, who tries to argue that Vanger was a victim of horrible circumstances – most especially, a father who was himself a serial rapist and killer, and who taught Vanger to participate in his crimes from the age of sixteen. Lisbeth, however, brushes this aside and hisses back at Blomkvist to stop talking about victims: Vanger had a choice, as does everyone, and the reason for his behaviour was simply that he was a pig who hated women (Figure 2.1). In this discussion, Blomkvist voices the official Scandinavian view, calling attention to the effects of Vanger's upbringing and thus suggesting that he too should be helped. Lisbeth's response is one of righteous anger and vindictiveness, typical of a violent avenger. Their discussion is an explicit articulation of the clash between the vengeful Lisbeth and a reasoned, normative view articulated by Blomkvist.

The Millennium trilogy is a changing mix of genres that includes aspects of detective, thriller, fantasy and espionage novels and films.[4] Notably, Lisbeth is a composite character borrowing from all these genres, and evokes clearly fictional associations. In the second instalment Lisbeth breaks free from the constraints of realism. When she tracks down her father, Zalachenko, who is at the root of all of her problems, the story about her transforms into an action film. The portrayal of Lisbeth in the Swedish adaptation of the trilogy (for example, her black clothes and her hard, muscular body) arguably derives from Hollywood female action heroines. Philippa Gates maintains that whereas the Swedish film began an '"internationalisation process" of the character of Salander by enacting many mainstream (that is, Hollywood) tropes', the 'American [remake of the first instalment by David Fincher] pushed Salander firmly into the role of superhero and action babe' (Gates 2013: 210–11).

[4] See, for example, Fister (2013); Leffler (2013); and O'Donoghue (2013).

However, Gates overlooks the many action heroine elements present already in the original Swedish novels, which refer abundantly to fiction film whenever Lisbeth takes centre stage. For instance, when she decides to find her father: 'She was talking to herself. And in a voice she had heard once in a film, she said: *Daaaaddyyyy, I'm coming to get yoooou*' (Larsson 2015: 498).

Indeed, Lisbeth recalls the Daughter, another of the female archetypes identified by Schubart in popular cinema, whose prototype is found in *La Femme Nikita* (Luc Besson, 1990) and its American remake *Point of No Return* (John Badham, 1993). Although transgressive and violent, the main character learns to use her feminine attributes as assets, thus transforming from a girl with a 'wrong' masculinity to an acceptable, conventionally feminine woman. Lisbeth's debt to the Daughter archetype, as well as her deviation from it, is apparent in her transformation at the end of the first instalment. Here Lisbeth masquerades as Irene Nesser, taking on a traditionally feminine persona to travel internationally and put her hacker skills to use in a massive con operation that leaves her a billionaire. But contrary to forerunners such as Nikita, Lisbeth only transforms externally. She knowingly masquerades as Nesser.[5] When she returns to Sweden with a fat savings account, her blonde wig, high heels and designer miniskirt are gone, and the old Lisbeth in her black hoodie and skinny jeans is back; she has not really changed in the way that Nikita changes.

In many ways, Lisbeth epitomises the action heroine, playfully taking up a number of conventions in the wave of action films with strong, violent female characters in the 1980s and 1990s, a trend to which I will return in Chapter 6. As Jeffrey A. Brown points out, one of the distinguishing conventions of the action heroine in film is her relationship to her father (Brown 2011: 76). Schubart also explores how the Daughter's strength stems either from her relationship to her father, on whom she has had to rely excessively, or from masculine qualities that are the result of fending for herself in a distorted upbringing (Schubart 2007: 210). Lisbeth's strength can indeed be tied to her troubled childhood and to her father, who takes on the monstrous features of the super-villain in this story. He even shoots his own daughter several times and buries her (alive, as it turns out). It is when Lisbeth faces her father and his ally, Lisbeth's half-brother Niedermann, that the trilogy is most similar to action film.

Niedermann brings to mind 1980s and 90s action heroes, especially those of Arnold Schwarzenegger, most prominently in the *Terminator* films. Niedermann is a blond giant, presented as an almost robot-like fighting machine; he has a neurological disorder rendering him incapable of feeling pain. Lisbeth's

---

[5] Similar to Schubart's claim that the Daughter stereotype does not subvert traditional gender roles is the often ambivalent reception of Lisbeth among feminists. See, for example, the essays collected in King and Smith (2012). For a discussion of masquerading female characters as subversive, see Brown (2011: 20).

strength is presented as biologically related to this villain and his equally evil father. Perhaps it is this kinship that enables her to rise from the grave in which her father has dumped her and, as the last survivor, or Final Girl, of the horror film, seek out the monsters for a final confrontation (cf. Clover 1992). Half-dead from numerous injuries, she attacks her father with an axe in a sequence that is far removed from sober, politically minded social critique: this is the Millennium trilogy turned slasher film. Even in the novel, she is described as looking 'like something from a horror film' (Larsson 2015: 560). Indeed, in the novel (but not the film), the fictional elements are carried one step further in Niedermann's distorted vision of the seething Lisbeth, covered in her own blood and dirt, as a vicious mythological creature:

> the creature on the floor was no girl, but a being that had come back from the other side of the grave who could not be conquered with human strength or weapons known to man.
>
> The transformation from human being to corpse had already begun. Her skin had changed into a lizard-like armour. Her bared teeth were piercing spikes for ripping chunks of meat from her prey. Her reptilian tongue shot out and flicked around her mouth. Her bloody hands had razor-sharp claws ten centimetres long. He could see her eyes glowing. He could hear her growling low and saw her tense her muscles to pounce at his throat.
>
> *He saw clearly that she had a tail that curled and ominously began to whip the floor.* (Larsson 2015: 561, emphasis original)

In addition to action and slasher film motifs, the story also draws on other genres and conventions. Lisbeth alludes to Pippi Longstocking, for example, a popular Swedish child superhero with superhuman powers – she can even lift a horse! There are direct references to the Longstocking stories in the trilogy. For example, when Lisbeth buys a luxury flat under a false name, the doorbell says V. Kulla; Pippi's house is Villa Kulla. Additionally, the characterisation of Lisbeth borrows from the countercultural hacker chick of science fiction film as well as the first feminist private investigators, models of 'independence and resistance', as Barbara Fister argues (Fister 2013: 42; see also Bergman 2012 and Povlsen and Waade 2009). In sum, Lisbeth's characterisation, even in the novels and the Swedish adaptations, draws on myriad conventions from a range of fictional genres, such as rape-revenge, action, slasher, as well as science fiction and crime stories.

These fictional conventions stand in contrast to the realism typical of Swedish crime fiction. The trilogy as a whole can be said to be a work of social realism, and makes claims to truth as social realism typically does (Vaage 2017). For example, the Millennium trilogy is a critique of the welfare state, revealing its corruption and, in particular, doing so in its focus on violence toward women in contemporary Swedish society. Yet in spite of the critical edge of this trilogy, its fictionality is flaunted through the character Lisbeth. The range of allusions to clearly fictional genres constitutes a self-reflexive element through which this work advertises its status as fiction. Thus, the spectator is encouraged to enjoy the extreme retribution for which Lisbeth is responsible: fictionality is what supplies a licence to do so.

LISBETH SALANDER AS A FICTIONAL RELIEF

However, we are still in need of an explanation: why is it important to make the avenger undeniably fictional in this context? Perhaps it is because when viewers engage with a story that they know is fiction, they rely heavily on moral intuitions and emotions and bracket the principled moral reasoning they feel obliged to make use of in real life (Vaage 2013, 2016).

The theoretical backdrop to the point I am making here is the commonly held view in cognitive film theory that there is a difference in the communicative act of a non-fiction and fiction film respectively: when we watch a non-fiction film, we are invited to believe what we see, to accept it as truth claims about the world, whereas a fiction film invites imaginings. The model can be labelled an intention-response approach to fiction and non-fiction (see, for example, Carroll 1997; Currie 1990; Plantinga 1987, 1997). I have expanded on this model in previous work, teasing out how the difference is also relevant morally and affectively (Vaage 2013, 2015, 2016). Indeed, even within the huge category of fiction film there are important differences between genres, for example between social realism and fantasy (Vaage 2017). When watching a fantasy film, for example, spectators do not tend to question magical turn of events as unrealistic, as they pick up on an intention to depict a storyworld that is quite different from the real world. This is very different from the way one engages with social realism in film, where any magical turn of events would be deemed inappropriate and unrealistic. My use of the notion 'realism' in this discussion should thus be read as related to 'social realism' (see, for example, Hallam and Marshment 2000), and the main point is how a fiction film's categorisation as either fantasy or social realism (to take two very different genres) will cause a distinct attitude on the part of the spectator.[6] Specifically, I argue that the spectator is probably willing to bracket more real-life beliefs, including moral principles, to a greater extent when engaging with

---

[6] Film studies sources drawing on psychoanalysis may emphasise that fantasy is not opposed to realism, see, for example, Horeck (2004: 4–5). But drawing on an intention-response model of fiction, I argue that various types of fiction do invite distinctly different types of engagement.

fantasy than when engaging with a work of social realism, and even more so when compared to a non-fiction film. So the question of fictionality is central when considering the spectator's ongoing moral evaluation of characters and events in a film.

Furthermore, according to the so-called dual-process model of morality in moral psychology, there are two routes a moral evaluation can take: a quick-and-dirty intuitive route and a slower and more cognitively demanding route forged through rational deliberation (see, for example, Greene 2013; Haidt 2012). I suggest that when engaging with works neatly categorised as fiction, people rely heavily on the intuitive route. Indeed, the difference between moral evaluation in real life and in relation to fictional stories is emphasised by revenge stories such as the Millennium trilogy. Whereas the majority of Scandinavians support the humane penal system in principle, in fiction, perhaps, they allow themselves to be stirred to righteous anger against the wrongdoer and to enjoy punishment in the subsequent justice sequences. Making the avenger a clearly fictional character facilitates enjoyment of severe punishment. Lisbeth constitutes what I elsewhere label a *fictional relief*: fictional elements that relieve spectators of the obligation to evaluate rationally, allowing them instead to rely on moral intuitions and emotions (Vaage 2013, 2016).

These might not be moral emotions of which we are particularly proud. The relative lack of literature on antipathy towards the villain in stories and the enjoyment of punishment of such characters, as compared to the literature on sympathy for the hero, is one indication that this is an aspect of our emotional engagement with fiction that we are not keen to acknowledge.[7] Carol Clover makes a related point in her discussion of rape-revenge films such as *I Spit on Your Grave* (Meir Zarchi, 1978), reminding us 'that lots and lots of the movies and television dramas that we prefer to think of in higher terms are in fact funded by impulses we would rather deny' (Clover 1992: 151). As discussed in the previous chapter, she suggests that *I Spit on Your Grave* forces us to face these impulses. Stripped down to its grim two-part structure, this classic rape-revenge film viscerally exposes the horror of rape and the protagonist's retaliation. Another way to put this is that it is difficult to escape from extreme emotions and intuitions, such as the pleasure of witnessing violent punishment, when watching rape-revenge films. Thus rape-revenge films likely confront the spectator with intuitions and impulses ordinarily unacknowledged or denied.

---

[7] See, for example, Smith (1995) for a classical account, concentrating on sympathy for the hero but also including antipathy for villains, and also Carroll (2008: 182–4). Kjeldgaard-Christiansen's work on villainy (2016, 2019; Kjeldegaard-Christiansen et al. 2021) are some notable recent exceptions. I also discuss strong feelings of disgust and antipathy towards rapist villains elsewhere (Vaage 2015, 2016: 120–49).

Claire Henry agrees in her discussion of *The Girl with the Dragon Tattoo* that this film encourages enjoyment of Lisbeth's revenge (Henry 2013). However, she is critical of this feature of the film, and argues that we should not take up this specific invitation (ibid. 176–7). The film should ideally have induced ethical reflection rather than encouraging us to take pleasure in her revenge. Such ethical reflection would be what she discusses as ethical spectatorship, which is to take a reflective attitude to what we see and to question its moral nature. Films ought to encourage ethical spectatorship in Henry's view, but *The Girl with the Dragon Tattoo* does so only to a very limited extent, she argues. And it is Lisbeth's revenge in particular that Henry finds problematic, because the spectator is encouraged to accept the rape-revenge convention (or moral framework) that violent revenge is deserved. She cites Michelle Aaron here, an influential film theorist who works in a Brechtian tradition: films should try to distance (or alienate) the spectator in some form or another, and by doing so, encourage us to reflect on what we are seeing rather than merely being caught up in it emotionally (Aaron 2007). I will return to Henry's account, and the theoretical framework offered by Aaron, in Chapter 7, where we will see that this vein of theory is labelled estrangement theory by Carl Plantinga due to its emphasis on the necessity of distancing the spectator from emotional immersion in film and encourage critical reflection (Plantinga 2018). This is the ideal spectator position discussed in relation to this film as ethical spectatorship.

In opposition to this, there is moral spectatorship, which in Henry's account is described as emotionally reassuring or intuitive. Moral spectatorship is encouraged when the film suggests we can allow ourselves to let go, to go along with it, such as when enjoying Lisbeth's revenge. And Henry argues that this film does slip into moral spectatorship rather than making us stay in the much more troubling, reflective position of ethical spectatorship. Henry backs up this claim through careful analysis of both the rape of Lisbeth and her ensuing revenge rape (ibid. 187–8). An array of filmic techniques is used to mirror how Lisbeth was raped in the very same room, thus reminding us of the horror of having witnessed this and making us root for Lisbeth's revenge in what Henry discusses as a perverse allegiance, running counter to what we would normally see as morally good or right (cf. Smith 1999). This prevents ethical spectatorship, allowing us to stay in moral spectatorship mode in her analysis (ibid. 189–90). She also argues that it is problematic that this film portrays revenge as the victim's responsibility: this is part of a post-feminist, anti-victimisation ideology which is deeply problematic in nature, she holds (ibid. 178–9).

I agree with Henry that the first instalment of this trilogy encourages enjoyment of Lisbeth's revenge. However, the aim of this book is to contest the idea that this moral spectatorship – as she labels it – is necessarily wrong or less valuable. I also disagree that the lone avenger should be read as an expression of individual responsibility.⁸ Henry underestimates how Lisbeth's revenge is a social critique: Lisbeth only takes the law into her own hands because she has repeatedly been let down by the law and its representatives. She has no reason to trust the law. It is unavailable to her. This is the fundamental political critique in the Millennium trilogy – it is no mere celebration of the strong individual enacting revenge. Moreover, in addition to this, I am going to argue that the gist of the rape-revenge film is that the female rape-avenger embodies vindictive anger, and that as such, its affective structure is at the very core of its political potential. She is a representation of an emotion, and a representation eliciting an emotion, that can have an important function personally, culturally and politically, as I will explore in Chapter 4. Henry and I thus agree that the film elicits moral spectatorship (sticking to her vocabulary), but I am going to argue that this can be valuable. And at the very least, a reader who is sceptical of this claim should agree that we need to understand what moral spectatorship is before critiquing it. The point I want to make in this chapter is that we need to understand our enjoyment of punishment in fiction to a greater extent rather than merely denying and condemning it.⁹

The transformation of the rape-avenger

We have seen how enjoyment of punishment is facilitated by fictional conventions in the Millennium trilogy. Indeed, I will now argue that making the avenger a clearly fictional character is a convention in rape-revenge film, and in this second half of this chapter I will explore this convention. Lisbeth's flaunting of fictionality can be said to be typical of the rape-avenger. After the rape sequence the rape-avenger typically goes through a transformation before, or as, she emerges as a violent avenger. This can be done either by referencing other fiction films, or by making use of magic, clearly fantastic or seemingly mythological features. There is not one set trope of transformation in the

---

⁸ For a careful discussion of representation of rape and individualism, see also Projansky (2001). She criticises many rape narratives (what she labels post-feminist rape narratives) for portraying rape as individualised crimes and women as empowered when overcoming that individual rape. However, in her analysis of *Thelma and Louise* (Ridley Scott, 1991) as a rape-revenge film, she denies that this film falls into this category of post-feminist rape narrative because it represents rape as pervasive and tied to a toxic culture of male harassment, and also rape law as ineffectual – she sees this as feminist potential in this particular rape-revenge film (ibid. 121ff). The point I am making about *The Girl with the Dragon Tattoo* is similar. See also Clover's discussion of responsibility in the rape-revenge film (Clover 1992: 143).

⁹ Many thanks to Nancy Easterlin for numerous helpful comments and suggestions on an earlier version of this part of the chapter, which included an analysis of Eli in *Let The Right One In*, published in *Poetics Today* (Vaage 2019).

rape-revenge film. She changes, but this can be portrayed in different ways. In her analysis of *I Spit on Your Grave* Barbara Creed points out that after the gang-rape sequences, the narrative takes an unrealistic turn as the protagonist Jennifer appears near mythological as avenger. Jennifer takes a religious pledge before setting out on her revenge mission. Creed observes how each death is portrayed like a ritual, with Jennifer wearing white robes, appearing like a priestess. Furthermore, as Jennifer transforms to this otherworldly figure, she also takes on superhuman powers:

> Jennifer's revenge is terrible, exact and executed in perfect style. She is transformed from a friendly, likeable but ordinary woman into a deadly and powerful killer. There is no suggestion that she will fail in the execution of her plans. From the moment she picks up her gun, dresses in black and asks God for forgiveness for what she is about to do, we know she – like the hero of the western – will hunt down each man and wipe him from the face of the earth. Filled with a terrible but perfectly justifiable wrath, Jennifer becomes [...] all-powerful, all-destructive, deadly (Creed 1993: 129)

This portrayal of Jennifer's change can be said to establish as a convention that the protagonist goes through some kind of transformation after the rape, suddenly rendering her a highly skilled killer, executing her revenge perfectly and without hesitation: she has transformed into an all-powerful avenger, as if by magic.

However, Henry notes about this change that 'the closer Jennifer moves to myth, the further she moves from our identification' (Henry 2014: 48). She sees this as a way of distancing the spectator from her revenge. Contrary to this I argue that the transformation the rape survivor often undergoes in rape-revenge film serves to help her step out of the painful confines of realism after the rape and facilitate engagement with her. Indeed, in her discussion of female action heroes, Lisa Purse points out that powerful female characters appear most frequently in films with a fantastical setting, thus setting 'the potentially culturally disturbing possibility of female agency and physical power at a distance from our everyday contemporary reality' (Purse 2011: 81). I explore Purse's account in more detail in Chapter 6. The important point here is that the female avenger is about to break radically with acceptable female behaviour, so she transforms, as in the classical example of *I Spit on Your Grave*, into a larger-than-life, clearly fictional character to secure sympathy with her – making her so clearly fictional, almost mythological, is a way of making it easier for the spectator to enjoy her violent revenge.[10]

---

[10] For an overview of related points made about *Thelma and Louise*, see Projansky's literature review of the 'fantasmatic identification' invited by the film (Projansky 2001: 148ff).

The protagonist's transformation evokes a clearly fictional attitude – a fictional relief – reassuring the spectator that there is no need to fully consider the consequences of what it is one sees, such as the consequences and many pitfalls of vigilante justice in real life. Few would probably condone such violent retribution in principle, and there are many good, rational reasons why we should not. However, in this clearly fictional context, we can allow ourselves to enjoy watching revenge. Thus the protagonist transforms to allow these feelings and desires for revenge to emerge. My analysis here is arguably an expansion of the observation made by Creed and others about the rape-avenger's transformation, and more importantly, an explanation for this effect – what it is that makes the revenge sequences feel more like fantasy, and what difference it makes for the spectator's engagement.

The transformation as fantasy space and inversion of conventional femininity

The transformation of a female character is a well-known trope in various film genres. Yvonne Tasker discusses the transformation often found in action films, comparing it to the established convention of the make-over of the male bodybuilder, where physical change signals a new status. When female characters take centre stage in action film, Tasker observes that this character often takes on conventional masculine features such as a muscular appearance 'in order to function effectively within the threatening, macho world of the action picture' (Tasker 1993: 149). One example where this very transformation is portrayed is the change Sarah Connor goes through towards the end of *The Terminator* (James Cameron, 1984), coming into full fruition in *Terminator 2: Judgement Day* (James Cameron, 1991). In the first Terminator film, Sarah is presented in the opening of the film as a conventionally feminine waitress at work in a peach dress, and playfully getting ready on a Friday evening in front of the mirror with her housemate. Inexplicably, someone seems to be after her, and she is in need of male help to escape the danger. When she learns that a killing machine sent back from the future is hell-bent on 'terminating' her in order to stop her from giving birth to a boy who will later be the leader of mankind in a fight against the machines, she needs to change, and at the end of the film she has stepped into the role of a soldier, no longer incapacitated by fear but fully prepared to fight to the death to save her son (ibid. 138). Sarah Connor transforms into an action heroine, and the first glimpse the spectator gets of her in the sequel is a close-up shot of her sweaty, muscular arms as she is doing pull-ups in a cell in a psychiatric ward. When she turns around to face the camera, her long, unkempt hair and aggressive stare at the hospital doctors signal her new, hard fighter persona, far removed from the soft femininity with which she was first introduced.

Tasker discusses how the two main characters in the rape-revenge film *Thelma and Louise* also transform from conventionally feminine women at the beginning of the film, neatly made-up with red lipstick and Thelma donning a summer dress, to avengers free from make-up and dressed in dirty dungarees and white T-shirts. As they try to make it to Mexico in order to escape conviction for killing Thelma's rapist, they turn more relaxed, shedding conventional femininity as they become more independent and active. As Sharon Willis points out in her discussion of this film, their body language – their posture, gait and gestures – also change (Willis 1993: 127).

Indeed, the transformation trope is found in many rape-revenge films. A recent example is found in *Revenge* (Coralie Fargeat, 2017). Jen is flown into the desert on a helicopter in order to spend a weekend with her rich boyfriend Richard in a luxury house in the middle of nowhere. However, it turns out that they are not alone – two of Richard's friends also show up in order to join him hunting. The following day Jen is raped by one of them. When Richard finds out what has happened, rather than feeling outrage and empathy with her, he quickly tries to cover it up by offering to set her up as an actress by drawing on some of his powerful contacts (clearly stirring up associations to the Harvey Weinstein scandal). When she disagrees, a quarrel ensues and as she is trying to escape Richard pushes her off a cliff. She falls on a dead tree, one of its branches penetrating her stomach and leaving her hanging there, seemingly dead. Realistically she would have died there, but like a zombie she awakens, and from there on the film leaves realism behind. While still stuck to the tree, she manages to light a fire in order to burn it down while she escapes unharmed from the flames. The three men are now looking for her, and she has to kill each of the men in order to make it out of the desert alive. She drags herself unseen into a cave, where she magically heals her wounds overnight in a drug-induced trance from chewing peyote.

Notably, Jen's appearance is changing. Jen's 'before' is girlish (Figure 2.2). She is wearing pastels and white, as in the skimpy white dress she wears the night before the rape, when the group of four get drunk and where she is dancing temptingly with the man who later rapes her. After she emerges from the cave, she is wearing only a sports-bra and briefs, both of which are black. She is holding a rifle, and around her shoulders are draped an ammo belt and a pair of binoculars, which she took after her first killing (Figure 2.3). The avenger Jen has changed from youthful, hyperfeminine seductress to action heroine, resembling Lisbeth the avenger and action heroines such as Sarah Connor. Becoming a warrior, taking on conventionally masculine features such as physical strength, reflected in both her clothing and her body language, allows the female avenger to emerge as omnipotent, a character in full control and with near superhuman powers. The avenger's revenge is secured when she

Figure 2.2 Jen before the transformation into an avenger (*Revenge*, 2017).

Figure 2.3 Jen after the transformation into an avenger (*Revenge*, 2017).

is in this powerful state: she does not hesitate, she shows little fear, grief or trauma. All of a sudden, she is a fighter, determined, focused and strong as she hunts the rapist(s) down.

This transformation is similar to the ones discussed by Tasker in the action film. In her now black outfit and battle-ready appearance, she has changed into an action heroine figure, looking more like Lara Croft in *Tomb Raider* (Simon West, 2001) than the young seductress from before the rape. The camera is circling around her, slowly mapping her entire body from her feet up. It is muddied and bloody from multiple cuts and wounds, her hair and eyes also darker. The chase for the rapist, and finally, also her treacherous boyfriend, can begin, and it is excessively bloody, as analysed by Patricia Pisters (2020: 37ff). The one remnant of her former persona as she is chasing barefoot through the desert is a pink star earring she is still wearing.

However, although her resemblance to the action heroine can explain her strength and determination, there is more to the rape-avenger's transformation. Take for example the way the avenger Jen is revealed to us, the camera circling around her, mapping her scantily clad body. As observed by Peter Lehman and others, the revenge is often eroticised in rape-revenge film (1993). Indeed, Jacinda Read points out that rather than being masculinised, the rape-avenger is often eroticised (Read 2000: 35). She argues that the rape-avenger should be seen as closely related to other eroticised, transgressive women in a historically specific cycle of erotic thriller and neo-noir films, such as *Basic Instinct* (Paul Verhoeven, 1992). She points out that the characters labelled as fatal femmes and the rape-avenger are typically portrayed by actresses widely celebrated for their beauty. The characters they play transform into deadly but irresistible femme fatale figures.

Notably, Read argues that what is offered by this female character is 'the fantasy of being conventionally feminine and strong' (Read 2000: 49). In her analysis, it is therefore essential that the female avenger is living out a contradiction experienced by many women as they try to make sense of femininity and feminism (as articulated in statements such as 'I'm not feminist, but ...') (ibid. 6–7). The avenger is living out one version of this very contradiction, as she refuses to live in fear, or to succumb to a position as passive victim, and refuses to get back in place (ibid. 33). Read points out that this is why feminist theorists like herself are drawn to the figure. She is critical of accounts where this aspect of the avenger is left unexplored, such as when Clover only emphasises the avenger's masculine features. Read thus argues that to understand the female avenger the feminine must be put back into play: this is the way to begin to explore how rape-revenge film is popular culture making sense of femininity and feminism, opening up a space for negotiation (ibid. 8–12). Thus it is of central importance to note that the female avenger's strength in this fantasy space not only stems from masculine features, but is also from what is conventionally feminine.

In order to examine how and why this is so, it is helpful to turn to the transformation of female characters in more conventionally feminine spheres. In her study of the transformation of female characters, Tamar Jeffers McDonald points out that although also found in thrillers, neo-noir and war film, the transformation trope is most commonly found in genres traditionally associated with female audiences such as romantic comedy and melodrama (Jeffers McDonald 2010: 8–9). Although Jeffers McDonald concentrates on romcoms and melodramas – which at first sight might seem worlds apart from the horror film, the action film and rape-revenge film – her study will be helpful in considering the implications of the rape-avenger's change. Whereas the action heroine is often conceptualised as stepping into a masculine sphere, Jeffers McDonald's study will help me articulate what is at stake in terms of conventional femininity.

Jeffers McDonald maps the tropes commonly used in the transformation of the female protagonist, which she argues are remarkably consistent across time (ibid. 39). A typical example that she starts with is *Date Movie* (Aaron Seltzer and Jason Friedberg, 2006), in which the protagonist Julia has to change in order to find a man to love her. She needs to be rendered beautiful, and is transformed from an alleged overweight woman in a baggy sweater and flowery skirt to a slim woman dressed in a classy black tight-fitting dress and high heels. The transformation has the function of making her desirable to men, and is often depicted as taking place in a fantasy zone, emphasised through use of montage sequences for example (ibid. 42, 70). The transformed character who emerges is the beautiful and graceful woman she probably was all along, her true self that was hidden behind her glasses and unflattering clothes (ibid. 82ff).

The rape-avenger can put the transformation of the female protagonist in romcoms and melodramas into play in a number of ways. She can wilfully masquerade as the conventionally attractive woman, the seductress, in order to get revenge, as in *Ms. 45* (Abel Ferrara, 1981), a film I will go on to discuss in detail. But she can also leave the conventions of femininity behind altogether, as Thelma and Louise increasingly do. Either way, whether making deceptive use of conventional femininity or discarding it completely, the rape-avenger emerges like its dark shadow. The transformation can be completely inverted in the rape-revenge story. The transformation is used in order to celebrate conventional femininity in the films analysed by Jeffers McDonald: these female characters typically move from being undesirable (to men) to desirable. But the rape-avenger changes from a woman who is desired, which is portrayed as leading to violation, to a woman who openly scorns any and all conventions of femininity and desirability.

Mary-Anne Doane points out that the transformation of the woman is often the moment the character takes off her glasses: look, lo and behold, she has been beautiful all along, and we, the audience, and they, the other characters in the fiction, see it now (Doane 1982). Doane discusses the glasses as representing the power to look, and this is what is now removed, in a sequence in which the woman emerges as passive, as someone to be looked at, in line with filmic conventions. By transforming, the female protagonist can thus be said to conform both to conventional femininity and filmic conventions – turning into an object to be desired rather than someone who acts and looks. Again, the rape-avenger can be said to be an inversion of this: it is as if she angrily puts her glasses back on, symbolically speaking, and by doing so she insists on the right to turn radically active and to control the gaze.

Ms. 45 is an interesting case in point. The protagonist Thana is portrayed in the beginning of the film as an overly shy, mousy low-level worker in a fashion house in New York. The city is filled to the brim with male creeps – the men we see are either catcalling tormentors lining the streets, hurling obscenities at all passing women, men who sexually harass such as her sleazy boss, or actual rapists or would-be-rapists. Thana is raped twice at gunpoint, first by a stranger in a back alley on her way home from work and then immediately following this by a burglar in her flat whom she walks in on. She kills the latter and chops up the dead body in pieces she disposes of throughout the city. It is after this that Thana starts transforming.

Thana's 'before' persona is very proper, dressed in a long, wide skirt, a white blouse and flat black comfortable shoes (Figure 2.4). She wears no make-up, and moves around in the world timidly, almost apologetically. The actress portraying Thana (Zoë Lund) was only nineteen when the film was made, and Thana appears with childlike innocence. She starts changing visually only after she shoots a man who runs after her as she is disposing of a plastic bag with a piece of the dead rapist. Killing her pursuer with the rapist's gun seems empowering. The next day we see her going to work wearing a black beret, bright red blouse, a more figure-formed skirt and high-heeled black boots. After shooting another man, who pretends to be a photographer in order to convince Thana to come back to his studio with him for some wine and a 'photo shoot', we see Thana apply heavy make-up in a long close-up shot reminiscent of make-over sequences in the films Jeffers McDonald discusses. She has emphasised her eyes with black eyeliner and is now applying a thick layer of shiny, bright red lipstick. Similar sequences are also found in action films, such as in *La Femme Nikita*, previously discussed in relation to the Daughter archetype, in which Nikita is portrayed as slowly applying lipstick in front of a mirror, just as Thana is doing here.[11] Brown discusses Nikita as masquerading womanliness in this film in order to become an effective killer: she is trained to feign conventional femininity so as to use it strategically to lure men (Brown 2011: 22ff). Thana is similarly masquerading to punish men. Thana's clothing continues to change, making her at first look sophisticated, elegant and confidently glamorous, with the flat shoes replaced by black pumps and her waistline highlighted by a black belt, and increasingly also raunchy when she sports tight-fitting black latex pants. Thana's body language is also changing from timid to confident: where the old Thana seemed always to avert her gaze when talking to people, the new Thana confidently holds the gaze of the men about to die (Figure 2.5).

---

[11] Adding to the rich film historical connotations of Thana's transformation, in her discussion of this film as a women's cult film, Alexandra Heller-Nicholas discusses Thana's transformation as one into a femme fatale (Heller-Nicholas 2017: 64). Heller-Nicholas discusses many interesting features of this film that I cannot include here, such as the significance of Thana's muteness (ibid. 46).

Figure 2.4 Thana before her transformation (*Ms. 45*, 1981).

Figure 2.5 Thana after her transformation (*Ms. 45*, 1981).

She goes on a vigilante killing spree in the city, similar to the father's revenge of his daughter's rape in *Death Wish* (Michael Winner, 1974), also taking place in New York-turned-lawless frontier. Thana explores this dark city space at night-time, performing what could be said to be a catalogue of actions women are standardly told to avoid: she gets into a stranger's car (who of course pays with his life for the assumption that she is a sex worker). She ventures into a park at night soon to be surrounded by four menacing men, circling her like a pack of predators. They are all shot. It is as if Thana is mocking all advice to women on how to keep safe: she was, after all, only on her way back from work in the afternoon, and simply locking herself into her own home, when she was raped. Being a good girl did not keep her safe. Now Thana is breaking all the rules, walking the city streets like an avenging angel. Towards the end she is also wearing a long, black hooded cape that makes her look like a character in a fairy tale.[12] Thana's transformation from shy, young girl dressed in white and soft colours to enraged avenger dressed in black, all illusions lost, is in many ways an archetype for the rape-avenger's transformation.

Such an archetypal female avenger is seen more recently in *Game of Thrones* (David Benioff and D. B. Weiss, 2011–19), for example, where Sansa Stark changes in a similar way over the course of eight seasons. In the beginning she is a blue-eyed young girl dutifully working on her embroideries and dreaming of marrying a handsome prince, embodying the very essence of conventional femininity (see also Larsson 2016: 31). In the end she has changed to a darkly clad woman who finally unleashes punishment on one of her tormentors after years of abuse and rape.[13] Arguably, the long duration of a television series can make her revenge all the more satisfying, as the pain of witnessing her suffering has been going on for so much longer.[14]

But let us stick to the analysis of Thana here. The degree to which Thana's transformation resembles typical cases discussed by Jeffers McDonald is striking. Her analysis of Sandy in *Grease* (Randal Kleiser, 1978) is a good example for comparison. As Jeffers McDonald observes, Sandy is at first portrayed as a stereotypical 'good girl' or pure maiden, with a blonde bob, pastel dresses and ankle socks. After a quarrel with her boyfriend Danny, Sandy approaches her friend Frenchy for help. A transformation that the spectator is not privy to ensues after which Sandy's new 'raunchy-looking vamp' persona, with 'curly perm, skin-tight black trousers, off the shoulder top and red high heels' emerges as a surprise both to Danny, his friends and to the audience (Jeffers McDonald 2010: 53). Jeffers McDonald describes her transformation as one which makes her look sexually experienced, indicating to Danny that she is now willing to go 'all the way', as he has wanted. These signifiers of desirability are thus tied to sexual experience, preparedness and availability. Sandy's transformation is one from 'prude to vixen' (ibid. 54). In a similar way, Thana is transformed

---

[12] Thana is punished at the end when she starts gunning down all the guests at a Halloween party. However, this ending is not my main interest here.

[13] Published before this final season, see also Gjelsvik (2016) for a general discussion of the portrayal of rape in *Game of Thrones*.

[14] This is in line with my reasoning elsewhere in writing about the strong emotional response to television series because of their long duration (Blanchet and Vaage 2012; Vaage 2016).

to sexually alluring woman through use of make-up and black, more revealing clothing and high heels. However, in this rape-revenge context, this change is used to lure men to their death. This is a mere display facilitating her revenge against whomever takes her willingness and availability for granted.

In the romcom and melodrama, the transformed protagonist's desirability is clearly what is at stake. The rape-revenge film can very much be said to show the dark side of the woman as desired object. Here, the male gaze as objectifying is taken to its extreme in the rape sequence where the man insists on his right to have her, to fully dominate her. She is near eradicated as a subject, and truly reduced to an object, a body to be used by him against her will. Because the woman as desirable is the crux of these films, the focus on desirability is often maintained in the revenge, as it is in *Ms. 45*. Thana is increasingly portrayed as conventionally attractive and this exterior enables her eroticised revenge: she uses this mask in order to ensnare men as they all make assumptions about her availability. So, in contrast to a film such as *Grease*, in which the transformed woman-as-vixen is celebrated as a woman finding her form and revealing her true self, which is attractive to men and therefore to be emulated by women in the audience, as argued by Jeffers McDonald, Thana takes on a similar appearance as sexually liberated seductress, with its connotations of sexual agency and status, but only in order to punish men. Whereas the transformation in romcoms and melodramas is often a making-clear of her true self rather than make-over, the rape-avenger's transformation should not be read as a similar revelation of her true self.[15] The transformation takes on a critical edge: this is not Thana as sexually experienced, racy vixen, qualities somehow released in her by the trauma of rape – an obscene point that I hope may seem obvious to most readers. The transformation is rather used as a tool: she takes up the role as seductress in order to get revenge. As the violation represented male insistence on femininity as complete subordination, and male agency as total control, so the rape-avenger uses the conventions of femininity in order to turn the tables – the man is fooled by her appearance but punished for his assumptions about her availability. She makes herself conventionally desirable in order to communicate that she is still in control of her body, not him.

Thana's transformation thus makes reference to the well-known trope of transformation in romcoms and melodramas. By doing so, its fictional nature

---

[15] Projansky discusses how some rape stories can portray rape as a painful but ultimately positive event that brings out latent feminist views and independence in a woman, and analyses this as one of the problematic features of rape stories as post-feminist liberation narrative (Projansky 2001: 100–1). Here I argue that the films I explore – which are not the same ones she examines – should not be read as liberation narratives in this sense. She does discuss the feminist potential in some rape stories that I also discuss, namely in *Thelma and Louise* and some rape-revenge films. I return to her account in the last chapter.

is emphasised through intertextual awareness, and connotations to conventional femininity and its signifiers are also explicitly evoked. In *Revenge*, Jen's transformation resonates both with the transformation in action film, and with the transformation tropes discussed by Jeffers McDonald. In the film's opening, Jen is already highly desirable from a conventional point of view: this is a portrayal of a very young, beautiful blonde 'babe' with a body like a model, which she shows off willingly, thus fully embodying the conventional feminine ideal of desirability. She knows that men desire her and she uses this in order to flirt with her powerful, wealthy, handsome and fit boyfriend, who is also married and older than her. Although in her mind she is showing off for him, she is unaware or unconcerned about also being desperately desired by his two much more ordinary-looking friends.[16] Her clothing is girlish yet her behaviour explicitly sexual, thus making her for some men a porn-style sexual fantasy, which is inaccessible to most of them. Elements of the biblical story about Adam and Eve are used to portray her as the original temptress: in this undisturbed wilderness, a seeming paradise, Jen is innocently eating an apple when the two friends arrive. She represents the temptation, and rape – knowing a body intimately against a woman's will – the original sin.

We have seen that desirability and the role this plays in conventional femininity is very much at stake in the rape-revenge film. In *Revenge* too the rape-avenger continues to be excessively eroticised, as in the continued focus on her body and in particular her buttocks, praised in the beginning of the film by her boyfriend, touched against her will by the rapist, and often in the centre of the framing in the revenge sequences: this film does not hide the fact that this is a battle over Jen's body as sexually attractive, but rather insists on it. Her transformation is used in order to emphasise this, serving as a link between this convention in conventionally feminine romcoms and melodramas and the female character's transformation in the context of traditional masculine genres such as action, horror, slasher and Westerns.

In Jeffers McDonald's discussion, the transformation is typically a fantasy space, and in the rape-revenge film, a transformation is used in order to move the entire remainder of the film to a realm of fantasy. The rape survivor's transformation represents a fictional relief, inviting the spectator to unleash intuitions and emotions relating to punishment and revenge. Her transformation into a clearly fictional figure also puts the conventional delineation between what is masculine and feminine into play: the implications and limits of conventional femininity are explored in this critical space. Moving far

---

[16] In contrast to the blond boyfriend, the dark hair and dark eyes of these two friends, one of whom is the rapist, can be read as a racialisation, as in Tanya Horeck's discussion of the rapist Cliff 'Scorpion' Albrecht's 'swarthy complexion' in *The Accused* (Jonathan Kaplan, 1988) (Horeck 2004: 103). I discuss race further in Chapter 5.

beyond acceptable femininity, indeed, beyond what most would see as normatively and morally acceptable, the revenge sequence should rightly be seen as a revenge fantasy where the rape survivor leaves her conventional self behind, and her new shadow self emerges as pure vindictive anger.

I have shown how a key trope in rape-revenge film historically is the avenger's transformation, and how this is maintained in a recent rape-revenge film made by a woman. However, some other contemporary rape-revenge films made by women break with this convention by sticking more closely to realism. In line with my argument here, maintaining realism in the revenge sequences can arguably be used to problematise revenge. One such example is *Violation* (Madeleine Sims-Fewer and Dusty Mannicelli, 2020). The rape sequence is the violation of a close relationship, as the protagonist Miriam is raped by her sister's partner Dylan late at night as they sleep outside after having enjoyed a nice summer evening by the fire, getting merrily drunk together while the sister is sleeping. Miriam only wakes up as Dylan is raping her, and her shocked response telling him to stop ('Don't. Stop') is interpreted by Dylan as encouragement ('Don't stop'), or so he claims. Miriam later confronts Dylan, who laughs it off, insisting that she wanted it, in spite of her attempts at explaining that she really did not. Miriam then turns into an avenger, seemingly to get revenge but also perhaps to protect her sister, but without any difference in appearance or any other clear-cut change in her characterisation. Miriam pretends that she wants to have sex with him, seduces him and attacks him only after he is undressed and placed on a chair, waiting for her with an erection. However, what is starkly different in this rape-revenge film is that the revenge sequence sticks to realism, in the sense that Miriam has not transformed and does not take on the all-powerful characteristics Jennifer and Jen did. She responds in an altogether human way to killing a fellow human being and mutilating his dead body to hide the crime. After the seduction a nerve-rackingly prolonged fight between the two emerges. It is nothing like the neatly choreographed Hollywood fight scene, but the naturally clumsy movements of two people who are not trained to fight. Having finally got the upper hand, she straps him up by his ankles, and slits his throat in order to drain the blood from the body. However, Miriam is overwhelmed by disgust at doing so, and in a nauseating long sequence we see her retching and throwing up several times next to his naked body, hanging there from the ceiling as blood is draining from it. Miriam is standing on her hands and knees, groaning like an animal in severe distress and pain. This is probably what it would look like if one tried to take revenge on a rapist by killing him. And notably, watching Miriam's revenge is not very pleasurable: the visceral, bodily horror she is going through arguably prevents enjoyment.

Another example of greater realism in the revenge sequences is found in *Monster* (Patty Jenkins, 2003) in its focus on how the urge to take violent revenge is part of post-traumatic stress.[17] The protagonist Aileen is portrayed as a severely traumatised woman, facing a lifetime of abuse, first as a child who was sexually abused by a friend of her father's, physically abused by her father for attempting to tell him what was going on, and then as a sex worker from the age of thirteen. We see one of her customers turning violent on her and raping her in a graphic rape sequence, from which she makes it alive only because she gets hold of a gun and shoots him in self-defence. This spurs a killing spree where she kills men who pick her up for sex. However, Aileen's revenge never feels liberating or pleasurable to watch, arguably because of the film's realism throughout and also because Aileen is portrayed as terrified when acting it out: she is having flashbacks to the rape, dreading that the man presently in her car is about to turn violent on her. The revenge sequences invite empathy with Aileen, urging the spectator to feel the pain she is in, rather than enjoyment of the revenge.

I want to argue that these revenge sequences can serve to illustrate just how important it is that the avenger is cut off from reality for very violent revenge to be fully enjoyed: just as revenge is nauseating or terrifying for Miriam and Aileen, realism can take the pleasure out of revenge for the spectator. In some recent rape-revenge made by women filmmakers there is thus a careful negotiation of the realism in the revenge sequences, portraying them as painful rather than pleasurable.

Yet one of the most pleasurable revenge sequences in a film that can also be characterised as social realism is perhaps found in *Stella Does Tricks* (Coky Giedroyc, 1996). The teenage protagonist Stella has been sexually abused by her father in her hometown Glasgow, and she has run away to London. In the opening of the film we find her there with her pimp Mr Peters, who exploits and abuses her. This film explores fantasy sequences as Stella's imagination, into which Stella disappears in order to cope, and the film is as such a complex mix between realism and fantasy, and a clear break with the tradition of social realism in British film (Brunsdon 2000; Murray 2015). Stella's memories and fantasies are blended, giving careful access to Stella's state of mind as she keeps being retraumatised by sexual abuse and betrayal, using her imagination to process her ordeals, and as an escape. Mr Peters picks up on how her dreams and her fantasies serve as a site of resistance for Stella, affording her a sense of agency in an unbearable situation. He carefully manipulates her hopes and dreams as he understands that this is the way to control her.

---

[17] This film is based on a true story, where Jenkins used trial documents, documentaries and also private letters written by Aileen Wuornos, who was sentenced to death for the murder of seven men (Aitkenhead 2004). Knowing this context will probably also greatly affect the spectator's engagement.

The film's oscillation between realism and fantasy can perhaps be said to activate a fictional relief when watching the revenge sequences, where Stella actually takes revenge, and not just in her imagination. But importantly, the spectator has been made to witness the abuse of Stella. In the opening, Stella masturbates her middle-aged pimp in a park in London in broad daylight, with Stella dressed up as a young girl with pig tails, while he holds her ice cream, asking her to tell her about her dreams as she does so – and ordering her to lick clean her hands afterwards. This is only the first of several sequences where his abuse of her is made clear, culminating in how the spectator is made to witness the gang rape of Stella that he has orchestrated – and is watching – when she tries to break with him. The violence we witness in relation to Stella's abuse will evoke strong responses, especially because Stella is so young. This will arguably also allow spectators to enjoy her revenge more. Finally, Stella's revenge is less violent than most revenge sequences in rape-revenge film: she blows up the car of a man who raped her friend, she tips the police off on Mr Peters's paedophilia so that he is arrested, and she sets her father's crotch ablaze. As rape-avengers go, Stella's revenge is not very violent. In *Stella Does Tricks* the portrayal of abuse and rape of this young protagonist, in combination with her relatively speaking less brutal revenge on her abusers, secures enjoyment of Stella's revenge in spite of the film's realism.

Fantasy and clearly fictional elements are thus used to secure enjoyment of revenge in many rape-revenge films, but witnessing rape can also stir up a strong desire to see the rapist(s) punished even within a framework of realism. This brings us yet again back to the desire to see wrongdoers punished. Indeed, the desire to see wrongdoing punished can be remarkably strong, and in order to get clarity on the affective nature of watching revenge sequences, in the next chapter I turn to revenge.

3. ON REVENGE: RAPE-REVENGE STORYLINES AND THE EVOLUTIONARY ORIGIN OF PAYBACK

Revenge has played an important role in the arts from antiquity until today, and is at the very core of the rape-revenge film. It is striking, and a good starting point in this chapter, to observe that many an account of revenge in philosophy and psychology, and also discussions of honour – a notion intrinsically tied to revenge that I will also explore – typically either start or end with the observation that portrayals of honourable revenge in fiction are not only prevalent, but massively popular. For example, Tamler Sommers starts by asking who your favourite character is in *The Godfather* (Francis Ford Coppola, 1972) as an introduction to his book about honour (Sommers 2009). Susan Jacoby discusses *Death Wish* (Michael Winner, 1974) in the introduction to her book about revenge (Jacoby 1983). Jeffrie G. Murphy also points to the popularity of revenge entertainment, such as *Silverado* (Lawrence Kasdan, 1985) (Murphy 2003: 21). Peter A. French takes vengeance in the Western film as his main case study, using various films such as *The Searchers* (John Ford, 1956) as examples throughout his book on revenge (French 2001). It seems difficult to deny that portrayals of revenge in fiction are so prominent because they are appealing.

Yet, in spite of the prevalence of revenge in fiction, the view on revenge in real life in Western societies is probably first and foremost characterised by disreputation. Indeed, accounts of revenge typically at some stage encourage us at the very least to acknowledge this desire, and, in Nico H. Frijda's words for example, 'find ways to deal with desire for revenge beyond denying or condemning its existence' (Frijda 1994: 286). The link from revenge to justice is denied by many (French 2001: x), and revenge is seen as the very antithesis of civilised justice. Indeed, Jacoby starts her book on revenge by discussing what she labels the revenge taboo (Jacoby 1983: 1–13). But in her analysis of contemporary portrayals of revenge in fiction, she also points to the tendency for revenge to be glorified: modern avengers are not typically tragic figures, and the stories they appear in not cautionary tales, as in earlier dramas (ibid. 54, 174). These stories, she argues, are an indication that something is askew in the rigid justice vs revenge dichotomy (ibid. 178). There is a conflict between the idealised and glorified image of the avenger in mass entertainment and the revenge taboo:

> The powerful appeal of the revenge theme in mass entertainment is simply one more manifestation of the gap between private feelings about revenge and the public pretense that justice and vengeance have nothing, perish the uncivilized thought, to do with each other. (Jacoby 1983: 8)

She ends her book by urging us to stop dismissing the 'legitimate aspects of the human need for retribution' which would make us 'more vulnerable to the illegitimate, murderous, wild impulses that always lie beneath the surface of civilization' (ibid. 362). She makes a case for continuity between revenge and modern law, and she explores carefully how the desire for revenge was curtailed in the historical development from private revenge to public, third-party punishers in modern jurisdiction due to the need for more reliable forms of punishment.

In this chapter I explore revenge, and elaborate on what its functions have been, evolutionarily and historically speaking. I hold that this is relevant to an exploration of our feelings about what is just, without thereby arguing that revenge in real life is legitimate. Indeed, the move to impartial third-party punishers was an attempt to control the violent excesses of the human desire for revenge, and the many pitfalls in the psychology of human beings, including our biases and prejudices, as we shall see. There are good reasons not to trust the human urge to take revenge in real life – but equally so, there are good reasons for us to explore and understand vindictive feelings and the reasons they tend to be stirred up by fiction. I start with an overview of theories on the origin and evolution of revenge, and in particular paying attention to the reasons it fell out of favour.

An introduction to revenge

The desire for revenge is intrinsically tied to the propensity to punish. Sommers observes that 'every known culture features retribution in some form' (Sommers 2009: 37). As discussed in the previous chapter, a commonly shared hypothesis in moral psychology is that this is because it enhances evolutionary fitness: punishing wrongdoers enhances cooperation, so humans have evolved moral feelings to secure willingness to punish.

Yet, due to the disreputation of revenge, theories about its nature would typically include a rebuttal of the view that revenge is intrinsically irrational. Murphy, for example, argues that in order to understand vengeance, defined as 'infliction of suffering on a person in order to satisfy vindictive emotions or passions [...] felt by victims toward those who have wronged them' (Murphy 2003: 17), we need to understand the values to which it is tied: self-respect, self-defence and respect for the moral order. He proposes that 'resentment stand[s] as emotional testimony that we care about ourselves and our rights' (ibid. 19), an idea that is shared with philosophers defending anger, as we shall see in the next chapter.

French also sees revenge as tied to a person's self-respect, which he discusses in terms of honour (French 2001: 63–4, 93, 142). He draws on Jon Elster's discussion of norms of revenge in seeing honour as key to understanding revenge (Elster 1990). French argues that revenge cannot be understood without including the concept of honour, which, along with other seemingly archaic notions to which vengeance belongs, has almost been washed out of the Western moral lexicon. Nevertheless, arguably strong feelings of honour are stirred up by revenge narratives, suggesting that affronts to a person's self, their integrity and self-respect, still easily whip many spectators into a state of vengefulness. It is thus worth dwelling on this notion of honour.

French shows how honour is mirrored by shame, and shares some of the same characteristics (French 2001: 147). Whereas transgressions of moral codes or laws would trigger feelings of guilt, shame is a feeling of inadequacy or inferiority, tied to unwanted exposure of weakness. Feelings of shame make a person want to conceal or mask themselves: shame might trigger an identity crisis, or a disappearance of the sense of self. Defending one's honour is to avoid shame in this sense, and insist on one's right to self-respect. In other cultures, contemporary or historically, we find fully fledged honour cultures, in which vengeance is typically socially sanctioned – indeed, it might be mandatory for a person who suffers unwanted exposure of weakness to strike back at the offender, as we shall see. So there can be public honour in honour cultures, and revenge often takes centre stage in such cultures. Central to the function of revenge is to restore one's sense of personal honour – one's self-respect – in the face of experiences that are perceived as shameful and a threat to one's self.

Frijda also sees revenge as tied to restoration of damage to self-esteem, and argues that revenge can be seen as functional for humans in several ways. He points out that our desire for revenge evolved in order to stabilise society and secure cooperation in that the mere threat of revenge in response to a moral trespass might deter the trespasser in the first place. Frijda sums up five levels of gains yielded by revenge, namely deterrence, restoration of equality in suffering and gains, restoration of equality of power, restoration of one's sense of self and relief from pain. He sums up the main function of revenge as annulling power inequality. Humans are concerned about what he labels the law of comparative suffering: we compare our suffering to the suffering or well-being of others, and this affects how we perceive our own situation (Frijda 1994: 274). Revenge seeks to take away what is perceived as an offender's gain at the victim's expense. The wrongdoer is seen as having gained something, either tangible or non-tangible, illegitimately, perhaps in terms of increasing their own pleasure by inflicting pain on others, or profiting financially or otherwise from their wrongdoing. Revenge serves the function of annulling these gains by either inflicting pain, or extracting a fee from the wrongdoer, or whatever else might balance out the offender's gains. All of this might serve to alleviate the victim's pain by ensuring that the offender's gains are forcefully taken away. Revenge also serves as a power equaliser in the sense that it restores the victim's self-esteem and self-efficacy, easing the victim's feeling of powerlessness and helplessness, which is a cornerstone in stress theory, Frijda writes (ibid. 275).

David P. Barash and Judith Eve Lipton explain well how this is so. They explore the biochemical hardwired basis for what they discuss as redirected aggression, i.e. our tendency to seek retaliation or revenge – payback, in one word. Physiologically, payback first and foremost serves to alleviate subordination stress, that is, stress resulting from being socially subordinate. Being at the very bottom of the pecking order is a very unpleasant, and thus undesirable, state to be in (Barash and Lipton 2011: 17, 48ff). Blood pressure goes up, adrenaline levels increase, while hormones giving us a sense of well-being decrease. Whereas the hormonal response to stress is adaptive and helpful in the short term – increasing one's level of adrenaline, for example, in order to promote the will to fight – they point out that long-term effects of being in a state of subordination stress, for example from domestic conflicts or workplace subordination, is very harmful. Indeed, they sum up research demonstrating that 'prolonged stress can result in hypertension, lowered sex hormone levels, reduced immune responses, and autoimmune reactions' (ibid. 48).[1] The negative effects of subordination stress is why we are hardwired to redirect aggression, as they put it: by passing the pain of subordination on to someone else, the other will have to deal with the negative effects of subordination stress and I will feel better. This is the biochemical reason that revenge apparently is sweet: biochemically, meting out revenge will be perceived as more pleasurable than the painful experience of subordination stress.

---

[1] See also Maté (2019) for a related discussion of the adverse effect of stress on immune health, and repression of anger and autoimmune disease, affecting women more than men.

However, Barash and Lipton certainly do not endorse this tendency: their goal is to explain why payback seems so appealing, hoping that by understanding the phenomenon better we might realise that although it may have been biologically and socially adaptive, 'injuring and diminishing those around us' is a 'misguided' strategy (ibid. 52). In current studies, there is one line of empirical research on revenge in which the negative consequences of revenge are emphasised (for example, Carlsmith, Wilson and Gilbert 2008). Other studies find a mixture of both negative and positive consequences of revenge, where a positive consequence is seen as hedonic reward and a negative consequence would be lack of such reward, i.e. whether or not revenge makes us feel good (for example, Eadeh, Peak and Lambert 2017). The studies find conflicting responses to revenge, including both positive and negative feelings.

However, I will not examine this research in detail here: the question of whether enacting revenge in real life would actually make us feel good is not central to my exploration. I do not argue that the rape-revenge film is a recipe for us to follow in response to rape. Mine is a smaller project: I want to explore its affective qualities and what might be offered by this revenge fantasy. Indeed, in the next two chapters I explore how its main affective response is one of vindictive anger, an emotion that is generally considered a negative, not a positive, emotion, but one that might nevertheless have a function. What I am suggesting here, which is in line with the current research on vengeance, is that there is a sweetness to revenge – in the spur of the moment there is enjoyment of it – probably for evolutionary reasons: just as we have evolved a taste for sweet foodstuff because it gave us energy when resources were limited, we have evolved a taste for punishment. That does not mean that we should uncritically embrace the conclusion that enacting revenge is thereby healthy, any less so than a diet of sweet treats, or that it makes us feel all but good after consumption of either sweet food or a bloody revenge story.

The aforementioned theorists agree that evolutionarily speaking, revenge has served a function, and this is why humans have developed a taste for it. Frijda argues that the urge to take revenge served as a regulator in societies without central justice (Frijda 1994: 270). Whereas people in Western societies would now like to think that they have left this violent urge behind (see, for example, French 2001: x), scholars exploring revenge would typically emphasise the continuity between the law in contemporary society and this primordial vengeful urge. For example, Barash and Lipton argue that the legal system and our idea of justice satisfy the desire for revenge in a socially acceptable setting (Barash and Lipton 2011: 155). Punishment meted out by impartial third-party punishers is still redirected aggression, only shared rather than personal. Jacoby also argues that the law is legalised revenge (Jacoby 1983: 115). Mapping the historical evolution of revenge/justice, she explains how we have moved the response to wrongdoing from the private to the public sphere, and by doing so from norms of revenge to the law of third-party punishers.

Drawing on Hubert Treston, Marvin Henberg lays out various stages of retributive practices: from unrestricted blood feud between warring nomadic clans, to the adoption of strict retaliation or proportionality, such as in the *lex talionis*, to monetary compensation in lieu of exact retaliation, to a fourth stage in which wrongdoing is seen as a crime against the state, over and above private wrongs against individuals, and in which only state authorities are sanctioned to punish wrongdoers (Henberg 1990: 60–1). The first step in the development of retribution is that only exact, identical or mirroring punishment is sanctioned. We might now read the relevant passages in Exodus in the Bible as condoning surprisingly harsh punishment, but in its historical context the passage instructing us that 'if harm follows, then you shall give life for life, eye for eye, tooth for tooth, hand for hand, foot for foot, burn for burn, wound for wound, stripe for stripe' was actually a way of curtailing revenge – to limit it. The correct way to read this passage is that as punishment for an eye, you shall not take *more* than an eye.[2] Introducing the idea of proportionality in punishment was a way of making punishment more reliable, and also limiting punishment, as Jacoby argues (Jacoby 1983: 118, 129). Frijda also points out how the Law of Talion, or *lex talionis*, should be considered a major advance in lawfulness, and that 'curtailing personal vengeance is considered to be one of the major general sources of criminal law' (Frijda 1994: 264). The evolution of justice is a history of containing our vindictive impulses not just by prohibiting private revenge but also limiting public revenge through proportionality (Jacoby 1983: 139).

The transition to modern jurisdiction is not the topic of this book. What is more interesting in this context is the gendered aspect of the history of, and representation of, revenge. Jacoby discusses how in Aeschylus' *Oresteia* trilogy the vengeful passions manifest themselves as the female Furies, seen as an embodiment of the savage revenge instinct from tribal culture, needed to be reined in by the powerful male god Apollo (somewhat paradoxically, as violent revenge was a male prerogative in tribal culture, and not a duty typically carried out by women, a topic to which I will turn shortly). Jacoby argues that in these early literary sources, 'religious and social order are firmly linked to male power' (Jacoby 1983: 76). The transition from tribal revenge to justice is thus gendered. Another central female avenger in early fiction is Euripides' eponymous Medea. In revenge for her husband's betrayal when he leaves her for a younger woman, she kills his new bride as well as their own two sons. Jacoby denies the common conception that this play's portrayal of its female

---

[2] However, as William Ian Miller argues, one should not overdo this interpretation, as it is clearly also stated that neither should you take less than an eye (Miller 2006: 21).

avenger is misogynistic. Euripides is actually demonstrating that this is what is to be expected in a system where women are at a grave disadvantage and where there is no system in place to redress their grievances, she argues (ibid. 24–5). Jacoby discusses the distress that this female avenger evokes:

> the occasional appearance of an openly vengeful woman – like any rebel from a group without access to conventional power – carries enormous symbolic importance. It stimulates fear on the part of those in authority that others will follow the example of the avenger. Men tend to regard a woman who carries out an act of violent revenge as a kind of miner's canary, a warning of the suppressed rage that may lie beneath the surface of the good mother, good daughter, and good wife. (Jacoby 1983: 207)

A woman's revenge is therefore especially troublesome culturally.

Indeed, French also argues that masculine vengeance has enjoyed higher status in Western fiction than feminine vengeance, and points to the portrayal of the Furies too and their low status as feminine avengers of kinship murders and crimes of blood (French 2001: 15ff, 34, 61). He also makes a similar point to the one Jacoby makes about Medea. She is portrayed as a woman 'with nowhere to turn for redress but to her own murderous resources', and a character who 'plays on the terror the audience no doubt experiences from witnessing the lengths to which the disenfranchised, vengeance-minded female can go to rectify her perception of injustice' (ibid. 18). He argues that this very feature is taken as a model for later female avengers in Western films, such as *Hannie Caulder* (Burt Kennedy, 1971), a rape-revenge Western film he discusses.

Revenge in the rape-revenge film

What is interesting about rape-revenge film – indeed, about any vigilante story – is that it returns to other retributive practices in Western cultural history. The law is typically absent in rape-revenge film. This is indeed part of the attraction of any vigilante film, as Peter Robson points out in his study of the vigilante on-screen: the 'essence of the modern vigilante film is to pose questions about the nature of justice in a much clearer way than occurs in the traditional courtroom drama but in the context of a thriller. What we get is the revenge motif [...]' (Robson 2016: 175). As such, the vigilante figure can be said to highlight the 'problematic and contingent nature of legality' (ibid. 168). Robson is, however, more ambivalent about the rape-revenge film specifically, as compared to the other vigilante films he discusses, and he argues that whereas there is 'an ambivalent and shifting stance in relation to the justice system' in vigilante films generally, in rape-revenge films specifically the justice system is simply assumed to be irrelevant (ibid. 184). He ends up implying that what I discuss as revisionist rape-revenge films, drawing on Claire Henry's analysis (Henry 2014), are less problematic because their relationship to revenge is more ambivalent. We have seen that this observation about the complete absence or inability of the law in rape-revenge films has been made by others too – by Carol Clover, for example, who points to the 'nervous relationship to third-party dispute settlement' in the rape-revenge film (Clover 1992: 123).

Sometimes this is presented as an explicit critique of the inability of the law in Western societies to protect rape survivors, as in *Thelma and Louise* (Ridley Scott, 1991): Louise shoots the man raping her friend Thelma, and when Thelma argues that they should go to the police, Louise points out that plenty of people saw Thelma dance flirtatiously with the man and drink heavily – these will be seen as reasons not to believe their claim that Louise fired that gun to stop a rape. Statistically speaking, Louise is probably right: it is statistically unlikely that Thelma's rapist would be convicted, and Louise's killing him may not pass as defence of her friend. It is hinted in the film that Louise has prior experience with this – referred to as something that happened to her in Texas, which is the reason she refuses to set foot in Texas ever again – so Louise's firing that gun can also be seen as delayed revenge for her own ordeal.[3] So here, the law is explicitly portrayed as unavailable to the two women, and this is the reason they turn into outlaws.

The inability of the law to convict rapists can be said to be a backdrop to the rape-avenger's taking the law into her own hands in other rape-revenge films as well, even when this is not articulated explicitly. Sometimes turning to the law just is not an option, as in *Revenge* (Coralie Fargeat, 2017) where the three men will finish off Jen in the vast uninhabited desert unless she kills them first. Or, as in the rape-revenge Western film *Hannie Caulder*, there is no effectual law on the frontier, and she has to fend for herself. So the law is typically either unavailable or unable to help the rape survivor in rape-revenge film, and thus she reverts to revenge, as an ancient route to power equalisation.

The rape-revenge film is indebted to the Western film in this sense. As argued by Will Wright, a dominant theme in many Western films is indeed revenge, a variation he discusses as the vengeance tradition (Wright 1975).[4] French also discusses some of these Western films in detail in his book. Sometimes the Western film is cited reflexively in rape-revenge film, such as in the use of the desert landscape in *Thelma and Louise* and similarly also in *Revenge*

---

[3] See also Alison Young's discussion of this film (2010: 59).
[4] See also Read's discussion of the permutations of rape-revenge films with female avengers and the vengeance tradition in Western films (Read 2000: 125ff), and Heller-Nicholas's exploration of rape-revenge Westerns (Heller-Nicholas 2011: 69ff).

Figure 3.1 Thelma and Louise in the desert landscape of the Western (*Thelma and Louise*, 1991)

(Figure 3.1).[5] The lawlessness of the frontier is also portrayed in other cultural contexts, such as in the Australian post-colonial rape-revenge film *The Nightingale*, where an Irish lower-class woman and an Indigenous Australian woman both suffer repeated rapes at the hands of British officials. Although this film thus uses the frontier for a historically situated political critique of colonialism, the frontier and the wilderness also evoke associations to epics about human nature and what it is like beyond the reach of civilisation.

The rape-avenger is sometimes placed directly into this landscape, although at other times it is the big city that is portrayed as the frontier, just as lawless as the Wild West, sometimes even explicitly so, such as in *Death Wish* where the male avenger's killings make numerous newspaper headlines in which the city's lawlessness is framed as the new frontier, or less explicitly in *Ms. 45* (Abel Ferrara, 1981), where the protagonist experiences repeated assault and harassment on the streets of New York. The frontier, the wilderness or the big city are all portrayed as lawless, and this is what initiates the tale about revenge as a thought experiment in the rape-revenge film: how would one want to respond to this violation in the absence of the law? The rape-avengers, as the heroes in Western films, cannot rely on anyone but themselves for justice.

It is interesting to dwell on the revenge sequences in rape-revenge film in order to tease out what they implicitly reveal about rape as a violation. As will be remembered from the first two chapters, Clover argues that the rape-revenge film confronts the spectator with the *lex talionis* – indeed, that it relentlessly makes them stare at this law of retaliation unadorned. David Andrews also argues that the extreme violence of the revenge in rape-revenge film communicates the special nature of rape (Andrews 2012). He discusses the rape-revenge

---

[5] See, for example, Man (1993) for a discussion of this aspect of *Thelma and Louise*.

film in light of evolutionary theory, and emphasises the evolutionary costs of rape to female victims: it is a violation of the social structure allowing women to choose the male they bond and have children with, thus violating her ability to exercise agency and consent. He points out that 'the enormous pain of rape is predicted by sexual-selection theory', and that the special-ness of rape from the female point of view is emphasised in the horrific dual structure of the rape-revenge film (ibid. n.p.).[6] This is in line with Barbara Creed's observation that the rape-revenge film represents epitomised horror for the female audience, as discussed in the first chapter in this book.[7] Evolutionarily speaking, rape is destabilising both for the woman who is raped, her offspring and the group to which she belongs.

To see the rape-revenge film as representing *lex talionis* makes sense of the often eroticised features of revenge in rape-revenge films, as often observed in the literature: the rapist(s) is killed, but often only after he or they have been subject to prolonged pain and humiliation, often of a sexual nature (for example, castration or rape). As the rape victim was humiliated in the most fundamental sense, so should the rapist be. Andrews points out that torture porn imagery may be used to convey the special-ness of rape, and argues that 'reciprocal cruelty allows an avenger to teach a rapist what it feels like to be raped' (Andrews 2012, n.p.).

The extreme violence of the revenge thus casts light on what rape is and what it feels like. Sometimes this is literally the case, as in Lisbeth Salander's raping the rapist back, as explored in the previous chapter. Other times this is portrayed symbolically, as in the original *I Spit on Your Grave* (Meir Zarchi, 1978), where one of the rapists is castrated with a knife just as Jennifer performs fellatio on him in a bathtub where they are both bathing naked. In *Revenge*, the three men die but not before they have all symbolically been penetrated: the first one dies from a knife stabbed into his eyeball, a symbolic punishment for having walked in on the rape, understanding what is happening but doing nothing. He loses an eye, and then his life, for what he saw. The rapist tries to flee from Jen but steps on a glass splinter piercing his foot, and his bloodied attempt at digging it out of his flesh is portrayed in a lengthy close-up shot, truly lingering on the pain of having a foreign body perforate one's own body. It is Jen's own arm that penetrates Richard's stomach as she

---

[6] One problematic feature of Andrews's discussion is his uncritical inclusion of the rape adaptation hypothesis. Andrews does not explicitly support it, but remains agnostic. For a damning critique of the rape adaptation hypothesis, see Eva Dadlez et al. (2009).

[7] Evolutionary accounts of rape may seem completely at odds with feminist approaches, but see Vandermassen (2011) for a careful discussion of how the two approaches may be unified.

punches him hard in a shotgun wound she inflicted in the final battle between the two, as they chase after one another in a veritable bloodbath in the house where the rape took place. Richard's betrayal must literally have been felt by Jen as the ultimate punch in the gut.

However, the rape-avenger's punishment does not only portray sexualised torture and violence as a fitting punishment for rape. She also kills her rapist(s), and sometimes she only kills them, as Thana does in *Ms. 45*. Simply inflicting pain on the rapist is not portrayed as sufficient punishment in these films. He typically has to die. Why does he have to die, when her life has not been taken? One may be tempted to say that this makes Clover and Andrews wrong when claiming that the punishment in these films is talionic in principle: her revenge goes further than an eye for an eye. One explanation could potentially be that this is fiction: as discussed in Chapter 2, Raney found that we often expect overpunishment in fiction in order to enjoy the story. In this fictional context, the emotive nature of rape seems to call for the strongest punishment there is: death.

However, when considering the revenge sequences as symbolic representations, as pure revenge fantasy, one can also argue that one part of her has been violated so badly that it has been eradicated – the carefree, girlish, trusting part of Jen and Thelma perhaps. As Susan Brison writes in her philosophical reflection on her own experience of rape and attempted murder while on holiday in France, in its aftermath she kept wanting to say that she died last year in France (Brison 2002: xi). Nancy Venable Raine makes the same point in her autobiographical book about rape: that she died on the day a stranger attacked and raped her in her own home, and 'another person was born that day' (Raine 1999: 2). In the previous chapter I pointed out that the rape-avenger typically transforms: as she retaliates, it is as if her shadow self, enraged and dangerous, takes control. Whoever she was before the rape is gone – perhaps to return when justice has been served, though we would not know as rape-revenge films typically leave her as soon as the revenge has been completed. Sometimes she dies, as in *Ms. 45* and *Thelma and Louise*, as if reintegration of this new self into conventional society is simply impossible. One could argue that the rape has shattered her self. There has been a death of *a* self, and revenge allows another self to emerge. This new self sees the rapist's death as an entirely appropriate punishment. In the rape-revenge film it is thus typically conveyed that this is what it would take to restore her self-esteem and self-respect. This is how painful the rape was. In order for her to regain her sense of self-worth and avoid feeling shame, he has to die.

Furthermore, I want to argue that the fact that the woman who was raped is the one who punishes in rape-revenge film is of central importance, not just for these films as morality tales, but also to their affective structure and not least of all for their controversial nature. In order to get to the bottom of this controversy, we need to turn to the role played by honour in revenge.

Honour and revenge

We saw that French and Elster propose that revenge only makes sense in a framework of honour. The idea that honour serves an important function as a motivator, which pushes humans to truly care about and act on moral rules and principles, is central to some recent accounts on honour, such as Kwame Anthony Appiah and Sommers's respective defences of the continued relevance of honour (Appiah 2010; Sommers 2009, 2018). In order to fully understand revenge – and also the gendered nature of this phenomenon – we need to immerse ourselves temporarily in honour cultures.

Many studies of honour culture focus on its manifestation in various cultures in the Mediterranean region, but in their classical study of cultures of honour, Richard Nisbett and Dov Cohen explain that such cultures are found in many, often quite different, societies. They share one feature: 'the individual is prepared to protect his reputation – for probity or strength or both – by resort to violence' (Nisbett and Cohen 1996: 4). Nisbett and Cohen explain that cultures of honour are likely to develop if the individual is at risk of financial loss from his fellows, and the state is weak or non-existent. One prominent example is found in herding societies that can thus serve to illustrate how this works. The herder is at great risk of loss of livestock as he is operating in rural areas far from any kind of state or third-party control. It is easy to steal some sheep or cattle as they are roaming around freely in the wilderness with a lone herder to look after them. What will protect the herder is a reputation for strength: this might prevent anyone from even attempting to steal his sheep, and rather move on to the next herder. Nisbett and Cohen explain how this is manifested in the focus on insults in honour cultures. As a reputation for strength offers a herder protection, it is essential that he respond to any insult instantly and forcefully, as lack of a response might make him look weak. By extension, one can then see how the reputation for taking revenge for slights of any kind, big and small, and stopping short of nothing to set things straight, would be important for a herder in this cultural setting. This reputation – his honour – is what keeps his livelihood safe. Ideally, the herder is perceived as having sufficient power and strength to defend what is his. This is what it means to be an honourable man. Nisbett and Cohen postulate that this type of thinking is more prevalent in the American South than in the North, and tested this empirically. Indeed, they found that southerners are more likely to approve of violence in order to protect the self, family and home (ibid. 28). For example, stark contrasts are found when investigating responses to a scenario where a person takes violent revenge on his daughter's rapist: 47 per cent of southerners see this as 'extremely justified', compared to only 26 per cent of northerners (ibid. 31).

In the herder scenario, the person defending his honour through acts of revenge is undeniably male. Theorists discussing honour cultures point to the clearly gendered nature of the notion of honour. French, for example, argues that the responsibility for honour and shame is not distributed equally between men and women in honour cultures: 'honour is understood as an essentially male value, but it is measured by shame, understood primarily in terms of the chastity of women' (French 2001: 148). Elster makes a similar point: for women in Mediterranean societies 'the analogue of honour is "shame" (sexual modesty)' (Elster 1990: 867). A woman thus has the ability to severely damage a man's honour by being unchaste. French and Elster see honour as tied to men's reputation, and shame as something women can inflict on men by not being sexually modest. Appiah puts it differently: what behaviour is required to demand respect varies between men and women. For women, it is typically about chastity. Honour for women is about fidelity control: a woman is honourable or respectable if her fidelity is carefully controlled or curbed.[8]

In his book on honour Appiah discusses two grim examples, the first of which is foot-binding of Chinese women, seen as making her looking quintessentially feminine but basically also a way of curbing her movements and making her passive and thus enforcing sexual chastity, and the second, honour killings of women, where women who are seen as dishonourable, such as by choosing their own boyfriend, by being caught cheating or having been raped, are killed in order to secure family honour. Yet, while people in Western societies are quick to condemn honour killings, the shamefulness of being a rape survivor is not restricted to honour cultures. Appiah points out that:

> [e]ven in the industrialized West, in the United States and in Europe, it has taken an enormous amount of work to persuade women and men that rape should not be treated as a source of shame for the victim. It's not that women who have been raped believe deep down that they were 'asking for it'; the shame has, instead, to do with the powerlessness of being a victim. It is not guilt – the thought that they have done something wrong – that haunts them, it is the reminder of their humiliation. And that humiliation [...] makes it possible that she will lose the respect of those who know she was raped, however unreasonable this may be; indeed, it may undermine (once more, for no good reason) her respect for herself. (Appiah 2010: 145)

---

[8] The role played by women in honour cultures may be more complicated than this brief survey suggests; see, for example, Nisbett and Cohen (1996: 86–8), and some fascinating examples on women going to some lengths to get their male relatives to take revenge in Miller (2006: 91–2).

Furthermore, historically in Western societies women have had to rely on men to defend their honour, such as in cases of rape. Traditionally, rape was first and foremost seen as a violation of a man's property, and for many hundreds of years marrying the victim off to the rapist was seen as an appropriate absolution in England (Jacoby 1983: 201–3; see also Brownmiller 1975). In Western culture shame in terms of chastity is still very much seen as a problem for women, as with 'slut shaming' even of rape survivors, for example.[9] There is still a stigma of shame for the rape survivor.

The response to rape in honour cultures is not the topic of this book, but given the reprehensible nature of the practice of honour killings, a few more words about it are warranted. In order not to vilify entire cultures, it might help to understand what causes the practice. It is easy to jump to the conclusion that rape survivors in these cultures are killed because they are blamed for their own misfortune, or mistrusted in their account of coercion, so seen as responsible. However, as Sommers argues, we should be cautious about applying Western understanding of responsibility to these cultures. He explains how there is likely to be two very different ideas about responsibility in honour cultures as compared to cultures where punishment is institutionalised, such as in Western cultures. If we return to the lonely herder, if he is insulted, or if someone does steal one of his sheep, the onus is actually on the herder to react. He carries the moral burden. This is not to say that he is blamed for this wrong – but he surely will be blamed if he fails to react. The burden is on him to set things right, and he must do so. The insulter, or the thief, only has this retribution coming. So, in honour cultures, it is the offended party that ought to act (Sommers 2009: 44). In contrast, in Western society, the focus in moral theories and legal institutions is on the offender. The offender must be punished, and he is (or should be) seen as responsible and blameworthy. The focus in Western societies is thus how the offender ought to be treated. Sommers explains how honour cultures do not have the same notion of responsibility as Western societies have: it may almost appear irrelevant that the rape survivor does not in any way deserve to die. The intuition in honour cultures about blame and punishment are very different from Western intuitions.[10]

Indeed, the practice of honour killings is tied to honour culture through and through, and not to Islam, Appiah argues, which is another common misconception in the West. Appiah points out that 'honor killing is un-Islamic' (Appiah 2010: 153), a practice with roots in an honour culture far older than

---

[9] See, for example, Chemaly (2016).

[10] What might complicate Sommers's idea that there are two types of intuitions in two types of cultures, respectively, is why portrayals of honour cultures then keep recurring in Western entertainment. It is beyond the scope of this chapter to discuss the implications for the understanding of responsibility here.

this religion. Like the long-practised duelling among gentlemen in the UK, a case he also discusses, Appiah points out that honour killings are practised but are contrary to the official religion (i.e. as duelling went against the teachings of Christianity in the UK, honour killings go against Islam in countries in which honour killings are practised).

In any case, surely this is all the proof we need that honour is an outdated notion, intrinsically linked to misogynistic practices? This, however, is not the conclusion Appiah draws. On the contrary, in this thought-provoking book, he argues that what has, and will, enable change to these cultural practices is again honour. He analyses changing practices in a number of historical cases that can arguably be seen as examples of moral revolutions, the ending of Chinese foot-binding being one of them. He argues that when exploring the discourse in this era, the notion of honour actually plays an instrumental role in bringing the painful and degrading practice to an end. The rational arguments against this practice would have been well known, but what made a real difference is when the Chinese bourgeoisie became aware that this practice made Chinese culture appear shameful to foreigners: the practice ended because they wanted to save face, so to say, and appear honourable to others. Appiah argues that this demonstrates just how powerful honour is as a motivator. Human beings' concern for status, respect and recognition serves as one of the most powerful motivators there is (Appiah 2010: 96, 179, 204). Thus Appiah argues that what can be done in order to stop the abhorrent practice of honour killings, is to question to what extent it is honourable to 'open fire on an unarmed woman':

> In all the earlier revolutions, the motivating power of honor was channeled not challenged. The right way to proceed, it would seem, is not to argue against honor but to work to change the grounds of honor (Appiah 2010: 169)
> [...]
> [R]eforming honor is relevant, I believe, to every form of gendered violence; and, in particular, every society needs to sustain codes in which assaulting a woman – assaulting anyone – in your family is a source of dishonour, a cause of shame. (Ibid.)

As we will see, this is perhaps one of the roles that rape-revenge portrayals can play: in rape-revenge film, there is usually no question about the dishonourable and shameful nature of the rapist. The emotion that is elicited most prominently in order to communicate this is perhaps disgust. In *Revenge*, for example, Jen's disgust at the rape is communicated in numerous ways. Her revulsion at the man who walks in on the rape but does nothing, for example, is shown through numerous close-up shots of his open mouth as he is carelessly chewing a chocolate and marshmallow bar when seemingly contemplating what to do – as if deciding whether or not to participate in the rape, as he has been invited to do – but nonchalantly leaves instead. Later, in the cave, her recollection of the rape is portrayed in symbolic ways as she is dreaming, seemingly waking up from a nightmare again and again, experiencing the rape like getting one's head blasted off, and her hands on her boyfriend's buttocks when performing fellatio on him are now compared to an insect's claws on a worm.

The rapist is portrayed as disgusting and a source of dishonour. The rapist is typically portrayed as a loser, a pathetic and sometimes even degenerate figure, a weak and reprehensible creep – in short, as a dishonourable man. This depiction is often repeated in crime stories portraying rape, where the rapist is contrasted with the male detective, whose repulsion at this crime is used to portray him as representing good, hegemonic masculinity – an honourable man.[11] Mirroring this representation of the rapist as the one lacking honour, the rape survivor in rape-revenge film is not shameful. She insists on her right to self-respect, and taking revenge is a way of communicating this clearly.

This is not the only way rape-revenge film can be disruptive of powerful rape myths in our society. The female avenger also steps out of the limited role assigned to her in the traditional view on a woman's honour as tied to chastity and passivity. When she enacts violent revenge, she is stepping into what has been, and still is, very much a male domain. The honour of the rape-avenger is in many ways traditionally male: she insists on responding to rape as a man in an honour culture would respond to wrongdoing against himself. Ultimately, perhaps this is one of the reasons she is so unpalatable culturally. And this is also why there is a significant difference between rape-revenge films where the rape survivor takes revenge herself, and films where other characters – typically male relatives – take revenge on her behalf. This is of course the more conventional pattern, evident in some early rape-revenge films such as *The Last House on the Left* (Wes Craven, 1972), for example, where her parents take revenge, or the father's revenge in *Death Wish*.

This is also the case in some vengeance Western films, such as in *The Searchers*, which is one of French's main case studies in his book on virtuous vengeance. In *The Searchers*, Ethan Edward is on a quest for revenge for the brutal end met by his brother and his family: they are killed by Native Americans, his brother's wife Martha raped before she is killed, and their two daughters kidnapped by the Native Americans. One of the daughters is later found raped and killed too, so there is one daughter, Debbie, left to find. It is

---

[11] See Vaage (2015) and Chapter 5 in Vaage (2016) for further discussion, drawing on Cuklanz (2000). I return to these discussions of disgust in Chapter 5 in the present study as well.

worth dwelling ever so briefly on French's discussion of this case as it will reveal a problem in his discussion of revenge.

In French's first description of Ethan, he is described as a problematic avenger because he is racist towards Native Americans, and this is central to the topic of the film in French's analysis:

> A very convincing case can be made that John Ford uses *The Searchers* to indict and attack the racism that he identifies as an indelible feature of the American character and experience. That he does so through a character played by one of the most American of film icons, John Wayne, strengthens the interpretation, for Ethan Edwards is a dark, driven, antisocial, and brutal racist. (French 2001: 53)

Ethan is portrayed as horrified by Martha's violation, and is seeking revenge for her. However, for him, the daughters are also disgraced and dishonoured if they have been with a Native American – even if they have been raped. He thus sets out not only to kill Martha's rapist and killer, but to kill Debbie. French discusses this aspect of Ethan's quest for revenge as an expression of his racism and hatred of miscegenation, and also claims that it is 'bound up in barely repressed sexual jealousy' as it is suggested in the film that Ethan was and is in love with Martha, who instead chose to marry his brother – and Debbie looks just like her (ibid. 56). However, what French does not discuss is how Ethan's desire to kill Debbie can be said to be an honour killing. Debbie has to die, in his eyes, because she has been dishonoured. Most Americans would probably like to think that honour killings of women who have been raped are only found in other cultures, but in this American film from the not-too-distant American past, the protagonist Ethan is in effect on a quest to perform an honour killing of Debbie because she has been raped by a Native American.

However, in the sympathy structure of the film, arguably Ethan is ultimately revealed as morally flawed, in line with French's summary above. At the end, the spectator is supposed to recognise him as a flawed avenger, rooted in deep-seated racism. In his careful analysis of racism in this film, or what he discusses as White racialised disgust at Native American characters, Dan Flory argues that whereas Ethan and other White characters' racialised disgust throughout the film 'serve as cues for its intended audience to feel congruently', in an epistemological twist the film slowly but steadily also 'turns these feelings of racialized disgust against its audience' because Ethan represents such an extreme version of them (Flory 2019: 119). In Flory's analysis, the audience's recognition of Ethan's racism – and their own racist biases, which might be non-conscious – is thus intended to be dawning on White viewers over the course of the film. White viewers' allegiance with Ethan might thus be 'troubled and largely alienated by the end' of this film (Flory 2021: 475).[12] As such, Ethan ends up a strangely disturbing protagonist in a mainstream Hollywood film.

However, what is odd in French's discussion is that he later uses Ethan as an example of a virtuous avenger, focusing only on his revenge for the death of Martha by killing her rapist and killer, while not returning to the very problematic aspect of his desire to kill Debbie. French writes, for example, that Ethan has a 'very special target and very good reasons to pursue it' (French 2001: 165). The equivalent in the rape-revenge film would be portrayals of male relatives not just wanting to kill the rapist, but kill the rape survivor, due to the belief that dying is better than living with such shame. There is nothing progressive about the male response to rape as a source of shame and dishonour – this is entirely conventional, indeed, even in line with the response to rape in traditional honour cultures. As Flory points out, Ethan and other White characters see Debbie and other White women who have been raped by Native Americans as having 'forfeited their claim to whiteness by virtue of having been sexually defiled by Comanche men' (Flory 2019: 118). When Debbie is raped by a Native American she loses her White purity in this racist world view.

What I will add to Flory's point that Ethan is motivated by overpowering racism in his obsessive search for Debbie throughout this film, is that, for Ethan, it seems it is not only Debbie who has been dishonoured: his obsessive need to set things right suggests that more is at stake, and Ethan himself, and by extension, the entire family have been dishonoured. This Western film and its portrayal of vengeance can be said to be all about the consequences of rape for the masculine psyche, the head of the family, as if rape of female family members is first and foremost an affront to him, a source of dishonour and shame. In Ford's defence, the fact that Ethan is arguably portrayed as, and supposed to be recognised as, unsympathetic can be said to be intended to make the spectator recognise how flawed his response is – and make the spectator feel horror when he finally finds Debbie, and relief when he decides to let her live. Ethan's revenge could remind us of the moral tightrope a personal avenger will have to balance on, and how easily one can and will be led astray by biases and prejudices. But Ethan is not a good case study for someone who wants to argue that vengeance can be morally right.

French's account is problematic, as he argues that private revenge – even in societies where revenge is not sanctioned publicly – can still be virtuous. This is where I diverge from French: my exploration of these portrayals of revenge in film in no way suggests that this is a practical alternative we should hold

---

[12] See also Heller-Nicholas's discussion of this film in terms of roots in the racism of the 'captivity narrative' (Heller-Nicholas 2011: 71ff).

up, or even contemplate, in real life. There are very good reasons why private revenge must be off-limits, and among them is that human nature is in many ways flawed and biased, and an enraged person can very well go off the rails in a manhunt where meting out punishment might seem more important than getting it right. Third-party punishers are intended to protect the innocent and ensure that measures are taken to convict only those that are proven as guilty beyond doubt.

Indeed, the history of responses to rape has been badly tainted by vigilante cultures gone wrong. I have discussed rape and racism in relation to Native Americans. Another example is the lynching of African American men in the United States because of any claim, suspicion or loose rumour that a White woman had been raped. Angela Y. Davis carefully analyses the cultural and political context for the widespread lynching of Black boys and men in the US as this practice consolidated especially after the abolition of slavery (Davis 1981: 165ff). She argues that lynching as an institution formed only with the emancipation of Black people as a White supremacist measure to prevent equality. At first, various conspiracy theories about planned Black revolts and Black supremacy circulated, but drawing on the work of Frederick Douglass, Davis points out that 'the rape charge turned out to be the most powerful of several attempts to justify the lynching of Black people' (ibid. 166). The myth of the Black rapist was conjured up, as a distinct racist political invention.[13] So powerful was this myth that White resistance and opposition to lynching was effectively stifled. Who, Davis asks rhetorically, 'would dare to defend a rapist? [W]hite support for the cause of Black equality in general began to wane': indeed, the 'characterization of Black men as rapists wrought incredible confusion within the ranks of progressive movements' (ibid. 168–9). This historical example serves to illustrate just how effectively rape stirs up desire for revenge. The White people doing the lynching might have felt that they were doing the morally right thing to protect the honour of women in their White communities, but racism made them commit atrocities towards the African American community.

To be sure, there is institutional racism in third-party punishers too, as revealed in the ongoing trauma suffered by people of colour in the face of racist police behaviour and violence in the US, the UK and elsewhere. I will also discuss institutional racism faced by women of colour in the British legal system in Chapter 5. Racial injustice has been institutionalised for centuries, and this is going to be a long, arduous struggle. The law is far from flawless: made by and embodied predominantly by the humans in power, the law will

---

[13] I return to the myth of the Black rapist in Chapter 5, where I explore the implications for Black women. For more on the literary and filmic origins of the myth of the Black rapist, see Guerrero (1993: 12ff).

be marred by the biases and prejudices of these people. However, leaving each individual to set things right for themselves through revenge is even riskier – the chances of getting it wrong even higher. My emphasis is therefore firmly on the fictional nature of the representations of revenge in rape-revenge film.

A FUNCTION FOR REVENGE FANTASIES

I argue that as a thought experiment, rape-revenge films may reveal something about rape, and make us reflect on the response to rape. As one American attorney writes in a review of French's book:

> But French, I think, has it backwards when he argues that, as in the movies, we should tolerate or even encourage 'virtuous avengers.' Revenge plots in Western movies are emotionally satisfying because they humanize abstract, bureaucratic processes that are indispensable to our real-life system of justice. Movie plots simplify complex concepts such as due process, so that the fundamental moral message is accessible to their audience. They are morality tales, not practical alternatives. (Covey 2001, n.p.)

French argues that in order to discuss a suitable punishment for rape, one needs to imagine what it is to be raped. Imagining which punishment might fit the contours of rape he wonders whether

> it might involve continual torture and long-term incarceration, perhaps for life, in absolute solitary confinement. It might involve the forced feeding of substances that produce all manner of ghastly physical and mental reactions. *Such things are fertile grounds for fiendish imagination.* (French 2001: 226, my emphasis)

He points out how Dante set the bar on such inventiveness with his nine circles of hell with endlessly imaginative forms of punishment, meant to reflect the moral wrong, in his description of hell in *Inferno*. The response to rape, how rape is dealt with in the legal system and society more generally, is arguably unsettled. Perhaps this also then brings us to the core of the controversy of the rape-revenge story: these stories stir up numerous controversial questions about the portrayal of, and nature of, rape, and what is an appropriate response to rape, which are all unresolved questions subject to ongoing negotiations. The means through which the rape-revenge story does this is the vengeance narrative, which is another unsettling topic. The rape-revenge film is layer upon layer of cultural taboo. Rape is traditionally seen as near unspeakable and the most shameful of experiences, and this is the experience that the rape-revenge film explores. The film insists on the gravity of the rape through the act of vengeance that follows. And then the rape-revenge film allows a female avenger to step into this pinnacle of masculine honour, and seek to set things right for herself. At its most effective, rape-revenge film does imagine what it is to be raped, and forces the spectator to do the same, sometimes through portraying the actual rape, but importantly, also by exploring the revenge. If the harrowing nature of rape should be missed by anyone, this point is typically hammered in through the violence of the revenge sequences.

Ending French's book is a call for critical conversation about the fit of punishment, something in which 'a moral community should always take a serious interest' (ibid. 229). Rape-revenge stories do typically stir up controversy, and although critics might want to argue that they do so for all the wrong reasons, one could also argue that the rape-revenge story serves the function French calls for – they make us discuss rape, and what is an appropriate response to rape, as pointed out in the literature on rape-revenge film (for example, Henry 2014; Read 2000). I will return to a more critical discussion of the violence in the rape-revenge film in the final chapter in this book. The main point in this chapter has been to understand what revenge is, and how it is tied to notions of honour and shame that are fundamentally gendered. This inversion of conventional femininity is one of the reasons the female rape-avenger appears so contentious culturally – but it is also why it is so important to study the controversy she stirs up. She really does unleash quite a beast. She is no role model to be imitated in real life, or a solution to the practical problems in legal systems on how to respond to rape. But the rape-revenge film can nevertheless be said to be a fantasy with a function as a place of rage for women. This is what I will continue to explore in the following chapter on anger.

4. ON ANGER: A PHILOSOPHICAL EXPLORATION OF WOMEN'S ANGER AND ITS FUNCTIONS

Rape-revenge stories are prone to trigger anger. The female avenger is angry: these are stories about her vindictive rage in response to violation. The critics and the audience typically feel angry after watching these films – think back on the reception of rape-revenge exploitation films such as *I Spit on Your Grave* (Meir Zarchi, 1978), banned in many countries, or a more recent rape-revenge film such as *Baise-moi* (Virginie Despentes and Coralie Trinh Thi, 2000) that was deemed vile, worthless trash by critics, as explained in the introduction. Although the anger response to the rape-revenge film is common, arguably it can be difficult to pin down exactly what one is angry about. Anger could be an empathic response, through which one shares the protagonist's feelings. However, the spectator's anger is probably not limited to feeling with her: to varying degrees one may also be angry with the film and its creators, and question its portrayal of rape and revenge. Rape-revenge stories may also trigger feelings of anger about rape more generally. Sometimes one may wonder whether this real anger about rape as a crime, and the empathic anger in response to the protagonist's ordeal, are sometimes misplaced as critique of the representation of rape. I will return to the question of whether it is ethically wrong to portray rape and revenge on-screen in Chapter 7.

This is a chapter about anger as a response to moral wrongs, exploring this emotion and its potential function for the female spectator. What does it mean to be angry for women in particular? What does it mean that the rape-revenge film triggers anger? Anger is a contested emotion culturally, and this is also reflected in the philosophical literature – anger is defended as an important and productive emotion by some, but rejected as toxic and damaging by others. Part of the problem is who gets to be angry, and whose anger is deemed inappropriate. Unsurprisingly, women's anger in particular is controversial, and the onus has often been on women to forgive instead. In the latter half of the chapter I turn to two films, *Twilight Portrait* (Angelina Nikonova, 2011) and *Women Talking* (Sarah Polley, 2022), to discuss anger and forgiveness, and ultimately argue that the rape-revenge film can serve as an imaginary place of rage.

Feminists on women's anger

Soraya Chemaly recently published a thoughtful call for reflection on, and acceptance of, women's anger (Chemaly 2018). She starts by observing that girls are rarely taught how to be angry – they are not encouraged to explore what anger is and what to do with it. Anger is seen as unfeminine and unattractive, and girls learn to expect to be mocked, ostracised or gaslighted if expressing anger. Indeed, anger is a deeply gendered emotion. Culturally, Chemaly observes that White men's anger tends to be perceived as justifiable, whereas women's anger has traditionally been associated with madness (ibid. xiv). This makes men and women experience anger differently: men more frequently report feeling powerful when angry, whereas women associate anger with powerlessness. Furthermore, men are allowed to express anger whereas women are expected to express displeasure with sadness. Showing anger makes women feel ugly (ibid. xv, 4, 6, 31). Chemaly urges us to think and talk about women's anger, as this is 'the emotion that best protects us against danger and injustice': '[i]n expressing anger and demanding to be heard, we reveal the deeper belief that we can engage with and shape the world around us' (ibid. xxi).

Several of Chemaly's points resonate with discussions of anger in feminist philosophy. Lisa Tessman explains how anger is given a central and important role in some resistance movements, such as in feminist and anti-racist activism (Tessman 2005: 107–32). Here, anger may be seen as a forceful and necessary way to signal wrongness and a refusal to accept injustices and discrimination. Core to this line of thought is that to be angry is to demand respect. Anger is to insist on the right to assert one's self and resist the subordinate status of women and people of colour. As Chemaly puts it, 'you can't express anger without asserting *I* and your own perspective' (Chemaly 2018: 47, emphasis original). Marilyn Frye points to the claims inherent in a display of anger, and argues that

> [t]o get angry is to claim implicitly that one is a certain sort of being, a being which can (and in this case does) stand in a certain relation

and position *a propos* the being one is angry at. One claims that one is in certain ways and dimensions *respectable*. (Frye 1983: 90, emphasis original)

Being angry with someone is to insist on one's equal value and right to be taken seriously.

Feminist thinkers argue that anger has traditionally been off-limits for women for exactly this reason: being angry is a rejection of subordination. This idea is central to the philosophical defence of anger: anger is seen as a productive emotion in so far as it is status-maintaining for the subject – basically a way of insisting on self-respect and respect for those one cares about. Because anger signals a resistant self it has been discussed as an 'outlaw emotion' for women, i.e. conventionally unacceptable and incompatible with dominant values (Alison Jaggar quoted in Lugones 2003: 103). Frye observes that women's anger is often seen as hysterical or a sign of mental instability, and she can get away with anger only if it is within a feminine realm conventionally, such as being angry on behalf of one's children, or generally on another's behalf (Frye 1983: 91). Anger on a woman's own behalf is less likely to be understood by others (get uptake): for women 'it is safer to get angry about nuclear power than about one's own rape', Frye suggests (ibid. 92). María Lugones discusses a woman's oppositional anger as 'hard-to-handle anger', an anger that endangers convention. It is separatist in nature, rejecting a patriarchal world in which women are subordinate and not allowed to be angry about it. This is 'anger of a self different from the one who is trying to make sense within the confines of the official reality, a self who is doing the work of resistance' (Lugones 2003: 103).

An important predecessor here is Audre Lorde, a feminist and anti-racist activist who argued that anger can be used for growth (Lorde 2017: 107ff). When Myisha Cherry makes rage central to anti-racist activism in her recent book, she discusses this politically potent emotion as Lordean rage (Cherry 2021). Central to this tradition is a critical analysis of how Black women's anger is treated. Lorde, for example, points to speaking out of anger at an academic conference and being told by a White woman to '[t]ell me how you feel but don't say it too harshly or I cannot hear you' (Lorde 2017: 108). Lorde's anger, as an African American woman, is dismissed as unacceptable, effectively silencing Lorde and ignoring the point she is making.

Cherry points out how proper evaluation of anger takes time and effort, which is increasingly difficult the more distant someone is to us, i.e. the less familiar their anger experience is (Cherry 2018). The example Lorde uses would be a case of inappropriate anger evaluation in Cherry's account, or more specifically anger policing where the mere presence of anger is used as a reason to dismiss someone's view. Amia Srinivasan discusses this tendency to dismiss the anger of victims of oppression as inappropriate, and labels it an *affective injustice* (Srinivasan 2018: 127). The White woman in Lorde's example obscures the fact that Lorde's anger is apt, and explains away Lorde's anger as a sign of her inferior character, i.e. implying that she should be able to contain it, or dismissing her anger as pathological in a case of gaslighting. Cherry explains that 'gaslighting is directed at women, people of color and other minority groups' (Cherry 2018: 63). Being discriminated against is a first-order injustice, and having one's apt anger dismissed as inappropriate or counterproductive is a second-order, affective injustice, argues Srinivasan: not only is the person being discriminated against, she is also told that her affective response to this is unacceptable (Srinivasan 2018: 135). Affective injustice is a 'psychic tax levied on victims of oppression' (ibid.), disproportionately affecting those already disproportionately affected by first-order injustice. This is the oppressive feature of dismissals of anger, which Srinivasan sees as tied to social control. The norms of rationalistic justice are used to exclude the anger of those threatening the social order from the public sphere. This obviously serves those in power.

Chemaly points out that 'anger is usually about saying "no" in a world where women are conditioned to say almost anything but "no"' (Chemaly 2018: xix). In her philosophical reflection on her own experience of rape and attempted murder, Susan J. Brison observes that the hardest thing for women in her self-defence class was 'simply to yell "No!"' (Brison 2002: 14). She reports that she and the other women in her rape-survivor support group were hardly able to get angry with the rapists at all, and she was stunned to discover that this was not unusual (ibid. 13, 63, 74). For a long time, she only felt fear when conjuring up an image of the rapist, and she suggests that experiencing anger requires that one imagines oneself in proximity to him, and in the early stages of recovery this is too frightening. She found that her fear and feeling of powerlessness was assuaged only when she started taking self-defence classes, in which she learned to fight back and experience what she describes as a 'justified, healing rage' (ibid. 14). She suggests that self-defence classes might enable women to feel more in control, and enable survivors of rape specifically to 'put the blame where it belongs: on their assailants', 'facilitated by the ability to feel appropriate anger towards them' (ibid. 76). Indeed, she cites research on women in self-defence classes that found that these women discover 'feeling angry (as) an alternative to feeling fearful or helpless' (Louise H. Kidder, Joanne L. Boell and Marilyn M. Moyer quoted in Brison 2002: 142 n.23).

Brison ties the prevailing feeling of fear and helplessness in women to Iris Young's observation that girls are taught to move about hesitantly and fearfully in a constricted space, 'routinely underestimating the strength we actually have' (Young quoted in Brison 2002: 14). Sara Ahmed points out that '[v]ulnerability is not an inherent characteristic of women's bodies', but argues that 'it is an effect that works to secure femininity as delimitation of movement in the public and an overinhabitance in the private' (Ahmed quoted in Chemaly 2018: 129). In short, the curtailing of women's anger is tied in with a tendency to socialise girls into a feeling of vulnerability, restricting their movement and their sense of freedom.

One could thus say with Tessman that anger is a *burdened virtue* (Tessman 2005: 107–32). It may not lead to human flourishing in a just world, and ideally, it should not be needed. However, under oppression, character traits that may not ideally be virtuous may still be needed. So, as the world is not just, but rather systematically unjust, anger may be virtuous. What is at stake, then, when someone is not allowed to be angry? Let us turn to the discussion of the function of anger more broadly before returning to the question of women's anger in relation to film.

The functions of anger

The question about the value and function of anger lingers in the literature on anger in philosophy on emotions and moral philosophy. As the rape-revenge film typically stirs up feelings of anger, answering these questions is central to an examination of the purpose and potential function of this type of film. Notably, the literature on anger mirrors some of the questions and topics found in relation to revenge, which is not surprising as definitions of anger typically include a retaliatory component. This view dates back to Aristotle, who in his *Rhetoric* sees anger as pain at being unjustifiably harmed by someone coupled with a desire for revenge (see Flanagan 2018: xvii). Contemporary philosophical definitions of anger are usually more or less in line with his definition in that they include a confrontational, retaliatory action tendency. For example, Antti Kauppinen sees anger as a psychological and physiological response that prepares us for aggression towards someone who threatens our goals (Kauppinen 2018: 32). As Martha C. Nussbaum puts it, 'most traditional philosophical definitions of anger' hold that 'the idea of payback or retribution – in some form, however subtle – is a conceptual part of anger' (Nussbaum 2016: 15).

Philosophers would typically also point out that there is a group of anger emotions, from the relatively mild to the more aggressive, such as from feelings of resentment to absolute rage. And Cherry points out that anger might not always entail blame of someone – I might feel angry it is raining – and labels anger at a moral wrong as *moral anger*, which is 'an emotion of blame, is other-directed, and is associated with change or punishment' (Cherry 2018: 51). When I discuss anger in this chapter, I always refer to moral anger, but will call it anger for simplicity. The important point here is that anger is commonly seen as related to an action tendency to confront, retaliate or punish. The retaliatory feature of anger could in many ways be said to be what makes anger as an emotion so controversial: as revenge is off-limits, the vengeful aspects of anger are also deemed unacceptable.

By entailing an action tendency to want to respond to a past event, the angry person can be seen as intending to force the other to conform to some moral rule. This element of anger can be seen as forward-looking, intending to change something in the future or prevent something from happening again. But some philosophers reject anger because it also inherently entails retaliatory, backward-looking features. Nussbaum is one prominent example: she argues that anger is normatively problematic exactly because of its ideas about payback (Nussbaum 2016: 15). Assuming that payback will assuage one's own pain is flawed, she argues: retaliation will not right a wrong that has already been committed. To believe that it will is a kind of magical thinking (ibid. 21ff). Nussbaum only keeps a role in her normative philosophy for what she discusses as transition anger, which is only forward-looking in nature. I will explore Nussbaum's account in greater detail later on.

Related to Nussbaum's move to keep only transition anger, cleansed of backward-looking payback thoughts, others argue that anger is salvageable because it need not be retaliatory (see for example, McBride 2018: 5, 9). Yet, some tackle anger's retaliatory elements head-on, such as Kauppinen, for example, who argues that returning pain for pain is a central feature of anger – if one does not desire to bring about negative consequences for the target, it is not anger one is feeling. He nevertheless defends this response as having a valuable function (Kauppinen 2018: 32–3).

One value of anger can be to restore one's self-respect (see for example, McBride 2018: 9, Kauppinen 2018: 39). To be angry is to insist on one's self-worth, to restore one's self-confidence in the face of trespass. To be angry can be seen as a drive to maintain one's self and one's integrity, and demand respect for this. Being angry is a way of restoring the balance between a wrongdoer and oneself as one's angry response is a way of acknowledging that one has suffered a slight (cf. Shoemaker 2018: 82). This could be said to be the status-maintaining value of anger, and is in line with ideas in the literature on revenge, as we saw in the previous chapter, and also in line with the feminist writings on anger – anger is less accessible to women exactly because they are not supposed to insist on their own equal value. Indeed, Kauppinen argues that anger is part and parcel of valuing oneself, or valuing someone close to oneself. Not to feel angry when experiencing moral wrongs done to me or my loved ones should be seen as a moral deficiency, argues Kauppinen. This is in line with Aristotle's much-cited view on anger found in the *Nicomachean Ethic* (Book 4, Chapter 5): it is a moral deficiency never to feel anger – feeling anger in moderation in response to wrongdoing is appropriate.

Another feature in the discussions of anger in the literature on the philosophy of emotion, shared with discussions of revenge and again also the feminist discussions, is anger's motivating function. McBride, for example, describes how anger fortifies and emboldens a person and motivates them to resist (McBride 2018: 9–10). For example, Céline Leboeuf offers an analysis of anger felt by a person of colour who is using it to undo the bodily alienation felt due to racial prejudice; i.e. anger is used to embolden a person of colour to resist the White gaze (Leboeuf 2018).

Although this claim about the motivating function of anger might be controversial in the philosophical literature, the claim that emotions overall motivate human beings to act is a central idea in established cognitive theories of emotion.[1] The primary function of emotions is indeed to alert us to something of importance to our well-being, and make us ready to act appropriately. Fear, for example, alerts me to a threat and makes me ready to respond (freeze, flight, fight) in order to maximize safety and ultimately survival. Anger motivates me to confront and resist someone who has done me wrong. One might assume that it is not the idea that emotions overall motivate action that is controversial in the discussions about anger in moral psychology and philosophy. Rather, it is possibly the claim that anger is more motivating, or a better motivator, than other emotions, that is controversial, as we shall see.

Related to this motivating function is what is typically discussed as anger's epistemic function. The feeling of anger can draw our attention to something as wrong, and as such it can make us perceive something more clearly morally. This is again found in the feminist discussions of anger: not only is anger seen as motivating, but also as a source of clarification. This is typically seen as the 'epistemic productivity of anger', as argued by Srinivasan (2018: 126). In a critical discussion of anger, Glen Pettigrove counters this idea by pointing to research demonstrating that anger can adversely affect judgement.[2] This research is typically carried out by having respondents recall an episode in which they experienced wrongdoing that made them angry, or watch a clip in which a person experiences wrongdoing and responds with anger, or in similar ways trigger anger. The respondents are then asked to reason about a wide range of issues, and as Pettigrove points out, the results 'suggest that even a very modest degree of anger […] has a marked influence on our reasoning', i.e. an adverse effect (Pettigrove 2012: 362). However, this critique misses the point. Defenders of anger, including feminists and activists, do not claim that anger improves one's reasoning overall, or that an angry person is epistemologically superior to a non-angry person generally. The epistemic function of

---

[1] See, for example, Frijda (1986), and for a brief introduction to emotions, including their action tendencies, see Plantinga (2009: 53ff), and in relation to morality and film, Plantinga (2018), an account I will explore further in Chapter 7.

[2] His discussion also lists the proposed functions of anger and I draw on his neat summary of these functions here.

anger entails a lesser claim: it suggests that this emotion gives the angry person clarity on this situation specifically. The angry person may not be in a position to reason more effectively about any given matter, but experiences with clarity that this act is wrong because it makes them angry. It is a nagging reminder not to accept this specifically. This is more a charitable understanding of the claim that anger can be epistemologically productive.

Pettigrove points to a number of adverse effects of being angry as documented in this empirical research. For example, angry people tend to underestimate risk; they are more likely to see stimuli as hostile; they are less likely to perceive stimuli as ambiguous; they are more likely to see someone as responsible for an unpleasant event due to this person's personality traits and not accidental qualities in the situation; they are less likely to trust others and more likely to see themselves as exceptional and insightful; and finally, more likely to support punishment of others (ibid. 362–4). All of this should give the defender of anger pause for thought. However, although many of these effects can be negative – imagine how much of this might apply to hateful internet trolls for example – they can also be seen as positive, for example for people who are oppressed. It can be a good thing to underestimate the risk of speaking up against misogyny and racism, as someone needs to do so in spite of the risks this entails. Perhaps one needs to perceive the world as Manichean, and perceive some groups as very hostile and very blameworthy, in order to take this risk, unpleasant and dangerous as it is to speak up against, and break with, suppressing conventional norms in society. In order to turn activist and potentially take up unpopular positions, perhaps feeling exceptional and insightful can be a good thing.

Cherry maps these positive effects of anger carefully in her discussion of Lordean rage, a specific type of anger she explores that is directed at racial injustice. She points out that anger is motivating because it gives a person eagerness, self-belief and optimism (Cherry 2021: 66ff). Indeed, just as Pettigrove, as an anger sceptic, points to research on adverse effects of anger, anger proponents point to positive effects of anger. Shoemaker, for example, also points to studies in which it was found that anger tends to motivate greater success in getting what one wants; to make a person more optimistic; to promote psychological insight and self-improvement; and how anger can be empowering (Shoemaker 2018: 84). Huebner sums up a list of related beneficial effects: anger makes us vigilant about threats and harms, and optimistic about overcoming obstacles; it makes us motivated to restore fair and cooperative behaviour; it allows us to hold one another to higher moral standards (Huebner 2018: 90–1). Thinking back on the subordination stress discussed in the previous chapter, one can see how anger can be effective in counteracting the adverse effects of being subordinate and feeling helpless, and serving to help a person out of these conditions. However, it is easy to agree with critics that it would be wrong to say that anger is always positive, and that it should not be curtailed at all: making us more sure about ourselves, and more judgemental of others, anger is a strengthening potion that should clearly be used with caution.

Indeed, Cherry also discusses other, destructive forms of anger to delineate what makes Lordean rage different, giving it a clear political function. One such example is the 'rogue rage' of a White American neo-Nazi man, who feels anger at being marginalised and broken by injustices, but does not target his anger at the institutions that caused the injustice in the first place – so instead of working for new laws, police reforms, funding or other demands to authorities that would foster change, the rogue rager engages in random acts of violence at others who are not responsible for the injustices (Cherry 2021: 16–17). This is an important point about the difference between politically productive anger and the aggrieved entitlement of angry White men turning into racist terrorists and racist internet trolls: it is misdirected anger. One can add to Cherry's point here that what causes this misdirection of anger are ideologies such as racism, patriarchy and heteronormativity, putting the blame for one's experiences on someone who is not to blame.

The value of (properly directed) anger as an expression of self-respect, or respect for others, its motivating and epistemic functions, all add up to what can be said to be its core function: its communicative function. Srinivasan points out that anger as an act 'registers and communicates the badness of injustice' (Srinivasan 2018: 138). Shoemaker argues that anger's 'fundamental encompassing action tendency is *to communicate the anger*' (Shoemaker 2018: 74, emphasis original). This again makes sense in light of the previous discussion of revenge. The ultimate function of revenge can be seen as communicating that a moral trespass has happened and that it is unacceptable. This is exactly what Shoemaker argues about anger:

> Blaming anger's most fundamental encompassing aim is better described as communication, then. The motivation for retaliation is very often associated with it, of course, but that's essentially because retribution is perhaps the most effective and dramatic form the communication of anger can take. (Ibid. 75)

Anger thus has an expressive element crucial to its function for us: it communicates that a moral rule has been violated and that this person, with whom one is angry, is to blame. Later we will see that the alternative that Nussbaum holds up as a more morally praiseworthy alternative to anger, unconditional forgiveness, can be seen as inappropriate by the anger proponent exactly because it does not fulfil this communicative function.

To sum up this mapping of the functions of anger, feeling angry has a motivating function and an epistemic function for the person who has been wronged. Furthermore, in extension of this feeling of anger, this emotion also serves to communicate to others that the wronged person has self-respect, sees clearly that a wrong has been done to them and is willing to act on this in order to make this clear to others. This is anger's communicative function.

Tying this back to the literature on women and anger, and the observation that anger in women is not culturally condoned, one can begin to speculate on the effect this has on women, their self-respect, their motivation to act if they are wronged, and their ability to communicate to others that they have been wronged. In relation to rape-revenge film, one can also start to make sense of what it means to watch a woman respond to rape with vindictive anger on-screen. Her anger clearly communicates how violated she feels. She is not shameful, or blaming herself, but is directing her anger at the rapist. In rape-revenge film the moral structure is clear: he has wronged her, and he is to blame. She is insisting on her self-worth. Stirring up anger about rape through exploring this protagonist's vindictive anger could thus be said to be core to the affective structure of the rape-revenge film. This strong emotion can communicate something about rape and the violation it represents to personhood. Anger can give moral clarity on the horror of rape. Perhaps anger can even motivate moral change, at least if the film carefully harnesses the anger response in an argumentative context, as I will suggest in the final chapter. Many rape-revenge films cannot be said to have such a clear argument, but the question is whether some of them can, and whether this is the political potential in the rape-revenge film: an exploration of anger in response to rape can be valuable because this response to rape has been unavailable to women culturally. Indeed, rape may represent an extreme form of the humiliation, disrespect, powerlessness and helplessness that many women feel, as became evident in the outpouring of anger and pain caused by abuse and harassment in the #MeToo movement. Across the globe women widely shared their common experiences of injustices that they had not been allowed to respond to with anger. The rape-revenge film is an extreme dramatisation of wrongdoing against a woman, and an exploration of a response – vindictive anger – that is difficult to access for women in real life, and that clearly communicates the wrongness of the rape.

Anger eliminativists: on sadness and unconditional forgiveness as alternative responses

In this section I turn to those who are sceptical of anger, and examine the alternatives they propose. In rape-revenge films, revisionist takes on this type of story are found in films that complicate revenge, such as through unconditional love towards the rapist, as we will see in the film *Twilight Portrait*. Are such alternatives normatively preferable to and more ethically praiseworthy than classical cases of these stories where the protagonist takes revenge?

I will concentrate on two prominent anger eliminativists, Owen Flanagan and Nussbaum. Flanagan argues that in the West, most ordinary people are Aristotelians about anger: they 'think that anger can be a virtue if it is moderate and contained', as explained already (Flanagan 2017: 159). The cultural norm in the West is what Flanagan labels a containment view on anger. Flanagan disagrees with this view, and argues that it is morally better to extirpate anger: anger is bad because it is 'vengeful and spiteful. It does not seek to heal like forgiveness and sorrow [...]. It is ugly and harmful, and in the business of passing pain' (ibid. 203). Parts of Flanagan's defence of this elimination view rely on Buddhist metaphysics and does as such go beyond the scope of the present discussion. However, he also explicitly discusses some of the arguments for anger that I have outlined above (ibid. 180–1 for a summary). Most interesting here is his discussion of what he labels the injustice argument for anger: the idea that anger is the best vehicle to identify and overcome injustice. Here he discusses a story introduced by Nussbaum about Holocaust survivor Elie Wiesel, told second-hand to her:

> Wiesel was a child in one of the Nazi death camps. On the day the Allied forces arrived, the first member of the liberating army he saw was a very large black officer. Walking into the camp and seeing what there was to be seen, this man began to curse, shouting at the top of his voice. As Wiesel watched, he went on shouting and cursing for a long time. And the child Wiesel thought, watching him, now humanity has come back. Now, with that anger, humanity has come back. (Nussbaum cited in Flanagan 2017: 203–4)

In this earlier publication, Nussbaum defends this view, and argues that not to get angry is a moral shortcoming (we shall see that she has now changed her mind about anger). Flanagan disagrees. He asks us to imagine that

> instead of rage, the officer who was the first member of the liberating party to arrive at the concentration camp, had wept rivers of tears at what he saw. Suppose that instead of fury at the evidence of depraved racist inhumanity, he experienced compassion and solidarity and profound tearful sadness. One could easily imagine that this might have both diminished the young Wiesel's sense of hopelessness, allowing him to think that perhaps 'humanity had come back,' as well as served as a catharsis for the officer and his fellow soldiers. Imagine the soldiers shedding tears together; it is much easier to imagine than to imagine them all shouting and cursing. Could a contagion of tears rather than a contagion of rage be healing, could it restore hope in humanity? The answer seems clearly yes. (Flanagan 2017: 205)

This is relevant to my exploration of Pennsatucky's response in the aftermath of rape in *Orange Is the New Black* (Jenji Kohan, 2013–19), as will be remembered from Chapter 1 in this book: Pennsatucky and Boo set out to rape the rapist back, but stop halfway through when Pennsatucky admits that she does not feel rage, she merely feels sadness. This could be said to be a revisionist rape-revenge storyline, where the planned revenge is complicated and ultimately rejected. As a fictional representation of the response to rape one can question whether this response should be held up as normatively preferable, and morally more praiseworthy in fictional stories.

In a paper proposing that there is a role for anger in Buddhist philosophy, Emily McRae argues that although the sadness response in the Wiesel story does recognise the terrible suffering of Holocaust survivors,

> the expression of sadness does not properly recognize the *wrongdoing* of the Nazi guards because sadness is about loss, pain, and suffering. It is not sufficiently specific to track suffering caused by injustice (as in this case) [...]. One could have the same response to seeing the destruction caused by a natural disaster for which no person or group is at fault. [...] [I]t does not recognize an important aspect of the survivor's reality, namely that he has survived a grave *injustice* (and not simply a terrible misfortune). (McRae 2015: 471, emphasis original)

Sadness is not seen as fully appropriate as it does not mark out the death camps as *morally* monstrous. One way to rephrase this would be to say that sadness does not fulfil the exact same communicative function: it does not clearly mark something as moral wrongdoing, and it does not clearly mark someone as blameworthy – moral anger has an object, the wrongdoer, and this element can be absent when we feel sad. This is not to say that the two emotions cannot, and often do, co-exist, but my point here is what anger specifically brings.

Kauppinen proposes another argument for why sadness cannot always replace anger, namely that sadness does not carry the same 'must thoughts' as anger does: anger commands respect for me and mine (Kauppinen 2018: 44). He argues that 'other emotions won't suffice for affectively appreciating one's equal status in the face of attempted degradation, because they don't involve thoughts of justified self-defence' (ibid. 39). This relates to the status maintaining function of anger: I can be sad about an offence against me without clearly communicating that I should be seen as of equal status and value. Chemaly discusses the differences in terms of motivation or action tendencies: anger has a stronger action tendency, in terms of seeking change, than does sadness:

> [a]nger is an 'approach' emotion, while sadness is a 'retreat' emotion [...]. Anger, not sadness, is associated with controlling one's circumstances,

such as competition, independence and leadership. Anger, not sadness, is linked to assertiveness, persistence, and aggressiveness. Anger, not sadness, is a way to actively make changes and confront challenges. Anger, not sadness, leads to perceptions of higher status and respect. (Chemaly 2018: 5)

Sadness does not prepare us to act – beyond withdrawing – in the way anger does. One could therefore add to the reasons why the soldier in the Wiesel story was right in cursing and shouting that it might motivate action more effectively than rivers of tears.

To be fair to Flanagan, he does conclude by stating that he is not in a firm position to be against anger as he has never 'suffered racism or sexism, nor has anyone tried to rape or murder me. I have not been called on to heal from those kinds of awful injuries' (Flanagan 2017: 215). Interestingly, Flanagan discusses Brison's book about her own experience of rape, as introduced earlier in this chapter, and her claim that self-defence classes released a healing rage. He states that this is different from the Wiesel story, and argues that her rage is indeed healing as it helped her purge herself of fear, and perhaps also shame and guilt. However, he also argues that this rage is not punitive rage (ibid. 211). This latter conclusion, however, seems unwarranted: on what grounds can one claim to know that Brison's rage was not punitive? Brison's account of her own rage is accommodated by Flanagan without further explanation of why this rage is healing. Indeed, Brison's rage offers us a powerful counterexample to Flanagan's proposition that sadness is more appropriate than rage.

Perhaps Boo was right in *Orange Is the New Black* – not that the guard should be raped, but that Pennsatucky would be better off being angry with him. Sadness does not in the same way mark both to her and to him that what he did was morally wrong and that he is blameworthy. This rape storyline has a long aftermath for Pennsatucky as she keeps being drawn to him, an aspect of her storyline that was difficult to accept for many fans of the series. Arguably it is portrayed as a destructive relationship in which he takes advantage of her very low self-esteem, and it is quite a victory when she realises, several seasons later, that she will never be safe or feel confident with him. Blaming him for having wronged her earlier might have helped Pennsatucky restore her self-respect more quickly. Fortunately, though, she does get there in the end. The point here is obviously not to dismiss any actual rape survivor's response as less good. The response to rape in real life probably varies hugely, and whether or not real rape survivors should be angry or sad is not the topic of the present discussion. Pennsatucky, however, is a fictional character, and as such it is relevant to discuss this representation.

We have seen that Flanagan proposes sadness as a preferable alternative to anger. Nussbaum similarly dismisses anger as corrosive, and argues for unconditional forgiveness. She sees the core idea in anger as flawed: it is either incoherent or normatively ugly (Nussbaum 2016: 6). She sees the payback idea as an intrinsic part of anger, and this very idea is flawed, she argues, indeed, it is a kind of magical thinking (ibid. 24). What is flawed is the belief that payback is a way of assuaging one's own pain. Inflicting more pain on wrongdoers will not right a wrong. Furthermore, vindictive anger is flawed in that it makes everything revolve around relative positions, domination and control, which she discusses as a status error (ibid. 29). Although she does discuss the evolutionary origin of the payback idea and its coupling with status (ibid. 29, 36, 39), she dismisses this element of anger because we are simply wrong to value status in the way anger makes us do (ibid. 29). At several points in her discussion she does briefly sum up three more positive functions of anger, but she never addresses these more carefully. These are anger as a signal to others that wrongdoing has happened (mapping roughly onto what I have discussed as the communicative function), as motivation to address this (the motivating function) and as deterrent to others (ibid. 6, 37–40, 96). Instead, she proposes only one form of anger that is normatively appropriate and rational, and the only form of anger that should retain a role in normative philosophy, which is transition-anger. Transition-anger is only forward-looking, and rare in pure form, but normatively praiseworthy as a person experiencing transition-anger is not led astray by irrational payback urges but remains focused on creating future welfare (ibid. 6, 36). What remains unaddressed in Nussbaum's account is whether transition-anger retains anger's communicative and motivational functions, which Nussbaum sees as positive functions of anger. She also says relatively little on how anger should be overcome and turned into transition-anger, but thinks that in a rational person, anger realises its errors and 'soon laughs at itself and goes away' (ibid. 31). Will this rational person who has quickly dismissed her own anger as laughable still be motivated to act, for example to speak up against oppressors? Or will what caused her anger also be dismissed as a laugh, something not to be too upset about perhaps?

Nussbaum also dismisses what she labels as transactional forgiveness – in short, forgiveness with caveats such as that the perpetrator must apologise or repent before one can forgive. She sees this too as morally flawed because it involves the same errors as does anger. The rigid conditions set out maintains the payback error, and similarly the transactional nature of the process maintains the narrow status-focus (ibid. 74). Nussbaum holds up unconditional forgiveness and unconditional love as alternatives to both anger and transactional forgiveness, and as moral ideals (ibid. 75ff).

There are several arguments against Nussbaum's account. For example, if one forgives a wrongdoer who in no way acknowledges that what he did was wrong, this may be seen as failing to communicate clearly what was morally wrong and why. Shoemaker argues that if the wrongdoer acknowledges the wrong he has done to the victim, forgiveness can be appropriate because the nature of the wrongdoing – the fact that it was wrong – has still been communicated by the perpetrator's remorse (Shoemaker 2018: 81). Jacoby points out that justice is to restore some kind of equilibrium between the victim and victimiser, and sees acknowledgement of culpability and a feeling of remorse as central to this: 'forgiveness becomes impossible if a basic sense of fairness is repeatedly assaulted: the act is meaningless unless both parties realise there is something to forgive' (Jacoby 1983: 332). Without remorse, forgiveness is meaningless as a communicative act highlighting that a moral rule has been violated. Jacoby thus dismisses unconditional forgiveness as just because it may be as 'inappropriate and self-destructive a response to injury as overweening vindictiveness' (ibid. 352).

Here it is interesting also to note that in principle, in a system of third-party punishers, private forgiveness as a practical alternative for a person who has been victim to a crime is just as unavailable as is private revenge. The move to third-party punishing curtailed both (Jacoby 1983: 117). A crime is still a crime, punishable by the law, even if its victims have decided to forgive the perpetrator: it is not up to the victims to let the crime go unpunished, only the third-party punisher, or the legal system, is allowed to decide.[3] So although unconditional forgiveness may be a normative ideal, and a psychological attitude that one may see as better than vindictiveness in the face of crime, neither action alternative is accepted in lieu of state-sanctioned punishment.

However, let us return to Nussbaum's critics in philosophy. McBride points out that when defining anger as vindictive but seeing transition-anger as not being vindictive, it is confusing whether or not transition-anger is a type of anger at all. Kauppinen counters Nussbaum's claim that the retributive element in anger is a kind of magical thinking: Nussbaum sees the backward-looking payback idea as flawed because inflicting pain on a wrongdoer will not change the fact that a wrongdoing was committed, but Kauppinen points out that the payback element of anger is not at all magical and does help the victim because it insists and restores her equal status (Kauppinen 2018: 39ff). There is nothing irrational about this.

Another line of critique, found in McBride's discussion, is the suggestion that by deeming the garden-variety of anger wrong, Nussbaum is insensitive to those who suffer injustice: they are dismissed as irrational if they remain angry (McBride 2018: 8). This could be said to be a powerful critique against the anger

---

[3] Private forgiveness – or private vindictive feelings – may impact sentencing due to victim impact statements in court. For a discussion, see, for example, Murphy (2003: 27ff).

eliminativists. They seem to deem those who remain angry against injustices irrational. Cherry makes a related point, though not explicitly framed as a critique of Nussbaum (Cherry 2018). She discusses the morally problematic nature of what she labels as 'anger policing', which is to evaluate someone else's moral evaluation and decide whether or not they can be said to be entitled to their own response to any given situation (i.e. should they be angry). She discusses several reasons why anger in particular is difficult to evaluate, among them that sympathising with anger requires familiarity with the cause of the anger – if one witnesses an angry person and is not in any way familiar with the situation that has caused this anger, there is a tendency for the witnessed anger to provoke fear or disgust rather than understanding, basically because anger can be frightening and off-putting and does not invite intimacy (Cherry 2018: 52ff). We empathise and sympathise most easily with those familiar and similar to ourselves,[4] so Cherry is right to point to the potential for there to be a sympathy gap whenever we encounter angry people who are different from us. In a later book, Cherry turns to an explicit critical discussion of Nussbaum, and more specifically the latter's claims that revolutionary figures such as Martin Luther King show that justice can be achieved without anger. Cherry demonstrates how anger did play a role in fuelling King's political actions (Cherry 2021: 86ff).

Nussbaum uses several examples from literature to show how characters such as the father Seymore Levov in Philip Roth's *American Pastoral*, and psychologist Harriet Lerner's patient Maggie in *The Dance of Anger*, could be said to respond with unconditional forgiveness and love, and thus serve as exemplary cases for us to emulate (Nussbaum 2016: 102ff). I will not go into detail on these examples, but rather turn to a revisionist rape-revenge film that she does not discuss but that could be said to be in line with her argument. I am of course not suggesting that Nussbaum would in any way encourage unconditional forgiveness for rape instead of reporting it to the police in real life. However, in this story the law is portrayed as unavailable, as is so often the case in rape-revenge films, and the question is whether unconditional forgiveness should be portrayed as morally more praiseworthy than violent revenge in this fictional context. I will use this film as a thought experiment here to discuss the merits of unconditional forgiveness.

Unconditional forgiveness in *Twilight Portrait* and *Women Talking*

Twilight Portrait is a Russian rape-revenge film in which we follow Marina, who is raped by the police officer Andrei. She does not turn to the law to report the rape, as there is no reason to trust that her case will succeed in the legal

---

[4] See Maibom (2014), and also Vaage (2023).

system in Russia – indeed, the rapist is himself a police officer and the police is portrayed in other sequences as dismissive and disrespectful of women. So the question we are left with is what to do when the law does not protect women. Claire Henry discusses this as a revisionist rape-revenge film, challenging the conventions of the genre (Henry 2014: 169ff). At first Marina seems to seek revenge, as we see her follow Andrei to the building where he lives. She picks up a broken bottle as she sneaks in after him. But just as she seems to be about to attack him with the bottle in an elevator, she gets down on her knees and performs fellatio on him instead. This is the beginning of a love affair that she initiates, and where she is repeating again and again that she loves him in spite of his resistance, which is at times violent. Henry explores her own response of shock and disorientation in response to this storyline, yet suggests that 'Marina's response to rape is a radical and clever twist on the genre, where seduction and the redemptive power of love are used to seduce Andrei – and the viewer – out of the cycle of violence' (ibid. 179). In this interpretation, Marina's act of love is an attempt to 'cure or redeem Andrei', but also 'self-restoration' (ibid.). Henry does not discuss this in terms of forgiveness, but Marina could be said not just to embrace her rapist and show him love, but also – by doing so – to forgive him and to do so unconditionally: Andrei never shows any remorse for raping her, neither does he admit any blame (Figure 4.1). Marina's act of unconditional forgiveness could be seen as morally praiseworthy in Nussbaum's framework, exactly because vindictive anger is rejected and because forgiveness is unconditional. It seems reasonable

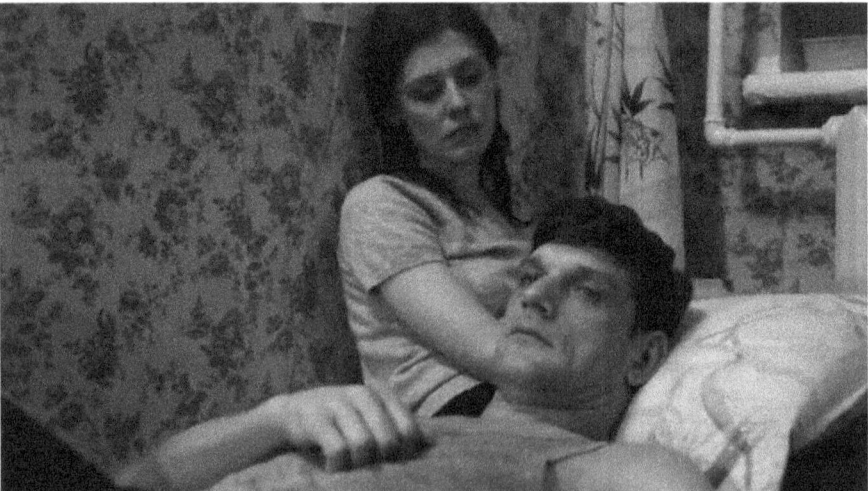

Figure 4.1 Marina forgives the rapist Andrei unconditionally and shows him love (*Twilight Portrait*, 2011).

to claim that the film invites us to see Marina's love as praiseworthy. So I will use this film as an illustration of what Nussbaum's alternative to vindictive anger might look like in the rape-revenge film, and point to a political problem with forgiveness in the context of the Anglo-American philosophical discussions of anger and forgiveness.

Adelaide McGinity-Peebles discusses related questions in her article on *Twilight Portrait*, which also offers analysis of the Russian context in which it was made and released. McGinity-Peebles points out that what we are witnessing is 'Marina's temporary loss of selfhood for the sake of Andrei's redemption' (McGinity-Peebles 2020: 21). She suggests the film symbolises the struggle for women's sovereignty in a patriarchal Russia, and compares Marina to Dostoevsky's heroine in *Crime and Punishment*, who demonstrates self-sacrifice, love and compassion with everyone, and through whom the main character Raskolnikov finds redemption (ibid.) I agree with McGinity-Peebles when she argues that 'this sentimental image of female martyrdom refuses the female protagonist any right to anger or justice against those who exploit her, and therefore Marina's trajectory cannot be seen here to follow a "conventional feminist narrative"' (ibid. 21–2). However, McGinity-Peebles continues by arguing that when Marina reclaims the space of Andrei's apartment, portrayed as a distinctly working-class masculine space, a beginning pathway opens up that enables Marina to occupy her own space within this city. The very end of the film, where Marina walks away from the camera followed by Andrei after he puts down his police badge, uniform jacket and gun, is read optimistically as a breakdown of state-sanctioned patriarchy.

Thus, although McGinity-Peebles discusses Marina's act of love as problematic, ultimately she too accepts that it plays a potentially progressive role in this film. This film's questioning of revenge makes it a revisionist rape-revenge film, and in the final chapter I will show how such films, making the spectator question revenge, are sometimes seen as morally preferable in the literature. I will argue that the reason for this celebration of revisionist rape-revenge films is that the film denies the spectator the emotional satisfaction of revenge, as if prevention of strong emotions such as vindictive anger in and of itself is always morally and politically more valuable. As will be clear to the reader by now, this book questions whether this is the case.

There is a fundamental problem with Marina's love and unconditional forgiveness. Conventionally, being loving and forgiving is not only more readily available to women than being angry and vindictive, but also the culturally expected response: women in particular have been and still are supposed to turn the other cheek. This is arguably intrinsically tied to injustice: all disempowered groups in society might feel a duty, or even need, to forgive as they are not allowed access to the feelings required to insist on one's self-respect (for example, anger), and they do not have any means to justice (for example, the legal system is less likely to restore their sense of justice). Any discussion of forgiveness should take account of power relations and how forgiveness may be more of a duty for the disempowered than a free choice.[5] If all other ways forward are closed, and forgiveness is near imperative, how can unconditional forgiveness be held up and celebrated as a normative ideal? This, then, becomes the fundamental problem in a film where the rape survivor's love and forgiveness are portrayed as redemptive.

The reason this is problematic is that if forgiveness and unconditional love are not a free choice but a duty or burden disproportionately expected of the disempowered, the systematic undermining of the disempowered sense of self might be aggravated. Nussbaum does seem to celebrate characters who can be said to make choices that impede their own well-being for the sake of someone else, like a saint or a martyr, and one problem this leaves us with is how to avoid self-eradication in this view. Furthermore, self-eradication is expected from some people more than others: the powerful are allowed to uphold their sense of self, draw boundaries and demand respect to a greater extent than the disempowered. The price Marina seems to pay is to put Andrei's needs over her own in a reversal of the conventional pattern in rape-revenge film: where the protagonist's vindictive anger in classic rape-revenge films can be seen as her insistence on a sense of self, in this film Marina erases her own self. The resulting problem is that this aftermath may not communicate the pain and horror of rape. Would it not be an emotional straightjacket if unconditional forgiveness and love towards one's rapist were the filmic convention, held up again and again as the way forward for rape survivors in lieu of justice? What would be the political potential of such a convention? In a cultural context where rape is near decriminalised, where there is commonly no justice to be found for rape survivors, and where unconditional forgiveness is perhaps the only culturally condoned response available to her, holding up unconditional forgiveness as an ideal can be seen as stifling and self-denying.

I want to argue that this alternative is not morally preferable. Preventing rape is also portrayed as Marina's responsibility, and something that is within her power: if only Marina loves Andrei, he will not rape again. The burden of love is on the woman, and if only she is loving enough, the world can heal. This film portrays Marina as leaving her own self and her own world behind when she moves into his flat, thus sharing his world and becoming one with him in her selfless act of love. However, arguably this is what many women have been doing for far too long, and it is entirely in line with conventional femininity and dominant ideology. An additional reason to be critical of forgiveness is that it may be a burden those already disempowered are made to shoulder,

---

[5] For example, Cherry discusses the pressure on Black people to forgive White people's racism (Cherry 2021: 102–3).

those unable to insist on their right to be angry, and through their anger communicate clearly their right to self-respect.

Indeed, a related argument about the unavailability of unconditional forgiveness is beautifully articulated in *Women Talking*. This is not a rape-revenge film per se, but anger and a violent uprising are explored as alternatives when the women in a secluded, strict religious community in the US try to decide what to do about the sexual abuse they have all faced for many years: the women are drugged and raped, waking up bloodied and bruised, their accusations that something has happened dismissed as the result of female imagination or Satan. The film covers the forty-eight hours they have to decide what to do after a young girl catches one of the attackers, who then names the others. The attackers are held in prison in town for their own protection but will be let out, and the women try to decide between three alternatives they have come up with: do nothing, stay and fight, or leave. The women in three families are chosen as representatives to discuss these alternatives, and their careful deliberation is what the film is about. Depicting a group of women actively explore available responses to rape allows this film to cover a wide range of emotions and approaches to trauma – from sadness, to anger, fear, and anxiety, to hope for change. The view that the only appropriate response is vengeance is also voiced: Salome, for example, is enraged as the women start talking, and argues that she wants to shoot each man and face God's wrath. Later in an outburst she lists what she is willing to do – killing the men, dancing on graves, burning in Hell – to protect her own children from experiencing the abuse she has experienced. Salome thus gives voice to the female avenger in this film, articulating the vindictive anger response that I argue is explored dramatically in the rape-revenge film. This violent response is covered by the alternative they have to stay and fight. Each of the responses the women voice is discussed or responded to by others, thus making the film a remarkable portrayal of human nature and a philosophical exploration of the response to violation. To stay and fight is eventually dismissed by the group as only leading to more violence, possibly making murderers of some of the women who might act out in anger, so they must prevent this and cannot stay, they agree. In this sense the film does dismiss violent revenge, but vindictive anger is nevertheless voiced, and in a flashback we see Salome attack one of the rapists with a knife – so Salome is already an avenger.

What is most interesting here is the careful discussion of the alternative of doing nothing: the women consider forgiving the rapists, but quickly dismiss it as unviable. The problem they point to is that forgiveness has always been forced upon them, and, as the loving and peaceful Ona puts it, is forgiveness that is forced upon us true forgiveness? This is accentuated further in the story of Mariche, a mother married to a violent drunk, Klaas, who regularly abuses her and the children, and who has now been identified as one of the attackers.

Figure 4.2 Greta apologises to her daughter Mariche for asking her repeatedly to forgive her violent and abusive husband (*Women Talking*, 2022).

Mariche is also one of the women who expresses anger most clearly throughout the deliberation, and she has much to be angry for, not least of all because she has had no choice but to forgive Klaas all of his trespasses, again and again. Her mother Greta apologises to Mariche for this, for being the one who has told her daughter to keep forgiving, as this has been their perceived duty and only option (Figure 4.2). This is part of the philosophical argument in this film, and its systemic analysis – how not just the young men are systematically taught harmful behaviour in the community, but how the women have been brought up to be complicit. Greta surmises that perhaps there is such a thing as misuse of forgiveness, and another elderly woman pitches in, suggesting that forgiveness can be confused with permission. These characters thus articulate some of the problems with unconditional forgiveness that I have discussed. The film also adds an important dimension in the focus on how women with various approaches and viewpoints can come together and talk openly about the abuse, thus supporting each other, and reflect on how they can support each other better – the firm focus on the women, their relationships and deliberations adds an important feminist perspective in the film.[6]

Indeed, forgiveness is dismissed as an alternative, and the women decide to leave. The film is an impressive philosophical exploration of anger and forgiveness, and also of the systemic nature of sexual abuse in this microcosm of a religious community. However, although the ending feels hopeful and moving, as they all gather and leave their homes behind, it is also a nervous ending, for where will they go? Is the wider world they are venturing into any better?

[6] When director and screenwriter Sarah Polley won an Oscar for best adapted screenplay from Miriam Toews's novel for this film, she famously thanked the Academy for 'not being mortally offended by the words "women" and "talking" so close together like that'.

And more broadly, as a solution to sexual violence, there is no female utopian elsewhere to which women can go. Yet the philosophical argument stands: the solution for these women is not to forgive, as has been the expectation, because forgiveness will not be chosen freely, and because forgiveness has run dangerously close to forgetting, ignoring and thus being complicit to a culture of abuse.

Rape-revenge film as a place of rage

Nussbaum sees the logic in anger as flawed, and a type of magical thinking, but we have seen there are potential gains from being angry – and for women in particular, for whom anger has been less accessible culturally. Jack Halberstam suggests that art and fantasy can serve as a ground of resistance when acting as a place of rage, 'a political space opened up by the representation in art, in poetry, in narrative, in popular film, of unsanctioned violences committed by subordinate upon powerful white men' (Halberstam 1993: 187).[7] Conventionally, it is powerful White men who are perpetrators of violence in art, often against women and people of colour. Turning this around, suggests Halberstam, and thus allowing the 'wrong' people to be violent, 'disrupts the logic of represented violence so thoroughly that (at least for a while) the emergence of such unsanctioned violence has an unpredictable power' (ibid. 191). Halberstam discusses the rape-revenge film *Thelma and Louise* (Ridley Scott, 1991) as one such example: the eponymous main characters' revenge was deemed toxic and immoral by some critics, but this can be seen as a film allowing women to imagine the possibility of fighting, of confronting their rapists and stepping out of the role assigned to them as mere victims in popular imaginings of violence.

Brenda Cooper's findings in an empirical study of student respondents writing about this film and their own responses to it by and large support Halberstam's claims about this film as a place of rage for women: her female respondents overwhelmingly applauded the reversal of traditional gender roles when Thelma and Louise take up a more active role and stand up for themselves against sexual assault and sexual harassment. This was described as enjoyable and empowering. Female respondents expressed a desire to be like them, that is, as having 'more courage, stand up to others, and be more aggressive', as one representative respondent put it (Cooper 1999: 27). Another respondent argued that 'the movie is an incredible vision of how every woman would like to feel at least once in her life' (ibid.) Susan Sarandon, the actress who plays Louise, observed that the film represented 'a little bit of every woman's rage' (Sarandon quoted in Cooper 1999: 28).

---

[7] Halberstam borrows the notion of place of rage from the poet June Jordan.

Halberstam argues that Thelma and Louise's imagined violence can serve to destabilise established truths and conventions.[8] Although he is careful to point out that we should avoid making easy assumptions about real effects, and that '[i]magined violence does not stop men from raping women', he nevertheless surmises that 'it might make a man think twice about whether a woman is going to blow him away' (ibid. 199). The main idea here is that fantasy might be productive exactly because it can help us imagine what is off-limits in real life, such as violent revenge, and by doing so, allowing a rage to form that can be destabilising in the real world as well. This could be an additional reason why the rape-avenger's violence is framed as so clearly fictional, as not real, as discussed in Chapter 2: this kind of rage is off-limits in real life, its potential destabilising.

In relation to revenge scenarios, Carl Plantinga examines the notion of 'narrative paradigm scenarios', defined as stories one tells oneself about how things typically go that have been appropriated and become conventions in screen stories. These conventions become standard ways to represents problems humans face and the solutions to such problems, and may thus become templates for action, 'ways of seeing and responding to the world' (Plantinga 2018: 233). Plantinga discusses the revenge plot as one such narrative paradigm scenario, but sees it as problematic because of its tendency to represent violent revenge as a solution to a problem (as I will explore in the last chapter). However, Halberstam emphasises how the role reversal in this film – which is the rape-revenge convention where women take up arms against male assailants – can perhaps serve a function in this film as a fantasy space:

> Women, in other words, long identified as victims rather than perpetrators of violence, have much to gain from new and different configurations of violence, terror and fantasy [...]. [W]omen are taught to fear certain spaces and certain individuals because they threaten rape: how do we produce a fear of retaliation in the rapist? (Halberstam 1993: 191)

What Halberstam is suggesting here is that perhaps such films can feed into, and even change, the narrative paradigm scenarios, to use Plantinga's term.

So, say that one narrative paradigm scenario is the portrayal of the helpless rape victim and the powerful rapist. These are the stories we tell ourselves: stay out of deserted parking garages, of woods and alleyways. But can a potential rapist be made to think twice because women are represented as lethal fighters who will stop short at nothing to get back at them? What would society be like if this were the narrative paradigm scenario? Would women feel more

---

[8] See also related discussions of the same film (Barr 1993: 21–9; Projansky 2001: 148–53, 232; Willis 1993).

confident in moving around in the world because the story they tell themselves is that they have the right to be angered and they have the right to fight back? Halberstam is careful to point out that they do not suggest that *Thelma and Louise* causes real-life effects in this direct manner, nor that the desired effect is that women actually turn violent: the argument is for imagined violence, not real violence. The question is whether fiction as a fantasy space can have an effect on the stories we tell ourselves, and whether rape-revenge film taps into a particularly difficult story about women's anger – as turns it into men's fear. Paradigm scenarios may change in productive ways because of the role reversal. This would potentially be the way the affective structure of the rape-revenge film can be politically productive.

Tania Modleski makes a related point in another context, in a discussion of the grindhouse filmmaker Doris Wishman, whose sexploitation films can easily be dismissed as a feminist's worst nightmare. She argues that films that fethishise and objectivise women and display violence towards woman can sometimes 'function counterphobically for women filmmakers and their female spectators'; she points to her own experience of watching horror films and violent films in a 'deliberate attempt to conquer the abject terror they inspired' (Modleski 2007: 62). Women's cinema can be counter-cinema yet working within the dominant filmic codes, as Claire Johnston postulated (Johnston 1999), and in Modleski's analysis, within women's cinema as counter-cinema there can also be an insistence on the right to 'politically incorrect fantasy' in women's counter-phobic cinema (Modleski 2007: 69). Perhaps the rape-revenge convention of a woman's violent response to rape can work counter-phobically for female spectators.

In line with this I want to suggest that the primary function of the rape-avenger's violent revenge is exactly that it may open up the rape-revenge film as a place of rage. Rape-revenge film as a place of rage can serve the epistemic function of anger: in spite of the tendency in real life to say that perhaps the victim had it coming, that she was asking for it, or that perhaps she enjoyed it, rape-revenge film can hammer in that the experience is simply and truly horrible for her and that she did not deserve it. This is how she is made to feel. There is moral clarity about rape in the universe of rape-revenge film, and the survivor's vindictive anger is central to this clarity. One might learn something about rape from the rape-revenge film – the horror of it – what society denies by shifting the blame to the victim, and again it is the survivor's insistence on punishing the rapist that calls out this all too common misattribution of blame. Finally, the rape-revenge film as a place of rage can be said to have a communicative function: communicating the full horror of rape through its portrayal of the rape survivor's vindictive anger and its insistence on the punishment the rapists deserve.

In this sense Tessman's discussion of anger as a burdened virtue is helpful, and I want to end this chapter by suggesting that rape-revenge film is a burdened viewing experience. It may not enhance well-being, and in an ideal world it might not be the kind of film that one would celebrate. However, in this world, where rape is prevalent and where cultural negotiations on how best to deal with this are ongoing, the rape-revenge film can be said to have the potential to fulfil a function. Triggering anger can sometimes be important. The rape-revenge story can bring us face to face with an affective injustice, unrelentingly, and force us to be in it, stay in that feeling. Feeling affective injustice is painful. On the other hand, watching a woman fight back can make some women feel more powerful. Perhaps at the end of the day, we want to dismiss these stories because the anger they communicate is so unpleasant. These films take the female spectator in particular to a place of rage that a subservient female self has been taught never, ever to go.

In the next two chapters I will examine the angry woman on-screen further by returning to film studies, and exploring how the female avenger first emerged in film, and how her presence in film has been carefully managed.

5. RACE AND THE RAPE-REVENGE FILM

In the previous chapters I mapped the functions vindictive anger and revenge can fulfil, and the reasons why this response has not been readily available to women. I suggested that the rape-revenge film can serve as a place of rage where this outlaw emotion is explored. With greater insight into the contentious nature of women's anger, in this chapter I turn to the history of the rape-revenge film to explore how a female avenger first appeared in film. In this and the following chapter, a main argument is that the exploration of the unconventional protagonist in the rape-revenge film has been contained in complex ways historically: this is a way to control the cultural threat posed by the female rape-avenger as a manifestation of a woman's vindictive anger. In this chapter I will build on the valuable work done by others on race in the rape-revenge film and rape stories historically, and show how this plays out in a contemporary film, *The Nightingale* (Jennifer Kent, 2018), and the television series *I May Destroy You* (Michaela Coel, 2020). However, first I will expand on the shared roots of the rape-avenger and the action heroine in Blaxploitation film, a historical feature that is sometimes ignored in the literature on rape-revenge film.

In her overview of female action heroes in film, Rikke Schubart discusses Pam Grier, the best-known actress in Blaxploitation films such as *Coffy* (Jack Hill, 1973) and *Foxy Brown* (Jack Hill, 1974), as the 'godmother of them all', as the film poster has it: she is the one who 'kicked the door open to future female action' (Schubart 2007: 63). Among the first female action heroes in

Western film culture were indeed Black women in Blaxploitation film, and they were typically on a quest for revenge. This brings us back to exploitation film, picking up on this discussion from the end of the previous chapter as well. Indeed, as I will go on to show, Blaxploitation films share storylines with rape-revenge films, and women-in-prison films, briefly touched upon in Chapter 1 in relation to *Orange Is the New Black* (Jenji Kohan, 2013–19). Stephane Dunn points out that a pivotal Blaxploitation film such as *Foxy Brown* follows the rape-revenge pattern found in other exploitation films (Dunn 2008: 126). But this point can be put more strongly, as it is by Mia Mask, who points out that Foxy Brown's retaliation against her rapist anticipates the revenge sequence in *I Spit on Your Grave* (Meir Zarchi, 1978). She argues that '*Foxy Brown* is a harbinger of rape-revenge films and ought to be considered a cinematic antecedent for its plot structure' (Mask 2009: 97–8). Pam Grier's characters in Blaxploitation film such as *Foxy Brown*, and women-in-prison sexploitation films such as *Black Mama, White Mama* (Eddie Romero, 1973), can be seen as 'a precursor to Clover's notion of the Final Girl' (ibid. 86), which I also discussed in Chapter 1. An important distinction Mask makes is that there is a difference between Grier's appearance in sexploitation films, such as *Black Mama, White Mama* and other women-in-prison films, and her role in Blaxploitation films, which engage more actively with Black politics through their camp aesthetics. The Black women vigilante-survivors portrayed by Grier are thus of central importance when establishing the female avenger, and Mask discusses Grier's characters as a cult cinema intertextual archetype that must be recognised for its radical paradigmatic effect in changing on-screen portrayals of Black women from passive objects to active subjects (ibid. 62, 95). However, as Claire Henry also points out, *Foxy Brown* tends not to be 'recognized as a canonical rape-revenge film despite being a popular early example that instituted some of the key conventions', and ties this to criticism against second-wave feminism for ignoring the experiences of women of colour (Henry 2014: 79). So let us explore the Black female action hero and rape-avenger as she emerged in Blaxploitation.

The Black rape-avenger

Blaxploitation is a subtype of exploitation film, earning its label by exploiting sex and violence, and in the case of Blaxploitation film specifically, though portrayal of Black characters in films made for a Black audience. In his overview of the portrayal of African Americans in American film, Ed Guerrero explains how Hollywood sought to target the Black audience with cheaply made Black-cast films in a cycle of action-adventure films in the ghetto from 1969 to 1974 (Guerrero 1993: 69–70, 82–4; see also Dunn 2008: 1ff; Mask 2009: 58ff). Guerrero shows how the emergence of Blaxploitation was shaped by several conditions, one of which was the rising political and social consciousness of Black people in the civil rights movement, and also the widespread dissatisfaction in this segment of the audience with the degrading portrayal of African Americans in most American film. Hollywood found itself in economic difficulties, so was keen to tap into the African American audience, which made up a significant part of those regularly found in cinemas.

Furthermore, as both Guerrero and Dunn are careful to point out, Blaxploitation film was first and foremost characterised by an exploration of Black masculinity: Guerrero argues that what was at stake was a rediscovery and liberation of Black manhood, leading to the absence of Black women's perspectives in the first cycle of male-led Blaxploitation films (Guerrero 1993: 91). Dunn describes this as the 'hypermasculine machismo at the centre of the genre', with a demonisation of Black women only as the heavily sexualised sex objects used by the Black male characters (Dunn 2008: 2). She also laments the lack of Black feminist exploration of these films, which has contributed to the 'dismissal of the films as so obviously cheap and exploitative of women that the politics therein do not warrant intense scrutiny' (ibid. 3). Her study seeks to rectify this, as does Mask's work, where Pam Grier is celebrated as a significant African American woman on-screen. They explore how Black female heroines – perhaps paradoxically – emerged later in this hypermasculine trend of Blaxploitation films. Indeed, Guerrero argues that these women protagonists were 'configured along the *macho* lines of the black action-fantasy heroes' (Guerrero 1993: 97, emphasis original). And this is my interest here.

Dunn labels the Blaxploitation heroines as 'baad bitches and sassy supermamas', giving her study its title. She describes them as streetwise and supertough, and as showing no fear: the Blaxploitation heroine never wavers in her quest for revenge for injustices not just against herself and her own family, but against the Black community. She is confident and cool, and above all an excellent fighter, giving the film its string of action sequences. Additionally, she is always portrayed as exceptionally attractive, making all men in the story immediately drawn to her. Indeed, she is excessively sexualised. Dunn points out how it is central to the figure of the baad bitch that she breaks with gender boundaries, not just because she 'plays the game' more successfully than her opponents and wins, but also because she is 'in charge of her own sexual representation', manipulating it for her own gain (Dunn 2008: 27). The Blaxploitation heroine thus takes up a difficult position in the history of the representation of Black women in American film, drawing on established racist stereotypes in one sense, especially in the extreme sexualisation, as I will go on to discuss, but also representing something new in that she is an active protagonist in an action film, a powerful, physical fighter: this was new not just in the portrayal of Black women, but for any woman on-screen in American film. This is how she paved the way for female action heroes.

Let us linger for a moment on an observation Jeffrey A. Brown makes: in light of this early history it is surprising 'how critical discussions often overlook the historical importance ethnicity has played in the development of strong female characters' (Brown 2015: 78). Yvonne Tasker argues that it 'is in part the blackness of these heroines which opens up, through notions of black animality, the production of an aggressive female heroine within existing traditions of representations' (Tasker 1993: 21). Elaborating on this point, Brown argues that part of the reason for this shift in American film of the representation of women generally, and of African American women in particular, was the marginality of the Blaxploitation film: mainstream Hollywood would not have wanted to take such a risk without it being tried and tested, but Blaxploitation film capitalised on everything that might be shocking (Brown 2015: 85). However, there are also other politically problematic reasons why the heroine in Blaxploitation film was the first woman in American film to step out of the helplessness and passivity to which she was conventionally confined in action film, and portrayed as active. These reasons are to be found in racist stereotypes about Black women, as pointed out by Tasker. Again, elaborating on this observation, Brown argues that:

> Historically, women of color have not been treated as reverently as white women; they have not been characterized and idealized as symbols of purity, as chaste, as civilized, as dependent on men, or as deserving or in need of protection. (Brown 2015: 112–13)

He sees this as one reason why women of colour were portrayed as 'more physical, more violent, more outspoken, and more likely to use weapons' (ibid. 112) Mask explains how Grier could be portrayed as an aggressive woman because racist myths about Black women were already in place: she points to the myth of the 'bitchy matriarch [that is] coterminous with the racist notion that black women are tougher, stronger, more masculine and more controlling' (Mask 2009: 69).

Dunn quotes Anna Everett's study of race where she sums up the exploitation and Blaxploitation director Jack Hill's work, which includes *Coffy* and *Foxy Brown*, as devising 'narrative situations that rely on race to authorize their speaking the unspeakable, performing the prohibited, defiling the sacred, and generally transgressing most sanctioned codes of social conduct' (Everett quoted in Dunn 2008: 121). Kimberly Springer argues that Black women were basically defined 'as everything that white women were not' (Springer 2001: 174). They could thus be said to serve a function as the Other of White womanhood, representing what would be deemed unacceptable in a revered White woman.

In American film, Black women had been portrayed on-screen only through some limited racist stereotypes, such as the passive and subservient maternal

Mammy, the domineering Sapphire character, portrayed as contemptuous towards the largely ineffectual men in her life, or the hypersexual Jezebel. It is the latter two stereotypes, and in particular the Jezebel, that are relevant here.

The Sapphire is never afraid to be loud and speak her mind, as observed by Springer. Indeed, being openly angry is one of her character traits (Springer 2001). However, the Sapphire is contained by the home context in which she is typically found, and the Blaxploitation heroine breaks free from this as she ventures out in the world on a violent mission. Coffy, for example, has her mind set on getting back at a drug cartel that was responsible for her sister's addiction. Dunn observes that although the Black action heroine is on a quest for revenge, she lacks legitimate means to power and must therefore rely on her sexual power, or what she and others discuss as 'pussy power' (Dunn 2008: 108; see also Alexander 2019 and Roach 2018). Yvonne D. Sims also observes that the Blaxploitation heroine's revenge can be seen as a way of reclaiming her body, tied to her use of sexuality in order to enact revenge (Sims 2006: 80–1). Coffy acts as a prostitute in order to get to the kingpins in the cartel, and this gives ample opportunity to see her in revealing outfits and sexualised situations. Her breasts are almost continually exposed. Dunn carefully analyses the racist nature of this extreme sexualisation of female Blaxploitation protagonists. The racist stereotype she is pointing to is the idea, which was prominent during slavery, that Black women were particularly sexually aggressive, excessive, deviant, promiscuous and wild: these are the roots of the Jezebel stereotype (Dunn 2008: 111ff). What is at stake here are the complex ways the Blaxploitation heroines thus tap into deeply racist stereotypes, such as the angry Black woman as Sapphire, and the Black woman as hypersexual in the Jezebel. Dunn is clear that films such as *Coffy* and *Foxy Brown* are a 'pornographic vision of the black female body through a racist, patriarchal narrative structure' (ibid. 117). Historically significant racial stereotypes are used to produce sensationalist action (ibid. 129).

Dunn points out that the threat of rape is ever present in Blaxploitation film, and in her analysis the rape sequence in *Foxy Brown* is this film's most troubling moment because it 'figuratively enacts the historic function of rape in slavery' (Dunn 2008: 126; see also Guerrero 1993: 99). Foxy Brown is taken to a ranch in the countryside, run by two White men who clearly are expected to rape her, and do so after capturing her when trying to escape, using a lasso to rope her neck and drag her inside while banjo music is playing. Black women's experiences during slavery are explicitly referenced in this rape sequence. Angela Y. Davis explains how racist ideas about the wild sexuality of Black people legitimated White supremacy and widespread sexual abuse of female slaves, which was an essential part of slavery (Davis 1981: 158, 163–4). She shows how this is also closely tied to the myth of the Black rapist, as discussed in Chapter 3: as Black men were seen to 'harbor irresistible and animal-like sexual urges, the entire race is invested with bestiality' (ibid. 163; see also 172). Davis quotes Gerda Lerner, who observes that '[t]he myth of the black rapist of white women is the twin of the myth of the bad black woman – both designed to apologize for and facilitate the continued exploitation of black men and women' (Lerner quoted in Davis 1981: 156). This element of racism was used in what can be seen as a systematic misattribution of blame in the politics of rape, in that the systematic rape by White men that Black women faced was naturalised, thus protecting the White male rapist from prosecution, and instead maintaining a myth about the Black male rapist as a continuous threat to White women in order to legitimate violence towards Black men.

Powerful ideologies are thus at work when delineating between rapist and rape victim along racial lines. Davis points out that this problematic is one of the reasons that Black women were absent from the anti-rape movement (at the time of writing her book): the second-wave feminist movement overlooked the circumstances of the Black woman, and failed to address how racism has both enabled rape and erased the Black woman as rape survivor (see also, for example, Gaines 1988). Davis also argues that the feminist anti-rape movement failed to understand a Black woman's awareness of, and sympathy with, the burden carried by Black men due to racist myths about them. For example, she includes a critical discussion of Susan Brownmiller, a White feminist who was pivotal in the anti-rape movement, for maintaining racist myths about Black men in her discussion, and for ending up sometimes only working for the interests of White women by failing to see how racism is combined with sexism (Davis 1981: 160, 178). Indeed, she points out that lack of convictions for rape is tied to anonymity as a 'privilege enjoyed by men whose status protects them from prosecution', pointing to White men who are 'employers, executives, politicians, doctors, professors, etc.' (ibid. 179). What protects these rapists is not just sexism, but racism, in that the myth is maintained that Black men are the more likely rapists.

Guerrero observes how the myth of the Black rapist is at work explicitly in the anti-Black and overtly racist *Birth of a Nation* (D. W. Griffith, 1915), where a White woman is depicted as jumping off a cliff in order to avoid the advances of Gus (portrayed by a White actor in blackface): a Black man's rape of a White woman is clearly alluded to here. Gus is subsequently lynched by the Ku Klux Klan, who are glorified and portrayed as heroic (Guerrero 1993: 11–17).[1] Guerrero demonstrates how the racism of this and other plantation

---

[1] See also Manthia Diawara's discussion of his own experience as a Black man watching American films such as *Birth of a Nation*. Diawara explores how such a film compels the Black spectator both to identify with and resist the racist representation of Black characters (Diawara 1988).

films established many of the racist stereotypes in American film, such as the previously mentioned Mammy. His main argument is how African Americans have systematically been contained in filmic representations by these stereotypes as racially different Other, and thus how film has also shaped the popular imagination as racist (ibid. 7, 40, 56).

Dan Flory shows in his careful analysis of cognitive theories of character engagement and a corpus of American film that villainy is very often racialised through eliciting what he labels as racialised disgust (Flory 2023a; see also 2005, 2016, 2019, 2021, 2023b). He rightly argues that cognitive film theory has paid far too little attention to race, and he represents one of the few scholars working in this vein of film theory and philosophy who has done so over a number of years. His main argument is that the moral disapproval of villains in film very often draws on forms of White supremacist racialised disgust – or put another way, that the sympathy with heroes and antiheroes, and antipathy toward villains, that are invited by film 'have been and continue to be deeply and recurrently affected by racialized disgust' (Flory 2023a: 23). He shows how this is very much still at work in contemporary film, and not just historically, with villains in revenge scenarios often being presented as foreign or in other ways racialised as racial and ethic Others (ibid. 20). This is in line with Guerrero's observation about the myth of the Black rapist at work in early American film (see also Flory 2016: 1–2). Flory contextualises this as a much broader tendency, and offers an analysis of the affective response that underpins such racist depictions, namely the affect of disgust.

This is an affective response towards out-group members that is easily stirred up by racism, and Flory's point is that American film makes use of racialised disgust to establish out-group characters – from the White creators' point of view – as antagonists, from Native Americans in Westerns, to South Asians and Africans in the colonial adventure film, Vietnamese and Japanese in war films, Arabs in a wide range of genres, etc. He also points to my work on how rape is used to mark a character as a proper villain in the morally murky antihero series (Vaage 2016: 120ff), where I too explore the emotion of disgust to explain the response that is triggered when a character rapes, evoking strong feelings of disgust, anger and antipathy. However, in a critical examination of my own writing on this, Flory rightly points out that film indeed 'often racialize the act' of rape (Flory 2023a: 19). Guerrero's analysis of the myth of the Black rapist at work in American film points to the historical roots of this racialisation of the rapist.

My focus in this book has not been on portrayals of the rapist in and of themselves, and a survey of portrayals of the rapist along ethnic and racial lines is beyond the scope of this book. However, in the classical sources on the rape-revenge film, class has been discussed more often in relation to portrayals of rapists in rape-revenge film. In Clover's classical discussion, for example, she examines how the rapists are often portrayed as threatening rural Others, indeed as 'rednecks', and she argues that this lower-class rural type is used to explore 'anxieties no longer expressible in ethnic or racial terms [that] have become projected onto a safe target – safe not only because it is (nominally) white ...' (Clover 1992: 135). Tanya Horeck also argues that class can sometimes 'function as a racialized difference', and points to the portrayal of the rapist Cliff 'Scorpion' Albrecht as not just a lower-class man but of 'swarthy complexion' in *The Accused* (Jonathan Kaplan, 1988) (Horeck 2004: 103). The racialisation of rapists is thus relevant to rape-revenge films as well, but here I will return to my main focus on the female avenger as she emerged in Blaxploitation film.

Guerrero quickly dismisses the mere possibility that Black women would like the Blaxploitation heroine, thus agreeing with the Black critic Donald Bogle, whom he sees as 'right to point out that black women could find little in their adolescent-male-fantasy-oriented roles to identify with' (Guerrero 1993: 99). However, in spite of the troubling political implications in the portrayal of the Black action heroine, and in contrast to Guerrero's assumptions about Black female spectators, Dunn calls for a 'reading beyond acknowledgement of this problematic sexualisation' (Dunn 2008: 4). Indeed, she points out how male reviewers would typically stop short of exploring how the Blaxploitation heroine might be of significance to the Black female spectator:

> Criticism addressing the blaxploitation genre by and large dismisses or ignores issues of black female spectatorial desire – how these fantasy narratives and character icons might both repel and appeal to generations of black female audiences given the films' patriarchal structure but unique 'fantasy' of baad black female action heroes. (Ibid.)

Bogle and Guerrero are later also mentioned explicitly, and Dunn writes that the

> problem with [their] dismissing reading is that it obscures how black women may negotiate the racial and gender politics underlying the narrative but still find various types of pleasure in viewing action cinema generally and the rare fantasies of a baad black women heroine. (Ibid. 16)

Contrary to Bogle and Guerrero's assumptions, Dunn uses several examples from her own friends and family to illustrate how at least some female African American spectators did appreciate the Black action heroine's strength while also being acutely aware of the racism in the portrayal (Dunn 2008: 85, 107). This can serve to illustrate what bell hooks discusses as the oppositional gaze that Black women may need to develop when watching the racist portrayals of

Black people commonly found in American film (hooks 1996; see also Dunn 2008: 17–18). While recognising and opposing the racist representation of the Blaxploitation heroine, the response Dunn describes also includes appreciating her as a fantasy (indeed, perhaps even a counterphobic fantasy, in line with Modleski's analysis in the previous chapter). The productive potential for fantasy genres to imagine difference is explored by both Guerrero, who argues that social anxieties can be explored in the subversive politics and countercultural critique sometimes found in sci-fi, horror and fantasy films (Guerrero 1993: 57), and Dunn, as she explores how the Black women fighters in Blaxploitation film served as fantasy (Dunn 2008: 5ff).[2] Characters such as Coffy and Foxy Brown may have appealed to some Black women's desire to see a strong, tough and fearless Black woman on-screen taking on powerful White men and winning. An additional background for this pleasure is that the Black action heroine stands in contrast to the portrayal of women in most male-led Blaxploitation films, where women were reduced to 'the cool hero's subordinate sex object' (Dunn 2008: 3), and in response to the lack of Black female protagonists in American film overall. Thus, in spite of roots in racist stereotypes, the Blaxploitaiton heroine also represented something new.

Silencing the Black woman's experience of rape

Although Blaxploitation film heroines paved the way for women protagonists in action film, when adopted in mainstream film culture in the Hollywood action film, with few exceptions the protagonist was to be a White woman. This is mirrored in the rape-revenge film as well, where the protagonists were mostly White after the initial founding phase. What I want to suggest here is that this is tied to the way conventional femininity is by no means inclusive: it is not class-less or race-less, but middle-class and White.

It is worth allowing for an aside here to note how these norms related to conventional femininity play out in the courtroom in order to demonstrate how these ideologies are at work in today's Britain. In her discussion of how women are treated in British jurisprudence based on her own experiences in the courtroom, lawyer Helena Kennedy QC points out how easily juries seem to perceive something as being 'off' when women take the witness stand (Kennedy 2018). She discusses how, implicitly, there are norms of the perfect witness, and observes how this ideal witness should be as close as possible to middle-class conventional femininity:

---

[2] These ideas about fantasy link back to my discussion of realism versus fantasy in Chapter 2, and also the discussion of the rape-revenge film as an imagined place of rage in Chapter 4.

> the nearer I could get to painting a female client as a paragon of traditional womanhood, the more likely she was to experience the quality of mercy. If a woman with a weakness for bovver boots could be persuaded into wearing pearls and a broderie anglaise blouse she might just tip the judicial scales in her favour. (Kennedy 2018: 25)

Taking the witness stand, ideally a woman should signal that she is a good wife and mother, a respectable woman. Women from troubled backgrounds, and from working-class backgrounds, are perceived as less credible. Women who have a history of promiscuity and acting out are less credible, as are women with a history of any kind of mental illness. However, the main point here is what Kennedy writes about 'the other woman' and how women from Black, Asian or other minority ethnic backgrounds (BAME) are treated (ibid. 191ff). In addition to mapping the ways BAME people generally face discrimination by the law, she argues that Black women in particular bear the brunt of the combined effects of racism and sexism: 'black women are penalised for failing to conform to "appropriate" notions of womanhood' (ibid. 199). For example, she explains how many of the Black women she has defended come to court angry because they are made to appear in a system that discriminates again Black people. However, in the court of law, their 'anger was rarely understood; it was taken for aggression, and as an unwillingness to show deference' (ibid. 200). Kennedy alludes to the racist stereotype of the angry Black woman here, as explored in the Sapphire stereotype in American film, for example, and how young Black women in particular must be cautious not to appear 'lippy' and assertive in order to be heard. The police tend to assume that Black women will be aggressive and violent, and deal with them aggressively; Black women are also assumed to be promiscuous (ibid. 202). The systematic racism facing British BAME women are at work in rape cases:

> In rape cases in particular, the black experience seems to represent an amplified version of the disadvantages facing women generally. When black women are raped they have problems having their allegations heard, because all the myths about women generally merge with those about black sexuality and aggression. In the eyes of many jurors, black women are not readily seen as fragile creatures in need of protection. (Ibid. 202)

This resonates with a discussion that emerged in Philip Schlesinger and his colleagues' empirical study of British women viewing violent content in film and television. There was a marked difference between groups of women respondents to the film *The Accused* (Jonathan Kaplan, 1988), where the White woman Sarah Tobias is raped by a group of men in a bar while many others were watching, and where some of the men who watched are convicted. British Afro-Caribbean women experienced the ethnicity of the main protagonist as the central challenge when watching, urging them to ask 'What if the victim had been Black?' As one respondent puts it, 'I know that the whole line of the story would've changed ... and I know that the verdict could have been different. And I know that the support ... the sympathy would've been very different' (Schlesinger et al. 1992: 141). What this respondent is pointing out is that the happy ending, where the main character Sarah is believed, would have been different if Sarah had not been White.

In her discussion of this film, Tanya Horeck points out that this respondent's reflection is actually 'uncannily accurate' (Horeck 2004: 104). Horeck examines the ways this film draws on a real-life rape case, known in the US media as the Big Dan rape case, named after the bar in which a woman was gang-raped, as she is in the film. In this real case, the woman who was raped was of immigrant Portuguese descent, and thus not the WASP character that actor Jodie Foster presents as, and although the rapists were convicted, two cheering onlookers charged with aiding and abetting rape were acquitted (Horeck 2004: 70–6, 91, 104). Horeck discusses the fictionalised version of the Big Dan's rape case in *The Accused* as an example of historical revisionism in two ways: through changing the legal outcome of the rape case in order to give the story a happy ending where the law gets it right in the end by sentencing those who were spectators to the gang rape, and by omitting ethnic tensions found in the media coverage of the real-life rape. In the media both the woman and the men who raped her were described as part of a community of immigrants from the Azores, and Horeck maps how this gave rise to much anti-immigration rhetoric in the media. Her conclusion is that a comparison between the media coverage of the Big Dan's rape case and *The Accused* 'brings to light cultural unease reading gender, race and ethnicity' (ibid. 115). Central to her analysis is the oft-ignored 'whiteness of the film's characters', which she argues is strikingly absent not only from the public discourse on this film, but from 'feminist readings of the film' (ibid. 102). The filmmakers thus nudged Sarah Tobias as a rape survivor closer to the perfect witness as discussed by Kennedy, although she is portrayed as working class.

Sarah Projansky points out that 'whiteness is by far the dominant racialization of rape in late-twentieth-century fictional film and television shows' (Projansky 2001: 161). She observes that Black women are systematically displaced in these representations of rape, or more precisely, that they may have high visibility in terms of explicit portrayal of rape, but yet the Black rape survivor is given no voice in that attention to the Black woman's response to rape is 'conspicuously absent' (ibid. 160). She maps how the rape of Black women is displaced in various ways, such as being written off as only a problem historically and thus no longer relevant, or as a problem that affects

Black men more than Black women in stories that explicitly challenge the myth of the Black rapist, for example (ibid. 162, 166). She does explore a few more nuanced representations of African American women's relationship to rape in films such as *She's Gotta Have It* (Spike Lee, 1986) and *Daughters of the Dust* (Julie Dash, 1991), and sees the latter as the most 'sustained, critical and feminist representation of African American women's gendered, racialized, and political relationship to rape' in the storylines about Eula and Yellow Mary's experiences of rape (ibid. 193). However, she argues that even in these films there is a tendency to focus on Black men's experience of rape, such as the focus on Eula's husband Eli and his response to the rape of his wife in *Daughters of the Dust*, thus contributing to the silencing of African American women.

Furthermore, in spite of the central role in establishing rape-revenge conventions, this silencing of the Black woman's experience of rape is found also in the representations of the female avenger in Blaxploitation film. In contrast to *I Spit on Your Grave*, for example, in *Foxy Brown* the focus is arguably not on the veritable horror of the rape to the same extent, or on her trauma. For example, when the eponymous main character is raped in *Foxy Brown*, this is merely portrayed as one of many slights from her opponents: the rape is not emphasised as an exceptional crime, and she is not portrayed as traumatised by it. She displays little emotion beside the determination and anger she has been displaying all along, and simply keeps on fighting, taking down the rapists and moving on in the narrative. This can serve to illustrate Projansky's point about how high visibility of rape can go hand in hand with silencing of Black rape survivors. The rape sequence stands in stark contrast to the rape sequences in *I Spit on Your Grave*, for example, where Jennifer's utter despair, pain and horror are continuously expressed. In her analysis of the rape sequence in *Foxy Brown*, Dunn points out how the narrative quickly moves on, thus denying 'any physical or emotional signs of Foxy's ordeal. The narrative returns to Foxy's mission of avenging her man's murder without missing a beat' (Dunn 2008: 127; see also Lentz 1993: 401–2 n.22). She is acting out her vindictive anger against male perpetrators unhesitatingly and confidently, and is no more fazed by rape than by any other obstacles thrown her way (Figure 5.1). In the rape-revenge film, as in most representations of rape in the media, the trauma of rape is thus most prominently explored through a White woman.

I have shown how the trend of action heroines and rape-avengers shares its origin in the Blaxploitation film. Yet, once the audience appeal had been tried and tested, and the formula of violent women proved successful, quickly Hollywood reverted to White women protagonists.[3] Even in alternative

---

[3] Sims discusses how after the Blaxploitation phase ended in the mid-1970s, the next major Hollywood action film with a Black woman protagonist would be *Catwoman*

RACE AND THE RAPE-REVENGE FILM

Figure 5.1 Foxy Brown makes her escape from the farm (*Foxy Brown*, 1974).

rape-revenge films at the fringes of film culture, White women were predominantly the protagonists, probably also due to the Whiteness of the film industry. There are a few exceptions to this in rape-revenge film, such as *Descent* (Talia Lugacy, 2007), a rape-revenge film with a Latina protagonist analysed by others in the literature on rape-revenge film. For example, Henry offers a careful reading of this film and the role racism plays in the rape sequence (Henry 2014: 79ff; see also Heller-Nicholas 2011: 161–3). I will turn to two other contemporary examples to expand on this important work.

THE NIGHTINGALE AS POST-COLONIAL RAPE-REVENGE FILM

The Nightingale is a historical drama set in the colonisation period of Australia, exploring rape-revenge conventions in a critical, postcolonial framework.[4] The historical context is different from the manifestations of White supremacy and racism in an American context, as explored above, but is of course related, in that the power relations at work in the colonisation of Australia were fuelled by

---

(Pitof, 2004) (Sims 2006: 22, 49). This absence does of course offer an important context for understanding the innovation and much-needed presence of powerful Black women on-screen in American action and superhero films such as *Black Panther* (Ryan Coogler, 2018) and *Black Panther: Wakanda Forever* (Ryan Coogler, 2022), serving to emphasise how they are few and far between.

[4] Both Heller-Nicholas and Henry offer an overview of rape-revenge films in an Australian context, see Henry (2014: 110–11) and Heller-Nicholas (2011: 107ff).

the same colonial, racist ideologies. My interest here is how a White woman – the protagonist Clare – is portrayed compared to two Indigenous Australian characters in the film, Billy and Lowanna. This will allow me to explore how the tendencies outlined above on race play out in this contemporary film.

Clare is an Irish convict who has earned her freedom and married fellow Irishman Aidan, but the man she has worked for and is still working for, the English lieutenant Hawkins, is abusing her sexually, raping her repeatedly and refuses to let her go. Aidan, unaware of the sexual abuse, loses his temper with Hawkins for not granting his wife freedom, and in revenge for this Hawkins brings along two of his soldiers to rape her in front of Aidan and their baby daughter in their cabin. In the long, graphic and claustrophobic rape sequence that follows, the husband is eventually shot and the baby, crying frantically, is killed by being bashed against a wall while Clare is raped first by Hawkins and then one of the soldiers, Ruse. The two rapists will tend to evoke strong feelings of disgust, anger and antipathy, as explored above. And the Englishmen in question here are not just portrayed as drunken rapists, but as filthy and cowardly, untrustworthy and mean even to each other. Furthermore, as rapist villains they are notably not people of colour, but rather the White men in positions of power that Davis argues have typically been granted anonymity and protection by the law. This is an important affective element in this postcolonial film, in contrast to the racism often found in portrayals of villainy, as mapped by Flory.

Clare is portrayed as a lower-class Irish woman who simply has no legal protection, and the film explores how lower-class women are at greater risk of rape than middle-class women. When Clare tries to report the lieutenant's crimes, she is instantly dismissed as unbelievable because she is a convict. The rape is thus used to highlight her lack of rights. Clare is not the perfect witness. Without any other means to justice, she takes off on a quest for vengeance. An important political theme and argument in this film is arguably the power relations in colonialism and how they play out in rape cases when it comes to gender and class.

The film takes the political critique one step further when she, at first unwillingly, teams up with an Indigenous Australian man, Billy, in order to track down the gang of rapists and murderers as they are heading up north in Australia. She needs a guide to get her there through the wilderness, and pays Billy to come with her. At first, she is dismissive of him and distrustful, caught up as she is in prevailing racism in this environment: Indigenous Australians are hunted and killed, men strung up and hung from trees as Clare and Billy are moving through the woods. Clare is presented as scared of Billy, vigilantly keeping her rifle pointed at him continuously. But the aggressors threatening Clare and Billy as they make their way north are all Englishmen, and they all instantly see Clare as someone they may rape, and Billy as a Black who should be shot. The misogyny and the racism of the English colonisers are portrayed as closely linked. The English soldiers represent the UK as imperial power and colonisers, and this culture of the White man and his flawed masculinity is ultimately what gives Clare and Billy a common cause in a shared quest for vengeance.[5] Billy takes up an important role in this film, and gives voice to the trauma of the Indigenous Australian people. However, in line with Projansky's observations in an American context, the focus is again on a Black man: it is an Indigenous Australian man rather than a woman who is given a voice.

However, the link between misogyny and racism is accentuated further as the Englishmen capture and repeatedly rape the Indigenous Australian woman Lowanna. The sequence where she is first captured mirrors the gang rape of Clare: Lowanna is out foraging with her toddler, and there she is captured by Ruse, who also raped Clare. Lowanna starts screaming, and her child crying, thus resembling Clare's ordeal in the cabin, and using the frightened crying of her child to emphasise her terror. However, it is also interesting to compare the rape sequences. The gang rape sequence in Clare and Aidan's cabin feels affectively unbearable, and arguably it is the tight combination of quickly edited shots emphasising strong affective reactions that has such an effect. There are close-up shots of Clare's face as she is pinned down to a table by the raping Englishmen, thus giving access to her absolute despair – from shock, to horror, to pain and, finally, to a state of limp and soundless trauma. She is actively struggling, trying to get to her baby, and this adds to the feeling of intense helplessness in the sequence. In addition to this continuous focus on Clare, we see the husband's screaming, his anger and his desperate fighting to try to help her, thus adding powerful affective feelings of despair, helplessness and rage from his point of view too. The baby girl is crying loudly in distress until she is violently silenced. Even the soldiers are portrayed as stressed, and especially the third one, who never rapes Clare but is the one who kills the baby. The gang rape is portrayed as a whirlwind of strong emotions, with the helplessness, despair and anger of several characters in sharp and unrelenting focus in a tightly edited sequence that rapidly moves between shots of the various characters in close proximity to each other, making the sequence feel claustrophobic, as if the spectator too is entrapped in that small, dark cabin with no escape. The whole sequence is also very long, seven minutes in total, adding to the feeling of entrapment. The killing of both Aidan and the baby

---

[5] An interesting parallel here is found in the miniseries *The English* (Hugo Blick, 2022), exploring rape-revenge conventions in a Western setting in the US, where a White woman rape survivor teams up with a Native American man in her quest for revenge, and where redemption is arguably portrayed as found in the trusting relationship that develops between the two.

is used to underline and strengthen the horror of the rape: it is used to communicate even more clearly Clare's helplessness and terror.

The rape of Lowanna as mirroring Clare's rape is arguably used to show the systematic misogyny of the English soldiers. It is also portrayed as racist, in that Ruse makes a case for taking Lowanna with them because he has always 'wanted to try one'. And the portrayal of this rape is horrific too. But arguably it is not emphasised as clearly stylistically as such. Whereas there was no break or escape from the close proximity the spectator is brought into when Clare is raped in the cabin, we see the rape of Lowanna in much shorter glimpses, less than thirty seconds twice, intercut with shots of the men around the campfire talking. Where the gang rape in the cabin was presented as a nightmarish turmoil, with rapid editing emphasising the terror and violence, the rape of Lowanna is stylistically calmer, with shots of Lowanna, from over the shoulder of Hawkins, who rapes her first, and her point of view on him before the camera follows him as he returns to the group of men chatting around the campfire and staying there with him: the focus shifts to a conversation between Hawkins and a little boy in the group, who asks him whether they are hurting her. We continue to hear Lowanna screaming, but off-screen and from afar. We then cut back to a short shot of her again as she is raped by Ruse, again a close-up shot of her face, as she is now pleading and praying softly for help, ending with her point of view on the night sky. The editing is much calmer, as if the camera does not channel her despair in the way it channelled Clare's through stylistic means. Furthermore, the rape of Lowanna is not characterised by the same emphasis on violent rage, on fighting and on her terror; it feels sadder, heartbreaking for sure, but not as claustrophobic, as the spectator is given respite from her ordeal with the switch to the men around the campfire, thus not staying with her as relentlessly. There is thus a difference between the portrayal of the rape of the White woman and the woman of colour in this film.

Adding to this, of course, is the fact that Clare is the film's protagonist and, enraged, she sets out to get justice: Clare's response gives the story its narrative trajectory. Lowanna is a minor character and is shot by the Englishmen without further ado (Figure 5.2). In this sense, Projansky's point about the tendency for the rape of women of colour to have visibility, but to not give them voice is still valid: this is Clare's story, and it is her response to rape that is explored. Lowanna is quickly killed. Again, the focus is on the response of a man of colour, Billy, allowing him rather than Lowanna to speak the trauma of the Indigenous Australian population.

Whereas Lowanna is shot and left behind in the story, both Clare and Billy get their revenge, thus affording poetic justice to the White woman and the Indigenous man. Picking up on the discussion of vindictive anger, it is interesting that in this film there is both violent revenge and a verbal confrontation.

RACE AND THE RAPE-REVENGE FILM

Figure 5.2 Lowanna is a minor character who is raped, and quickly killed (*The Nightingale*, 2018).

Clare kills the young solider, the baby killer, in a fit of bloody rage, in line with rape-revenge conventions. After this killing, Clare's bloodlust subsides, as if the shadow self, the enraged outlaw that I have discussed previously, has got what she wants, and Clare's full sense of self is yet again appearing more integrated. She is exhausted and portrayed less as driven by anger, but rather as vulnerable: she is a woman in mourning. Clare emerges as more conventionally feminine after killing the young soldier – being the avenger made her courageous and powerful, but now she is more hesitant and in need of Billy's help. When Clare and Billy finally reach Hawkins and Ruse, after a long ordeal in the wilderness, she uses words as her weapon: she confronts Hawkins in the soldiers' saloon, in front of witnesses, and spells out how he raped her and killed her family, and how she is not his to own. Her revenge is to ruin his honour, and the one thing he cares about, namely his career. And it is Billy who puts on traditional body paint and sets out to kill them both as a final act of resistance and revenge for having taken away his home, his country, and also killing the one man he had made family after his own family was slaughtered by the colonisers. Perhaps this is what saves Clare's life. It is her friendship with a good man that gives the film's ending a hopeful feeling for her. Although Billy is badly wounded and probably dying, in the very final sequence as she is watching the sunrise, singing, and the film ends just as she is drawing a breath, as if to say something – on the verge of something.

The friendship between Clare and Billy is unusual in the rape-revenge setting, and is used to highlight that there are alternatives to toxic masculinity. The beauty of their friendship is portrayed through bird metaphors: she is first presented to us as the nightingale for her beautiful singing voice, and he is a Mangana, the blackbird. Magically, a blackbird comes to Clare's rescue when they are temporarily parted towards the end of their quest in the wilderness, after she has killed and is more vulnerable. Accepting his ways has made nature safe for her, it is the culture and civilisation brought in by the colonisers that is portrayed as decayed and dangerous. Clare and Billy's friendship is used to emphasise how questions of gender, class and race are connected when it comes to rights and the law. They are both lawless, neither of them enjoying protection from the law written by the White male powers that be.

The Nightingale is a contemporary rape-revenge film in which some rape-revenge conventions are intact, including the violence of both the rape and the revenge sequences, although this rape-revenge film also includes a forceful verbal confrontation. It arguably puts these conventions to good use to portray the horrors of the colonisation of Australia, as suffered by the Indigenous Australian and convicts. Indigenous Australians are given voice in the film, and the misogyny in the rape of the White woman Clare is mirrored in the rape of the Indigenous woman Lowanna, but, in line with tendencies in the rape-revenge film and its emphasis on the White woman's trauma, Lowanna is not given a proper voice in the film – rather, it is Billy as an Indigenous man who voices his trauma.

CRITIQUE OF CONVENTIONS: *I MAY DESTROY YOU*

I May Destroy You is a notable recent exception to the displacement of Black women in rape stories in its exploration of the Black British protagonist Arabella's response to rape. As Arabella is working on a book manuscript she is due to publish, she slowly realises through traumatic flashbacks that her drink was spiked and she has been raped after a night out. Like a rape-survivor turned detective, she sets out to investigate, to find out what happened and who did it. This storyline is revisited occasionally as the television series progresses, but instead of following this one path narrowly, the series makes good use of its small ensemble cast of Arabella's friendship group, and the longer duration of a television series, allowing its narration to expand in a complex portrayal of additional cases. For example, Arabella also experiences how Zain, hired by her publishers to help her with her book but turning into her lover, unbeknown to her removes the condom when they have sex, but also other characters' experience relating to deceit, consent, sexual assault and victimhood. In her analysis of this series, Caetlin Benson-Allott concludes that it 'is a monumental meditation on race, rape, and their televised combinations that offers searing insights into the culture it critiques' (Benson-Allott 2020: 105). She argues that it is an innovative and unique critical interrogation of the narrative conventions of stories about rape on television, in particular police procedurals, and even other innovative series such as *Unbelievable* (Susannah Grant, Michael Chabon and Angelet Waldman 2019). It is the Whiteness of the latter television series, as in most rape stories on TV, which fails to explore the intersections between gender and race in relation to rape. Through its exploration of how not just Arabella but also her close friends Kwame and Terry all experience sexual assault, *I May Destroy You* reveals how rape culture is a systemic issue. It also explores the position of rape victim, and who it is available to, in several storylines in addition to Arabella's. When her friend Kwame, a gay Black man, tries to report a sexual assault, the police officer is portrayed as homophobic and deeply uncomfortable by having to take down the details in this case (episodes 4 to 5). The series thus interrogates the heteronormativity of most rape stories, as carefully discussed by Benson-Allott as well.

The series actively explores how race enters the picture through the portrayal of Theodora, a girl we get to know in a flashback sequence from when Arabella and her best friend Terry were adolescents (episode 6). In this flashback, we see that Theodora has consensual sex with a fellow student, Ryan, but he starts taking pictures without her knowing. And then he offers to pay her. Theodora sets a plan in motion where she accuses him of raping her: she cuts herself with a knife and claims he did that to her when he forced her to have sex. This is her way of getting back at him. Arabella and Terry, however, get access to pictures that they use to inform the head teacher that the sex was consensual. In their analysis of the situation, Theodora is a White girl guilty of using her White privilege to accuse an innocent Black boy of rape – and there is a long cultural history to this, with Black men's sexuality seen as a threat to the purity of the White woman, as explored above. Arabella and Terry surmise that the White girl's tears have too high a currency, and that their own tears, had they tried to report a rape, would quickly have been dismissed. As Arabella puts it, their tears, as Black girls, would have been seen as 'weapons of mass destruction'. These girls are in effect discussing institutional racism and how it plays out in rape cases. The episode points to the importance of race in the discourse on rape, and how the rape victim has often been only seen as White. The storyline is effectively used to comment on how White feminists have failed to address how race enters the equation, and how Black women can feel solidarity with Black men, and identify with their struggle against racism, and that the White woman can thus be an oppressor rather than an ally. In this sense Theodora can be seen as a representation of what has come to be known as 'the Karen' in public discourse – the entitled White woman who is oblivious to her own privilege as White,[6] in spite of Theodora's troubled working-class home context. Theodora is portrayed as racist, hissing racist slurs as she is shown away from school after her ploy is revealed.

However, in the series' present time Theodora serves as a friend for Arabella: the adult Theodora is running a self-help group for rape survivors. The episode opens and ends with Theodora's statement to the participants in the group about wanting to help other survivors of sexual violence. As Benson-Allott points out, the creator's choice here is arguably a way to demonstrate 'how white privilege dominates and distorts conversations about sexual violence' (Benson-Allott 2020: 103). Arabella participates in Theodora's rape survivor group and finds Theodora supportive, but Terry remains sceptical, seeing Theodora as simply posing as a rape survivor. Benson-Allott argues that Arabella is struggling to make sense of her own relationship to Theodora, and that this 'shows viewers how difficult it is to understand oneself or others in the face of intersectional oppression' (ibid.) In Benson-Allott's reading, Arabella's friendship with Theodora is thus not meant to exonerate Theodora, but serves to illustrate just how difficult it is for Arabella to recognise that Theodora's positioning of herself is politically problematic.

In the final episode, *I May Destroy You* explicitly explores rape-revenge conventions. The main plot about Arabella and the aftermath of rape reaches a forking path point where multiple possible endings are explored. This is an ending befitting the series' complex examination of responses to rape. There is anger, and Arabella vents some of that anger through social media, directed towards Zain, and towards her other, unknown rapist who spiked her drink on a night out. There is trauma, which is skilfully portrayed through subjective narration, where we experience Arabella's flashbacks with her, as they keep intruding with disturbing vividness in her everyday life, often first introduced by a dreadful high-pitched sound, followed by imagery – a man pounding away at someone, at Arabella – in a stall in a restroom somewhere. In line with what is by far the most statistically typical outcome, her case is closed by the police without identifying a suspect: there is no justice for the rape survivor through the law.

Arabella starts to hang out with her faithful friend Terry at the bar where Arabella's drink was spiked in the hope of seeing something that might help

---

[6] Myisha Cherry defines Karen as 'a trope that describes white women who police others (and call the police on them) over minor inconveniences. Karens also weaponize their white womanhood in ways that are dangerous to non-whites' (Cherry 2021: 109). She points to the real-life example of a White woman jogger in Central Park in New York who called the police on a Black male birdwatcher, claiming he was threatening her when he asked her to put her dog on the lead in an area that prohibited off-lead dogs (ibid. 108).

RACE AND THE RAPE-REVENGE FILM

Figure 5.3 Arabella's imagined revenge on the man who raped her (*I May Destroy You*, 2020).

her remember more – perhaps even spotting the rapist. This is where we find her in the very last episode. And we are seemingly presented with various alternative endings to this story. First we see Arabella recognise the rapist in the bar and proceed with a plan she has hatched to take revenge on him, taking on the fantastical and clearly fictional features of the rape-avenger that I have explored in this book. With Terry and Theodora as her henchwomen, Arabella drugs him and follows him and ends up beating his face to a pulp and killing him (Figure 5.3). Theodora plays a notably active role in this revenge scenario, serving to highlight how the trend of female avengers has been dominated by White women. Arabella is also sporting a blonde wig, as a nod to the transformation of the protagonist in rape-revenge film.

As they discuss how to get rid of the body, we are suddenly back in an earlier sequence, where Arabella is at home with her flatmate Ben, in their rooftop garden, listening to a loud bird, before venturing out to the bar. Then we see the same events unfold, except this time around Terry has a plan: they set him up and intend to call the police in order to put him away in prison after having been caught red-handed when attempting to rape Arabella. In this version the rapist is indeed arrested, but he also turns much more fragile, a vulnerable person who is himself clearly haunted by trauma.

Then there is a third version, much more dreamlike in nature, in which the gender roles are seemingly reversed and where there is a love story between Arabella and the rapist. In between these versions we see Arabella working on her wall of Post-it notes, a writing strategy to finish her book, suggesting that these are endings Arabella is working through in her imagination. Then there is a final, fourth version, where she is in the garden with Ben and never ventures out to track down her rapist at all. Arabella has worked her way through various stages of trauma and grief: from fear of the rapist in post-traumatic stress, to explosive anger in the rape-revenge scenario, to a more nuanced, revisionist take on the rapist where she is exploring empathy with him – trying to understand what might make someone do something like this. Imagining his reasons and his background also makes him appear less powerful. The rapist is now also a victim, which is not used to justify or excuse what he has done to Arabella, but is portrayed as one step towards her peace of mind.

For the present purposes, it is interesting that the first two alternative endings represent two traditions in the portrayal of rape in on-screen stories, the rape-revenge film and the revisionist rape-revenge film, the latter as defined by Henry (Henry 2014). Notably, in this complex series they are both there, portrayed as steps in Arabella's recovery. Before she is able to feel empathy with her rapist, perhaps there needs to be anger. Her vindictiveness is portrayed as a way out of post-traumatic stress, in which the rapist is threatening, frightening and all-powerful: he was the one in control, taking control away from her. Her imaginary scheme is one first step in confronting him and taking back control. The first thing she imagines when having that control is losing it in a fit of violent rage. And for the spectator, there is closure in this: it is affectively rewarding to watch a rapist, whose case is closed by the police and who will probably never be caught, be punished. However, there is also something unsettling in this revenge sequence, highlighted by the use of music, for example, which is strangely upbeat and light-hearted, making the sinister nature of this plot turn seem eerie and out of place. This is a cue that this should not be the ending to Arabella's story. As a series tapping into the real complexity of contemporary discourses on sexual assault and consent, this is not in fact a befitting ending. This is the revenge fantasy, which serves a role, but Arabella must go further.

The second version of the ending revises rape-revenge conventions: Arabella takes the perpetrator out of the perpetrator, so to say, exploring him as a victim with his own trauma. In the fight against rape culture, understanding what makes men rape in the first place is essential. However, in the fight against rape culture, the hurt, trauma and extreme violation of rape also needs communicating, and this is where *I May Destroy You* notably gives voice to the Black rape survivor, making sure her voice and her response is the focus of the story. And in dramatic form, confined to a fictional setting, the rape-revenge film can do this too. It is significant that even in this complex series, the rape-avenger is given a role.

By way of conclusion, it is worth dwelling on the force of this representation of Arabella's imagined revenge, and how rarely it has been seen on-screen since the Blaxploitation film: a Black woman is taking her anger out on a

White rapist. The Black woman's anger is given dramatic expression in this fantasy justice sequence. *I May Destroy You* actively examines and critiques notions of victimhood, consent and the response to rape, effectively commenting on and revising tendencies in rape stories in film and television, putting an intersectional focus on race firmly into the picture. However, Arabella's violent revenge is contained as fantasy.

This is in line with Guerrero's analysis of the containment of Black characters, and I will expand on this analysis of containment strategies in the next chapter, where I turn to Lisa Purse's exploration of the containment of all violent women in action film.

6. CONTAINING THE THREAT OF THE FEMALE AVENGER ON-SCREEN

I have explored various genre contexts that feed into the rape-revenge convention, such as horror film (Chapter 1), Western film and its vengeance tradition (Chapter 3) and Blaxploitation films (in the previous chapter). The rape-revenge convention draws from a wide range of genres, as argued by Alexandra Heller-Nicholas (2011), and as epitomised by Lisbeth Salander, one of my case studies in Chapter 2. I now turn to the literature in film theory on the female action hero as she appeared from the 1980s onwards.[1] Taking the contentious nature of women's anger and aggression into consideration, it is not surprising that this figure stirred up a lot of controversy. In film theory, this has been framed as the 'gender trouble' that the action heroine causes, as she transgresses what is conventionally feminine and is often perceived as too masculine. This is explored explicitly in *Blue Steel* (Kathryn Bigelow, 1990), a film where the action heroine and rape-avenger merge, as I will show. My interest here is twofold: first, I want to examine how the action heroine stirred up gender trouble, and how various filmic techniques were used to ameliorate the threat that she posed. Second, I want to examine

---

[1] An important predecessor to the American action heroine that I will not explore here is the female fighter in Asian martial arts film (or wuxia). These films became very popular in the West in the 1970s and were another important influence when the action heroine emerged in this film culture. See, for example, Brown (2016: 93ff) and Schubart (2007: 123ff) for analysis.

how some of these filmic techniques can also be found in rape-revenge film, as the female rape-avenger is probably even more controversial culturally than the female action hero. My main aim in this chapter is therefore to discuss how the threat that an angry avenger poses is managed in the films in which she appears.

I turn to a recent rape-revenge film, *Promising Young Woman* (Emerald Fennell, 2020), to discuss whether a female avenger is now perceived as less threatening. I argue that this rape-revenge film does not allow its female avenger to be as angry, aggressive and powerful as is conventionally the case in rape-revenge film: indeed, *Promising Young Woman* is not by any measure an action film, thus toning down the violent aggression typically found in rape-revenge film. Cassie in *Promising Young Woman* does arguably not stir up much gender trouble, but stays within a conventional feminine sphere. I take this to back up the point I am making in this book that the rape-avenger's unapologetic vindictive anger is the focal point of the threat she poses culturally, and that her aggression is still carefully managed in manifestations of the convention that succeed in mainstream film culture.

Gender trouble: *Blue Steel*

In the previous chapter I outlined how the trend of action heroines took off in mainstream film culture only after early explorations in Blaxploitation film, and that Hollywood turned to White actresses as protagonists. This trend of action heroines stirred up a lot of media attention, as mapped carefully by Yvonne Tasker (Tasker 1993). Whereas the Blaxploitation heroine was heavily sexualised, the new Hollywood action heroine was often taken to be rendered symbolically male (see also Clover 1992), seen as taking on masculine features – indeed, as really being a man. The character evoked a 'suspicion of gender cross-dressing' (Brown 2011: 21). This can be framed as 'gender trouble', drawing on the theories of Judith Butler ([1990] 2007): gender trouble is the anxiety stirred up when someone does not fit into conventional gender roles. This is part of Butler's theory about the performative nature of gender, where an 'internal essence of gender is manufactured through a sustained set of acts, posited through the gendered stylization of the body' (Butler 2007: xv). According to Butler, this gender performativity is tied to careful control of sexuality: gender is repeatedly produced and maintained 'in the interests of the heterosexual construction and regulation of sexuality', which Butler seeks to overturn (Butler 2007: 185).

Tasker argues that the muscular woman that appeared in action film, such as Sarah Connor in *Terminator 2: Judgment Day* (James Cameron, 1991), illustrates the difficulty of securing gender identity in binary terms. Schubart points out that the action heroine triggered both pleasure and unease because she was difficult to identify: 'the less identifiable a body is as a *gendered* body, the more troubling', she observes (Schubart 2007: 7, emphasis original). She borrows from Jack Halberstam the notion of 'in-betweenness' to account for this. Halberstam uses this notion about female masculinity as embodied by a person whose gender identity is contested and ambiguous, and can therefore be a site of subversion. Nevertheless, Halberstam would not include Connor in this subversive category: indeed, he argues that Connor is presented as 'approved female masculinity' because of her 'resolute heterosexuality' (Halberstam 1998: 28). In other words, the gender trouble stirred up by the action heroine was limited because she was still, for the mainstream at the time, reassuringly heterosexual and not queer. More radical exploration might thus be needed to truly undermine traditional gender categories in Halberstam's analysis.

Indeed, there are few queer characters to be found in this trend of films. One is found in the portrayal of the soldier Vasquez in *Aliens* (James Cameron, 1986), the most masculine soldier in the entire, mostly male, crew: she is the one allowed to take up the traditional male gaze on Ripley when the latter appears as the new woman on the crew, in a tongue-in-cheek remark questioning who Show White is; she is the one with the biggest weapon, pointing domineeringly from her hip in an almost parodical phallocentric fashion as they go to battle. This supporting character is allowed to challenge heteronormative gender conventions more radically than is the protagonist Ripley. Indeed, Halberstam analyses Vasquez as part of his survey of the portrayal of butches on-screen, and argues that racial stereotypes about Latina women are used in the portrayal of this tough, lesbian character (1998: 181, 205).[2]

Furthermore, Lisbeth Salander is described as androgynous in the Millennium trilogy. She takes both male and female lovers, which makes her one of few protagonists in action films and in rape-revenge films who is not presented as firmly heterosexual. Jessie Daniels analyses some posts about Lisbeth written by feminist bloggers, who identify with Lisbeth's appearance (skinny, tattooed, pierced, punk-inflected feminist resistance). Daniels observes that 'Salander's appearance is also regarded as a marker of bisexuality, and thus another kind of resistance' (Daniels 2012: 183). For example, she quotes one blogger who explains that she is interested in this character 'as the androgynous (and very queerable) girl hacker' (ibid.).

There were also readings of *Thelma and Louise* (Ridley Scott, 1991) as a story about two lesbians coming out over the course of the film (for example, Griggers 1993). And Boo in *Orange Is the New Black* (Jenji Kohan, 2013–19), as analysed in Chapter 1, is of course a strong butch character, although Pennsatucky, the rape survivor, is heterosexual. It is interesting that it could be

---

[2] However, Vasquez is played by a White, and not Latina, character.

said to be the women-in-prison film conventions that this series self-reflexively draws on that afford a more radical exploration of sexualities. As a subtype of exploitation film, one central trope in the women-in-prison film is indeed its exploration of lesbianism, which can be seen as speculative, but also progressive (see, for example, Ciasullo 2008; Mayne 2000: 115; Walters 2001). The rape-revenge film and the women-in-prison film thus have a shared origin in exploitation film, where the protagonists did sometimes break with heteronormative conventions.

Boys Don't Cry (Kimberly Pierce, 1999) is perhaps one of the most radical explorations of gender and rape. Based on a true story, it portrays a trans man, Brandon Teena, who is raped by a group of young men for 'passing as' a man and taking a girlfriend. In an extreme case of transphobia, the rape is an act of revenge for what is perceived as gender transgression.[3] It is important to point out here that whereas I argue that the female avenger's anger can have a legitimate and productive political potential, these men's revenge is misdirected aggression. The female avenger takes revenge for crimes against her, but Brandon has committed no crime at all. My account cannot be used to legitimate their revenge. Trans- and homophobia have also tainted rape-revenge films such as *Descent* (Talia Lugacy, 2007). This rape-revenge film has been praised for the rare woman-of-colour protagonist, but discussed critically for the explicit homophobia in the revenge sequences (for example, Heller-Nicholas 2021: 161–3; Henry 2014: 79–108). I also discuss homophobia in *Irreversible* (Gaspar Noé, 2002) in the final chapter in this book. The British film *Femme* (Sam Freeman and Ng Choon Ping, 2023), still due to be released when I write this, is about a homophobic attack on a drag queen and the subsequent revenge, and promises to explore conventions from rape-revenge film in innovative ways.[4]

This very brief survey is merely intended to illustrate the important point that by and large, in spite of her roots in exploitation film that portrayed lesbianism, the rape-revenge film has been dominated by cis-gender, straight White women's revenge. The gender trouble offered by female avengers and action heroines should thus not be exaggerated – they clearly did shake up gender expectations, but their female gender identity and heterosexuality are

---

[3] See also Horeck's analysis of this film (2004: 111–13).

[4] There are also other more inclusive choices in relation to supporting characters in some of the films I discuss, for example the inclusion of the trans character Melvin in *Women Talking*, a film that I discuss in Chapter 4, and the trans actress Laverne Cox who plays Gail in *Promising Young Woman*. Joy McEntee offers an intriguing suggestion about the closing moments of *Promising Young Woman*, suggesting it 'passes the baton of revenge from a cisgender white woman to a trans black woman. *Promising Young Woman* sends rape-revenge in a new direction' (McEntee 2022, n.p.). I return to a discussion of this film later in this chapter.

not usually contestable or ambiguous. For a trend that was seen as characterised by gender trouble, films with female avengers and female action heroes are neither particularly inclusive nor diverse. In short, when she entered the mainstream, presenting an otherwise fairly conventional, heterosexual White woman as angry and aggressive seemed threatening enough.

Blue Steel is a film made in a wave of action and thriller films with strong female leads in the 1980s and 90s. It is a particularly interesting example as it explicitly explores and comments on the trend of female action heroines and the alleged gender trouble they stirred up, as argued by Tasker and also Christina Lane (Lane 2000: 113–17; Tasker 1993: 147–8, 158–62). Kathryn Bigelow is a notable woman director in that she has made use of a range of so-called 'male genres' in her filmmaking career, thus being one of the few women in Hollywood who made action films, thrillers, and cop films at the time, and her work serves as a central case study for both Tasker and Lane. And *Blue Steel* is indeed a mix of these genres. Furthermore, it also draws on the rape-revenge film, and can be said to continue the merge between the action heroine and the rape-avenger found in Blaxploitation films. Megan Turner, the newly graduated police officer protagonist in *Blue Steel*, is raped as the culmination of stalking and harassing by the villain in this film, Eugene. Other action films make allusions to rape, such as when the protagonist Sarah Connor in *Terminator 2: Judgment Day* is restrained while sectioned in a psychiatric ward and a guard licks her chin slowly in sadistic delight. But it is in a film made by a woman filmmaker – in *Blue Steel* – that rape is explicitly included.[5] Tasker observes how the possibility of rape always threatens the action heroine, but generally rape is only implied, such as through images of bodily penetration in *Terminator 2: Judgement Day* and *Aliens* (Tasker 1993: 151).

The context for Tasker's analysis of *Blue Steel* is her observation that female action heroes challenged conventions that women should be represented through codes of femininity, but were rather represented through a transgressive iconography where she takes control over weapons, cars and technologies, and often also displaying a muscular body, all conventionally signifiers of masculinity in contrast to the passivity and soft, curvaceous body as conventionally feminine (Tasker 1993: 132ff). This masculine iconography is the means of her empowerment, and often how she transforms over the course of the story, as in *Thelma and Louise* and the Terminator films (ibid.).[6] Tasker observes that

---

[5] See also discussions of rape sequences in another Bigelow film, *Strange Days* (1995) (for example, Horeck 2004: 105–11). Horeck discusses the rape sequences in *Strange Days* and *Boys Don't Cry*, and also comments on how it is 'interesting to note that women directed both' (ibid. 105).

[6] I discuss the transformation in detail in Chapter 2.

Blue Steel is an exploration of the roots of women in action cinema, teasing out 'the implications of the sexualised gloss' of the action heroine (ibid. 147). This is evident in the weapon fetish that the film explicitly explores: at the start of the film, Eugene witnesses Megan's shooting of an armed robber in a grocery store, and becomes obsessed with her. He takes the dead robber's gun, thus causing Megan's suspension from the police force as she is unable to prove that the robber she shot dead was armed. Eugene then starts stalking Megan, initiating a love affair with her, and turns violent when it is revealed why he is seeking her out. He kills her friend, and several other people, and keeps tormenting Megan, who is struggling to be believed by fellow police officers. He also rapes her, which is when Megan stops playing by the law and takes matters into her own hands. It is in the final shoot-out sequences that *Blue Steel* can be said to finally deliver on what is a key pleasure of the action heroine trend in Tasker's theory, found in the protagonist's empowerment (ibid. 161).

Lane carefully analyses the first five sequences in this film to explore how the film 'toys with the gender expectations embedded in the genre', such as by coding the gun as feminine in the opening credits, by the camera slowly tilting up a supposedly male body in a police uniform that turns out to be female, and where Megan in her uniform surprises two women she passes (Lane 2000: 114). Expanding on her analysis, I want to argue that, throughout the film, Megan is walking a tightrope between being empowered and disempowered: for an action film, and in spite of the playful, empowered introduction of Megan as police officer, this female protagonist is victimised and in danger, unable to act or respond, for most of the film.

After Megan shoots the robber, she is suspended from the force, disbelieved and frustrated. This is where this thriller intriguingly borrows from a more conventionally feminine genre, the love story, and explores her relationship with Eugene. Megan is single, and the men in the film are repeatedly portrayed as confused and threatened by the role she has taken up as police officer. Time and again she is questioned as to why she wanted to be a cop. A man she is introduced to at a party is provoked and put off by her when he learns about her career choice. The film thus seems to pre-empt a male response to its protagonist by explicitly having male characters on-screen interrogate her about her role, and reject her because of it. The film suggests that it is men in particular who are disturbed by Megan's masculine position: more specifically, they seem threatened by it. Or, as it turns out, Megan's masculine position is what attracts the deranged Eugene to her. In contrast, women in the film are generally portrayed as intrigued by Megan's power when in uniform, pleasantly surprised by it, as are the two women she passes on the street in one of the first sequences, who turn back to look at her in smiling admiration. The film thus arguably anticipates a gendered response, where women admire her, and men are intimidated by her, or aroused by her for all the wrong reasons. One is reminded of the fight sequence in a bar in *Wonder Woman* (Patty Jenkins, 2017) where a male character, after having witnessed Wonder Woman fight, says he is 'both frightened and aroused'.

The love story between Megan and Eugene turns into a nightmare as it becomes clear to her, the first time they try to have sex, that it is her posing with a gun that turns him on. Because he has witnessed her using it, he sees in her someone who will understand his own desire to kill. Megan's aggression or ability to kill is portrayed as dangerous in this film, as related to this villainous madness, and what puts her in danger. Tasker points out that the film could thus be seen by some as a conservative film, punishing Megan's transgressive desires to become powerful (Tasker 1993: 160; see also Lane 2000: 117). And this punishment is explored in a more feminine sphere, pulling Megan back into a passive role as a helpless victim who is preyed upon.

However, Tasker dismisses this position because *Blue Steel* also offers images of Megan's transgression as pleasurable. This film is arguably characterised by continuous oscillation between the feminine sphere, in particular her love life and family context, and the masculine sphere offered by the action and thriller film. In her love life in the middle portions of the film portraying this, Megan is punished for the role she takes up and her position of power. She is disempowered and increasingly victimised, made vulnerable. This is accentuated also by the domestic abuse her mother faces from her father. Affectively, her vulnerability is accentuated by putting the spectator in a position of epistemological superiority:[7] the spectator knows how deranged Eugene is, because the film portrays his killings, so when Megan starts dating him, the spectator is encouraged to fear for her and not share her feeling of hope that this one – seemingly nice – man is finally interested in her. The discrepancy between what the spectator knows, and what she knows, makes her appear even more vulnerable and helpless.

However, at the end of the film Megan steps out of this passive role, venturing after Eugene on her own, stepping into the role as avenger. Before this, she also confronts her father, as a promise of what is to come. When she finally goes after Eugene, Megan is powerful, unhesitant and confident, as characterises the female avenger, and in contrast to the nervousness and hesitation that was emphasised when she shot the robber in the grocery store at the beginning of the film. The camera lingers in a close-up on her unrelenting, determined expression of pure anger as she aims the gun and shoots him (Figure 6.1). This is a scene of empathy, borrowing Carl Plantinga's notion, inviting empathy

---

[7] This is often discussed as Hitchcockian suspense, although Alfred Hitchcock also used other types of suspense in his films. For a discussion of Hitchcockian suspense, see, for example, Smith (2000).

THE THREAT OF THE FEMALE AVENGER ON-SCREEN

Figure 6.1 Megan takes aim to shoot and kill her rapist and tormentor confidently and unhesitatingly (*Blue Steel*, 1990).

with her (cf. Plantinga 1999). And it is her determined vindictive anger the spectator is encouraged to feel here. The final shoot-out probably feels all the more satisfying exactly because of the painful constraints she has been tormented by. There is a huge affective shift for the spectator, in that after fearing for her in the middle part of the film, one is now made to feel with Megan as she is active, angry, fighting back, competent and powerful. Be that as it may, in keeping with the oscillation between power and disempower, being in power or in danger, in the final shot of the film we see Megan lifted out of a car by another (male) police officer, again helpless, limp and traumatised.

Blue Steel explicitly explores the gender trouble stirred up by the action heroine not just by having characters in the film question Megan's desire to be a police officer, and not just by explicitly exploring gender reversals in the opening sequences, but by creating a tension between disempowerment and victimisation in a feminine sphere, and the pleasurable empowerment offered by the conventionally masculine sphere. And at the core of this tension is a rape-revenge story, in that it is when Eugene rapes her that Megan is pushed over the line, stops trusting the law or others for help, and steps into the role as lone avenger, offering the satisfaction of revenge in the final shoot-out.

THE ACTION HEROINE EXPLAINED AND CONTAINED

So, the action heroine stirred up some degree of gender trouble when allowing a woman to step into a conventional masculine role, and take on conventional masculine features. Drawing on an observation Tasker makes that the action heroine is usually found in narratives that 'repeatedly seek to explain her (and to explain her away)' (Tasker quoted in Purse 2011: 92 n.1), Lisa Purse maps the various narrative techniques used in mainstream films with action heroines in order to ameliorate the threat she was perceived as posing (Purse 2011: 76ff). She discusses some such techniques as explanatory devices, which are ways of explaining away her strength as exceptional. Ellen Ripley, for example, is the natural leader of her crew in *Aliens*, but is driven by a maternal drive in the need to protect Newt, a young orphaned girl she takes under her wing. The motherly desire to protect Newt can be said to give her licence as a woman to fight. This observation is mirrored in the literature on women's anger discussed in Chapter 4: a woman's anger is condoned only if it occurs in defence of acceptable aspects of womanhood – and motherhood is surely one such example.[8]

Affording the action heroine a reassuring maternal instinct is not the only explanatory device in Purse's account. Sarah Connor in *Terminator 2: Judgment Day*, for example, is presented as mentally unstable. And in the rape-revenge film, the female protagonist is presented as suffering from trauma, so her violent revenge can be seen as the act of a pathological individual. The action heroine is not allowed to be strong and violent without having her strength pathologised, Purse points out. Whereas the male action hero can simply be a professional, as is James Bond for example, the action heroine is often in need of further motivation, which can be seen as explaining away her strength.

Indeed, Purse argues that films with action heroines 'work to contain the threat embodied by the presence of the physically powerful woman' (Purse 2011: 81). She introduces four such techniques, which she discusses as containment strategies.[9] Again drawing on Tasker, one such strategy she proposes is to sexualise the action heroine. Marc O'Day also argues that after a wave of muscular action heroines in the 1980s and 90s, action films increasingly presented their action heroines though a lens of eroticisation: in this way, 'the physical beauty and alluring sexuality of the female stars and the characters they play embody traditional, patriarchally defined qualities of femininity' (O'Day 2004: 205). He names this contemporary action heroine an action babe, and points out that although she is eroticised, she is not 'pathologised or

---

[8] Motherhood in relation to Ripley in *Aliens* has been discussed widely in the academic literature; see, for example, Hills (1999), Kamm (2019) and Schubart (2007: 169ff).

[9] Purse points out that the notion is taken from Ed Guerrero's discussion of the portrayal of African Americans, but she argues that the notion is also relevant to analyse the portrayal of women (Purse 2011: 92 n.3). See my discussion of Guerrero in the previous chapter. Critics might say she has appropriated this term and wrongly uses it beyond Guerrero's original context. On the other hand, Guerrero draws on Bill Nichols, who discusses ideology more broadly as a constraint (Guerrero 1993: 220 n.21).

motivated by personal revenge or gain' (ibid. 208). In other words, although her active strength can be seen as contained to the degree that it is rendered sexually alluring, inviting what O'Day discusses as both 'have me' and 'be me' fantasies in the spectator,[10] her strength is not explained away by making her either conventionally maternal or on a quest for vengeance. Nevertheless, in line with Purse, sexualising the action heroine can be seen as a way of containing her strength and power within heteronormative ideology, or as taming her by making her a sexually pleasing display.

Purse draws on Tasker in suggesting that this sexualisation makes the heroine fit into a traditional 'fetishistic figure of fantasy derived from comic books and soft pornography' (Tasker quoted in Purse 2011: 79). Similarly, both Schubart and Brown discuss the sexualisation of the action heroine as dominatrix features (Brown 2011: 45; Schubart 2007: 24–7; see also Edwards 2004). Dominatrix features are perhaps most obviously present in her clothing. Wonder Woman, for example, wears leather corsets and leather boots, and uses a lasso. Brown proposes that these overly fetishised images exploit and contain the male fear of this powerful female figure: fetishising the action heroine is a way of making her both feared because she is powerful, but also desired for exactly the same reason. Indeed, Brown argues that 'the symbolic function of the dominatrix is at the root of all the images of tough women that populate action films' (Brown 2011: 59). To the extent that the action heroine borrows from dominatrix aesthetics, she could also be said to break a feminist taboo: as will be remembered from Chapter 1, Carol Siegler holds that female sadism has always been problematic for feminism because it constitutes a category crisis (Siegler 2007: 66). However, eroticising or fetishising the sadistic female character could be one way of making her power and her dominant position – as she punishes men and takes pleasure in it – sexually intriguing.

A second containment strategy Purse points to is the non-realist nature of the female characters and their physical achievements (Purse 2011: 80). She uses the Mongolia sequence in *Charlie's Angels: Full Throttle* (McG, 2003), in which we see the three action heroines rescue a male fugitive and fight their way out of a crowded bar in Mongolia, as an example to illustrate how this fight sequence is clearly presented as artificial. This containment strategy can then seemingly replace explanatory devices, as Charlie's Angels are indeed professionals, and not motivated by conventional feminine protective instincts or trauma. Purse points out how there is complete disdain for gravity, weight and momentum in this fight sequence. Furthermore, physical consequences of the action are downplayed: there is little pain or injury, no dirty faces, the

---

[10] Whereas the tendency has been to focus on the response of the male spectator to action heroines, O'Day is a notable exception for including a discussion of the appeal to various groups of spectators, such as queer spectators, albeit briefly.

action heroines' make-up remains perfect at all times and there is no sign of physical exertion. Purse concludes that these are 'sanitised versions of female physicality' (Purse 2011: 85). In contrast, action sequences in films with male protagonists would often use stylistic devices in order to 'produce a sustained, unambiguous focus specifically on the physically rigorous aspects (exertions, impacts, risks, consequences) of the character action' (ibid. 39). The realism of these latter action sequences thus encourages embodied engagement, according to Purse, and allows 'us to "feel" this mastery for ourselves through our sensorial connection with the body of the hero' (ibid. 45).

What is at stake here for Purse, then, is that the non-realist nature of action sequences with female characters may offer fewer opportunities for embodied engagement due to fewer cues to her physicality: films with action heroines would rather emphasise her to-be-looked-at-ness than encourage embodied engagement through which a spectator might imagine what it is like to be her. In Purse's view, realism or naturalism brings us closer to the on-screen bodies and their experiences. She sees a film such as *Kill Bill: Volume 1* (Quentin Tarantino, 2003), which includes more realistic fights between female characters, as defying the action babe category, enabling embodied engagement with the strong female characters (ibid. 85–91). Indeed, this film can come close to fulfilling the potential she sees in action film to 'offer fantasies of empowerment that allow us to rehearse our own dreamed-of escapes, our own becoming-masterful, in a fantasy context, allow us to "feel" this mastery for ourselves' (ibid. 45). She concludes that

> our memories of our embodied experiences of these women's physically empowered actions might help these representations outlive and exceed the containing frames that mainstream action cinema tries to impose, prompting less talk of gender switches and more space for women to be active in action cinema without their presence being qualified. (Ibid. 91)

Interestingly, in a study of violent female action characters from 1991 to 2005, Katy Gilpatric found that these characters became more unrealistic over time. *Kill Bill* might thus be a notable exception, and artificiality as a containment strategy seems to have been used increasingly in the period Gilpatric studied. Her findings largely support Purse's claim that containment strategies are widely used, arguably in order to make these characters more acceptable culturally. In addition to becoming less realistic over the course of this period, Gilpatric also found that they 'maintained feminine stereotypes of submission and affection, especially in relation to male heroes present in the films' (Gilpatric 2010: 743). She concludes that 'the majority of female action characters shown in American cinema are not empowering images [...] operating outside the boundaries of gender restrictions' (ibid. 744).

Purse also shows how the action heroine can be contained inside marriage, the heterosexual couple or family in the film's end, thus using this strategy to take away her independence and securely re-introduce her to a more traditional gender role. Furthermore, the action heroine can be supplanted narratively by a male one; for example, Trinity makes way for the male hero and dies at the end in *The Matrix Revolutions* (Lana Wachowski and Lilly Wachowski, 2003). Among other containment strategies she discusses is the use of comedy to further portray the heroine's actions as implausible, pulling in the same direction as clearly fantastical settings to 'set the potentially culturally disturbing possibility of female agency and physical power at a distance from our everyday contemporary reality' (Purse 2011: 80–1). In line with Gilpatric, who argues that the female action heroine can be said to be an indicator of gender equality only superficially, Purse's conclusion is that containment strategies make action heroines 'less progressive than they might first appear' (ibid. 84).

There are close links between the protagonist in rape-revenge film and the action heroine historically, as explored in the previous chapter: the emergence of both was linked in exploitation film, and eventually parted ways in the mainstream developments of action film. I have looked at *Blue Steel* as an early example where the two are still merged. This heritage is also made explicit in some recent films: Purse argues that the Bride in *Kill Bill*, for example, is a homage to the rape-avenger and Final Girl of the slasher film (Purse 2011: 89), in other words, to exploitation film and other low-form action and horror films. In Chapter 2, I have also argued Lisbeth Salander embodies a merge between the action heroine and rape-avenger. Indeed, in most rape-revenge films there is an element of action film in the revenge sequences: the female avenger typically steps into the role as fighter in her quest for revenge, as explored in Chapter 3. All of a sudden, she knows how to handle weapons, technologies or cars; she is a skilled fighter; she is unhesitant, confident and shows no fear. The important point here is, as Purse points out, that 'both the heroine of rape revenge and the vengeful Final Girl are inextricably linked by an anger that then enables their physical aggression' (ibid.). And as I explore in this book, this is dangerous territory culturally. So, to what extent are the containment strategies and explanatory devices Purse discusses used to make the rape-avenger specifically more acceptable?

Explanatory devices and containment strategies in the rape-revenge film: *Promising Young Woman*

We have seen that the strength of violent and aggressive women on-screen is often explained away by making her exceptional: she is traumatised or mentally ill. The portrayal of the rape-avenger could be seen as suffering from such explanatory devices in that the trauma of rape is what acts as a catalyst in transforming this woman into a warrior. This is probably one of the most problematic features of rape-revenge films for many: she is humiliated and violated in the worst possible ways in rape sequences in order for her to transform into an action heroine in the revenge sequences. One can say that this does in a sense explain away her strength. Yet there is much to learn from this in terms of the cultural acceptability of women's anger. In order for a woman to turn violent, not to defend her children, her family or the society in which she lives, but for her to go on a killing spree only as a way of standing up for herself, the most severe of traumas is seemingly still needed in order to explain.

Furthermore, as Myisha Cherry points out, it may be difficult to sympathise with angry people (Cherry 2018: 55–6), and with the cultural prohibition on anger for women, as discussed in Chapter 4, so also with angry woman on-screen. More is seemingly needed to explain the reason for women's anger than that of male counterparts in film. Furthermore, rape is taboo, traditionally a shameful and unspeakable experience: women who write about their own experience of rape report that there is widespread discomfort and inability or unwillingness to empathise with rape survivors (see, for example, Brison 2002; Miller 2020; Raine 1999; Winkler 2002). The portrayal of rape in rape-revenge film is often brutal and very graphic, and in Chapter 7 I will discuss whether it need be so and whether such graphic portrayals could be said to serve a function. It is worth mentioning here that one such function may be that spectators are aligned with the rape-avenger so forcibly that they might just understand her anger, and not simply dismiss her response as unwarranted, as is the tendency. Purse is right to point out that additional motivation is typically needed for a woman to turn violent, as compared to a man in an action film. Yet I am also suggesting that another way to look at one of these explanatory devices, namely the trauma of rape, is that its inclusion could be said to prevent the spectator from explaining away the female avenger's anger as flawed, making her an antagonist rather than a protagonist.

The first containment strategy discussed by Purse is eroticisation. The rape-avenger is often eroticised: as Jacinda Read notes, the rape-avenger was more often eroticised than masculinised in early manifestations (Read 2000: 35). Purse discusses the sexualisation of the action heroine as a way of taming her and containing her strength in heteronormative ideology. However, there is a point to the eroticisation of the revenge sequences in rape-revenge film: this type of film is all about desirability and availability. Her body as erotic spectacle to men who want to control it is at the very core of the film. So in this sense one can say that eroticisation plays a more fundamental role in the rape-revenge film thematically than in action film, as the rape-avenger's desirability to men is so acutely at stake. Although there can be such a critical edge to the eroticisation in action film as well, for example when the action heroine uses her conventionally attractive exterior to fool men into thinking she is weak, a strategy used both by action heroines such as Nikita in *La Femme Nikita* (Luc Besson, 1990) and a rape-avenger such as Thana in *Ms. 45* (Abel Ferrara, 1981), the very sexualisation of the female body can sometimes be accentuated even more unrelentingly in the rape-revenge film, and as discussed in Chapter 2, arguably there is a reason why this is so.

Moving on to another containment strategy Purse discusses, she worries that the non-realist or non-naturalistic portrayal of the female action hero offers fewer possibilities for embodied engagement with this character, thus possibly making her less threatening and more clearly cut off from real-world implications. I would rephrase this point in terms of the potential for embodied empathy with these women in action film (Vaage 2010). Purse is right to point out that cues to the physicality of the fighting may facilitate such engagement, in contrast to sanitised fight sequences that seem to invite the spectator to look at the women fighters rather than feeling with them. In Chapter 2 I argued that the revenge sequence is typically one step removed from realism in rape-revenge film: the protagonist transforms into a more clearly fictional character as she becomes an avenger. The question is whether the avenger's transformation somehow hampers the spectator's empathy with her. *Pace* Purse, I argued that the opposite is the case: that engagement with the avenger is thus facilitated. The fictional or fantastic turn the rape-revenge film often takes could be said to facilitate empathy with her anger as culturally repressed.

Thinking back on the feminist discussions of anger, it is interesting how María Lugones, for example, discusses women's anger as hard to handle, something like a fit, as if some other persona is taking over, and not fully of this world (Lugones 2003). Whereas the subordinate self will try to conform, this type of anger resists. In the rape-revenge film, a near otherworldly, raging woman takes control, refusing to submit. The transformation of the rape-avenger arguably allows for anger to appear. The rape-avenger is hard-to-handle anger impersonated. I have discussed her as the rape survivor's shadow self emerging in the transformation and taking control in the revenge sequences. That such a transformation is needed is again a symptom of the status of women's anger in the real world. Making her revenge clearly fictional may make it more rather than less feasible for female spectators to engage with this outlaw emotion.

What is emerging here is the idea that the rage triggered by a trauma such as rape is deemed so unacceptable that perhaps every explanatory device and containment strategy is needed in order to facilitate engagement with the female avenger. This is in line with Purse in the observation that violent and angry women are perceived as threatening, but whereas Purse calls for films without amelioration through explanatory devices and containment strategies, the filmic techniques at work in rape-revenge film are not bearing the brunt of my critique: what I want to emphasise is that a culture which deems women's anger unacceptable is flawed, rather than the filmic representations. In spite of this slight difference in emphasis, I believe we are broadly in agreement in our analysis of angry and violent women on-screen.

Although the rape-avenger is thus perhaps one of the most unacceptable action heroines, some containment strategies Purse explores in action film are present to a more limited degree in rape-revenge film. One of them is the use of comedy. As Heller-Nicholas points out in her discussion of rape-revenge film, comedy might seem inappropriate for such a serious subject, yet to illustrate her argument that rape-revenge films are found across a range of generic frameworks, she show how there are rape-revenge films that use comedy, including, for example, *Traps* (Vera Chytilová, 1998) (Heller-Nicholas 2021: 55–60, 160–1). *Prevenge* (Alice Lowe, 2016) could also be said to be satirising the absurdity of revenge. Furthermore, there is humour to be found in the revenge sequences in *Thelma and Louise*, as argued by Projansky (2001: 135). This film is one of the few mainstream examples of the rape-revenge convention, and I will argue later that humour can be used as a containment strategy in the mainstream.

Another containment strategy that is less common in rape-revenge film is to couple her up with a man at the end, thus turning to a happy ending celebrating the heteronormative union or family reunion. Again, there are exceptions: in *Dogville* (Lars von Trier, 2003) for example, the female protagonist turns to her mobster father in order to get revenge. Neither does the female rape-avenger normally simply pave the way for a male hero, who thus in the end gets to save the day.

However, one interesting case to look at here is a film that is, in addition to *Thelma and Louise*, one of the rare cases of a rape-revenge film that truly made it in contemporary mainstream film culture, awarded as it was with an Oscar for Best Original Screenplay, and highly praised by critics: *Promising Young Woman*. So, what does it take to portray a rape-avenger in the mainstream today? I turn to this film here to explore to what extent containment strategies are at work.

The first thing to note is that *Promising Young Woman* allows the rape-avenger to escape from exploitation film, horror B-films or alternative film in which she is most often found, and where more explicit and gory violence is usually on display than in the mainstream. This too is perhaps a sort of containment: this narrative convention is long-lived and found in numerous genre contexts and types of film, but predominantly the rape-avenger has thrived on the fringes of film culture. The genre setting of *Promising Young Woman* is very different, as we shall see.

The protagonist Cassie has dropped out of medical school and is living at home with her parents, working in a coffee shop, and with a relatively uneventful daytime existence until she falls in love with someone who she thinks is the right guy. This romcom storyline is only part of the story: she is also, at night, an avenger, as she goes to bars on her own and acts senselessly drunk, awaiting a man to take advantage of her by bringing her home in anticipation of having his way with her without her being able to resist, or perhaps even remember, the rape. But as these men are about to rape Cassie she confronts them instead: she has only been acting in order to lure them in. We learn that this is revenge for her best friend Nina, who was raped by a gang of fellow medical students when drunk at a party, and later commited suicide.

What is most notably different about this rape-revenge film is that there is little violence in the film: the rape is not portrayed explicitly, we only see Cassie watch a recording of it, and her revenge seems typically to take the form of words rather than violent acts. In the one confrontation of a man who picked her up in a bar that we as spectators get to see, she merely confronts him verbally. She goes after the people deemed responsible for Nina's trauma by seeking to force them to experience what Nina experienced, but without actually getting hurt: she sets up the dean of the medical school to imagine that it is her own daughter who is left alone with the group of men who raped Nina, to force her to question her own view that these are basically good guys. Yet the daughter was safe all along. A victim-blaming female friend is set up to awaken in a hotel room with a stranger after getting senselessly drunk herself, and left to dread what has happened, whereas Cassie has in fact ensured she would not be harmed. There is thus an elegant poetic justice in this film without actually hurting anyone physically – Cassie still teaches the dean and the victim-blaming friend what it feels like to dread that a loved one, or oneself, is raped, and how their assessment would change had it happened to them or someone they love. This confrontation too fulfils the communicative function that I discussed in Chapter 4.

Furthermore, what is effective in *Promising Young Woman* is the critique of rape culture, and how it is systematically enabled by both men and women. C. A. York carefully maps the systemic critique offered by the film, and sees this aspect of the film as a distinctive turn in rape-revenge film (York 2022).[11] She turns to Kate Manne's account on misogyny to show how *Promising Young Woman* makes a rare and valuable contribution to highlighting structural misogyny. The rape is reported to the dean of the medical school, who dismisses the accusation because she does not want to ruin a promising young man's life; Nina and Cassie's female friend blames Nina for being too drunk; the rapist keeps insisting he did nothing wrong. York offers careful analysis of

---

[11] However, other rape-revenge films also offer exploration of the structural problems behind rape. Henry discusses this shift from the lone victim-avenger to exploration of collective trauma and collective response as one of the ways revisionist rape-revenge film diverges from classical examples of the genre (Henry 2014: 143ff).

each of these sequences as manifestations of misogyny. And the tendency to dismiss the rape survivor's pain and rather focus on how horrible the consequences of a rape accusation are for the man in question – a promising young man – is of course what gives the film its title. Chanel Miller discusses this very tendency in her book about the Stanford rape trial, where she observes that her 'pain was never more valuable than his potential' (Miller 2020: 241).

However, there are problems with the portrayal of Cassie's revenge mission. First, when Cassie is confronting the soon-to-be rapist early on in the film, she interrogates his lack of knowledge about her. She is not addressing the criminal core of the situation, which is lack of consent, but rather muddying the waters by suggesting that the problem is that men just want to have casual sex, whereas women want intimacy and lasting relationships. The problem is not that these men only want to have sex: the problem is that it is rape because she is (seemingly) too drunk to consent. And Cassie dies when attempting to carve Nina's name on the rapist's stomach with a scalpel, which is her revenge on him, thus breaking with the rape-revenge convention that she gets to take revenge: Cassie is not portrayed as all-powerful and in control in this situation. Indeed, Cassie's death is actually the one explicit act of violence that is portrayed in the film, as he is suffocating her slowly with a pillow. It takes a long time for her to die, and we see her fight desperately for her life.

This ending could be read as a containment strategy: the transgressive woman has to die at the end. The two transgressive women in the other prime example of an American mainstream rape-revenge film, Thelma and Louise, also die in the end. Perhaps they have gone too far to return to conventional society: after breaking with gender roles so radically, how can they return to oppression? However, Thelma and Louise choose to die. And Cassie does not. She is killed by Nina's rapist. In this case her death seems more like punishment for her transgressions. Contrary to rape-revenge conventions, Cassie is not allowed to be powerful: when the rape survivor turns avenger, the convention is that she is in full control. In this film, we see her killed and then burned on a pyre. Her hand is sticking out and is carelessly stuffed back in there by the rapist's helping friend in a final act of disrespect. So it is not correct to say that this film is not violent – there is violence towards her, but she does not get to be violent. Perhaps this would be too troubling for the mainstream. The fact that Cassie is not overly aggressive, or violent, is indicative of how her anger is contained in this film, as compared to the violence typically enacted by female avengers. This rape-revenge film thus breaks with action film altogether.

Adding to the containment of the rape-avenger in this film, she is supplanted in the end by another hero, so to say, which in this film is the law. After she dies at the hand of the rapist it is revealed that she had made a plan for the recording of the gang rape of Nina to be sent to a lawyer, who thus ensures that the rapists (and Cassie's murderer) are all arrested. Ending with the law getting it right can be seen as another containment strategy, indeed, an exit door, as suggested earlier.

Furthermore, I want to focus on the mood of the film.[12] *Promising Young Woman* is overall a fairly light-hearted film inviting conventional enjoyment with little explicit violence, except against Cassie. The film appears as a rape-revenge film in a bubble-gum wrapping, making use of the pastel colour palette of the chick flick, and some of the tropes of the romcom. This is of course most prominent in the romantic storyline about the seemingly good guy she falls in love with. In a montage sequence this romantic coupling appears as an almost hysterical celebration of Cassie as conventional, love-struck woman: he is the active one, the one who is talking, and her contribution is mostly to laugh non-stop, in awe of his sense of humour. This is what a happy Cassie looks like; this is what being in love looks like. She is passive, admiring him. However, this storyline takes a nasty turn when Cassie learns that he watched the gang rape and found it amusing, as documented in the recording of the rape of Nina, so in this regard the film breaks radically with the expected coupling of the two in a happy ending and thus firmly undermines romcom conventions.[13] There is thus an interesting subversion, and critique, of romcom conventions in *Promising Young Woman*, not least in the revelation that the seeming nice guy egged the rapists on.

Cassie's home environment is also portrayed as kitsch, old-fashioned and stifling, as if her entire existence is stuck in another time, a misogynistic culture she desperately wants to change and that should have been left behind, but that continues to torment her. In short, *Promising Young Woman* is notable as a rape-revenge film because it sticks to and stays in a conventionally feminine sphere. Cassie steps out of this sphere only to a very limited degree – she is entrapped in it.

Furthermore, part of the romcom setting is the light-hearted use of comedy, and in *Promising Young Woman* it can be said to be used as a containment strategy, in that her revenge schemes first and foremost seem intended to amuse. Although there is an element of anger, since this clearly must fuel her revenge mission at some level, it is portrayed through acts we can smile at – reassuringly, no one is hurt. Projansky argues that the revenge in *Thelma and Louise* is also tame in confronting the spectator, compared to the rape-revenge films Carol Clover discusses (Projansky 2001: 153). Her analysis demonstrates how this mainstream film relies more on comedy, and is less violent, compared

---

[12] I draw loosely on Greg M. Smith's mood-cue approach in this analysis in emphasising how the general mood of the film is important for the spectator's affective response (Smith 2003).

[13] For a discussion of the ideological implications of happy endings more generally, see MacDowell (2014).

to the typical rape-revenge film. In the mainstream, what appears is a rape-avenger cleansed of rage and violent revenge. Although there are sequences where Cassie is aggressive to some degree, inviting enjoyment of her open display of anger that is typical of the rape-revenge convention, she is mostly portrayed as controlled and calm. One such sequence where she is more openly aggressive is when she smashes the tail lights and windscreen of a car: she has stopped her car at an intersection and the man behind her drives up and starts hurling abuse at her for doing so. When Cassie steps out of the car, picks up a huge wrench and starts bashing his car, she appears powerful in the enjoyable way the avenger usually does: this is what many women might dream of doing but never dare to. However, mostly Cassie's anger is curtailed compared to most rape-revenge films. This is the perhaps biggest break with rape-revenge conventions: Cassie is a fairly non-threatening avenger, wrapped up as she is in a conventionally feminine context and enacting revenge where nobody really gets hurt.

As pointed out by some perceptive critics, Cassie is portrayed as weirdly non-angry for someone who spends most of her free time on the act of revenge.[14] In an interview, director and screenwriter Emerald Fennell shares her dislike of anger, confirming that it was probably not her intention to portray Cassie as very angry at all:

> But the thing about anger in anyone – but I suppose more specifically in women – it's not sexy or glamorous, you know? [...] actual anger, real anger, makes me feel ill, really ill. It's not something I ... For me, it's not pleasurable and the release of it isn't pleasurable. It's frightening. (Fennell quoted in Bastién 2021, n.p.)

Fennell inadvertently voices the view here that anger is simply unfeminine: it is unsexy and unglamorous, and just frightening. This becomes a problem in a story where anger is apt. One sequence where the lack of anger is especially noticeable, and where it would be highly appropriate both dramaturgically and psychologically, is when Cassie is watching the video recording of the gang rape of her best friend. The recording is not shared with the spectator, the camera lingers in a close-up of Cassie as she is watching it. She displays shock and sadness (Figure 6.2). This, however, is the turning point that makes her go for that final quest for vengeance, from which, as it turns out, she predicts she might not make it out alive. It should be portrayed forcefully, and vindictive anger does seem to be the emotion that can explain this turn of events most straightforwardly, giving her the motivation to turn to revenge in

---

[14] See, for example, Sidiqqi's good analysis (2021).

Figure 6.2 Cassie watching a recording of the rape of her best friend (*Promising Young Woman*, 2020).

a psychologically realistic manner. Mere sadness would not make this woman go on a quest for vengeance, or indeed be prepared to die for it.

Her final act of revenge is portrayed as light-hearted and playful, emphasised stylistically in a montage sequence with non-diegetic music and quick-paced editing of numerous close-up shots of Cassie in a risqué faux nurse's uniform, a rainbow-coloured wig, chewing girlishly on bright blue bubble-gum. This masquerading sequence can be said to pay homage to the transformation of the rape-avenger, but the mood is not darkly subverted as is commonly the case in the rape-revenge film; it is comedy. This has an effect on the spectator's affective response, of course: the invitation is to find much of the film reassuringly amusing, a very different affective response to the anger most rape-revenge films evoke.

What happens when you take anger and violent aggression out of the rape-revenge film? You get an Oscar. In line with my analysis of women's anger as the core of the controversy of the rape-revenge film, it is notable how toned down it is in this film. So, adding to Purse's containment strategies, I want to suggest that downplaying a female avenger's anger and aggression is a way of making her less threatening: verbal confrontation is more appropriate, though probably still pushing it, in a feminine sphere. I have also suggested some additions to the way the end can work to contain her: Cassie does not get to be the all-powerful avenger whose life is protected by near superpowers in the revenge sequences. On the contrary, her death in the end can be seen as a way of punishing her for her transgressions and firmly driving home the message that she is in fact vulnerable after all. This nudges her closer to conventional femininity.

Thus, considering the roots of the female avenger in action film, a genre element that typically allows her to step into a role as fighter to embody her anger fully, *Promising Young Woman* is unusually non-angry and non-violent. *Promising Young Woman* sticks much more closely to a feminine sphere, and can be said to playfully subvert expectations in relation to the romcom for critical effect, and use this subversion to critique rape culture effectively. But there is little gender trouble in Cassie as a protagonist: she poses less of a challenge to conventional femininity. This can serve to illustrate the continued cultural thorniness of angry and aggressive women.

7. EMOTIONS IN CONTEMPORARY FILM THEORY AND RAPE-REVENGE FILM AS EXPLOITATIVE

In this book I have sought to understand the emotions stirred up by the rape-revenge film. While I have offered an analysis of why the anger explored and evoked by this type of film can be important, it is time to address explicitly some concerns about and arguments against the rape-revenge film. The rejection of these films often dismisses them as exploitative: their graphic violence is seen as excessive and gratuitous. The violence is thus deemed unnecessary, as serving no legitimate function. Both the rape and the revenge sequences in rape-revenge film are subject to this critique.

For some, it is the graphic portrayal of rape that is the most troubling aspect of the rape-revenge film. The main worry here is that by showing rape on-screen, the film is making a spectacle out of it, catering to the male gaze and inviting perverse enjoyment of the extreme humiliation and degradation of the female rape victim. I will refer to this as the exploitation argument, and the crux of the question is whether rape cannot and should not be portrayed explicitly in fiction film, and whether there is an ethically sound way of doing so. A related argument addresses the revenge sequences. As rape survivors cannot legally and should not morally take revenge in real life, what is the ethical value of these prolonged revenge sequences? In this case the main worry is didactic in nature, claiming that the rape survivor's revenge is a senseless and destructive act of anger, and that the rape-revenge film does not teach us anything valuable. I will discuss this as the didactic argument against revenge stories. Finally, another concern is that the rape-revenge film is too far removed from realism. I examine this as the realist argument against rape-revenge film.

Together these three arguments pose the fundamental question of *why* portray rape and revenge in a story, and least of all in such gruesome detail. I suggest there are ways to defend the graphic portrayals of violence in some rape-revenge films, including both graphic portrayals of rape and the survivor's violent retribution. In this book I have concentrated on revenge, and I will start by discussing revenge in this chapter too. However, the ethical problems inherent in depicting rape on-screen is a pressing topic, so in the main bulk of the chapter I will concentrate on outlining a position on the portrayal of rape. I start by contextualising my discussion of the rape-revenge film in contemporary film theory, and suggest that the fundamental question is the value of strong emotions.

THE DIDACTIC ARGUMENT AGAINST REVENGE STORIES

Let us return to Claire Henry's discussion of revisionist rape-revenge film, as introduced in Chapter 1. Henry writes about the revisionist rape-revenge film that it is 'typically self-aware of the ways it positions and challenges its spectators ethically' (Henry 2014: 11). She points to the use of reflexive techniques such as breaking the fourth wall in revenge sequences as a way of challenging the spectator: an 'ambivalent relationship to revenge is characteristic of the revisionist genre', she holds (ibid. 17).[1] In revisionist rape-revenge films, such techniques are used to challenge the pleasures of revenge, which have traditionally been core to the genre, as Henry points out. The question is whether the questioning of revenge in revisionist films is more valuable because it triggers reflection rather than merely strong emotions. In her analysis of the film *Katalin Varga* (Peter Strickland, 2009) she writes that 'the radical potential of the genre' is to be found in this film's exploration of 'alternative responses to rape' (ibid. 14). Henry starts and ends her book with an analysis of this revisionist rape-revenge film, in which the protagonist seeks out her rapist but does not kill him. Henry notes that she 'feels almost a sense of outrage'

---

[1] It does, however, remain unclear in her account whether questioning of revenge is typical only of revisionist rape-revenge films, and/or also typical of classical rape-revenge films: she finds distancing effects in the revenge sequences in the original *Last House on the Left* (Wes Craven, 1972) and *I Spit on Your Grave* (Meir Zarchi, 1978), whereas the remakes from 2009 and 2010, respectively, are seen as uncritically revelling in revenge to a higher degree although both are labelled revisionist films (ibid. 32–3, 38–9, 47–8, 53). Later in her discussion some of these assertions are contradicted (for example, 71, 149). It is thus confusing exactly what role questioning of revenge plays when differentiating classic rape-revenge films from revisionist ones.

when the protagonist herself is killed at the end of the film, going against genre expectations (ibid. 1). Returning to this film and her own disappointment with the ending again in the book's conclusion, she confirms that she was offended by the ending and that this initial response 'was only somewhat diluted by later reflection' (ibid. 176). Reflecting on her own response, she concludes that *Katalin Varga* is not a feminist film.

I want to pick up on Henry's interesting analysis of her own complex response to this film, and counter one assumption that seems to be at work in her discussion, namely that a film's breaking the expected affective structure in order to trigger reflection is by default more valuable. This assumption is more clearly articulated by Henry in her article about *The Girl with the Dragon Tattoo* (Henry 2013). Here Henry differentiates between two types of spectator positions, ethical and moral spectatorship. Ethical spectatorship is invited by rape-revenge films that question the pleasures of revenge. Henry is critical of the way *The Girl with the Dragon Tattoo* rather encourages enjoyment of Lisbeth's revenge in what she rejects as moral spectatorship.

Henry's reasoning here is typical of a tendency in contemporary film theory that Carl Plantinga criticises as an ethics of estrangement or estrangement theory, which is influenced by Bertolt Brecht and critical theory (Plantinga 2018).[2] Michele Aaron is an influential contemporary theorist working in this vein (Aaron 2007). According to estrangement theory, immersive film experiences enhanced by emotions are deemed ideologically suspect, Plantinga explains, and only reflexive films can short-circuit emotional engagement through alienation effects and elicit distanced, critical spectatorship (Plantinga 2018: 99ff). This trend of contemporary film theory is characterised by a deep-seated distrust of the emotional engagement elicited by film. There can be said to be a tension between Henry's embrace of reflexive film techniques in revisionist rape-revenge film, and the outrage she herself reports feeling when genre expectations relating to the pleasures of revenge are broken. Although Henry does state that she is 'convinced of the genre's potential for understanding (and helping audiences understand and feel) the experience and psychology of rape and response to rape, from vulnerability and desubjectification to rage and catharsis', the theoretical framework of estrangement theory may prevent her from fully exploring this affective response (Henry 2014: 14). I hold that the avenger's rage and revenge may not need to be undermined or neutralised for the rape-revenge film to reach its most radical potential.

Plantinga proposes an ethics of engagement as an alternative to estrangement theory, in which it is acknowledged that it is 'the *emotional power* of screen stories that makes ethical criticism vital' (Plantinga 2018: 1, emphasis original). Sometimes strong emotional engagement with a film can be just

---

[2] See also Smith (1996).

as valuable as being pushed away, out of immersion in the story, and being continuously reminded that one is watching a film through reflexive filmic techniques, all in order to ponder intellectual questions relating to what it is one sees on-screen. Emotional engagement is seen as a fundamental part of the attraction of stories in the first place – and not an ethical problem. Only careful scrutiny of the emotional experiences invited by each individual film rather than wholesale dismissal of emotional response can reveal whether or not the film and the response it invites are politically and morally harmful or beneficial.

Although Plantinga explores the ethical potential of emotional engagement with film, he too is nevertheless sceptical of the portrayal of revenge. He agrees that it is a reliable way to elicit strong emotions; indeed, he points out that it is one of the most recognisable 'primary narrative means of eliciting the desire for a violent outcome' (ibid. 232). The revenge scenario allows the spectator to 'revel in strong emotions', and Plantinga sees it as troubling from an ethical perspective because of its tendency to 'run rationality off the rails and for the desire for vengeance to lead to acts that are in fact unjust' (ibid. 235). In his discussion, Plantinga makes a clear demarcation between the retribution of revenge scenarios on the one hand, and justice proper on the other, and he argues that revenge scenarios are only secondarily about justice – they are about retribution (ibid. 234). By implication, the latter should be kept separate from ideas about justice, a claim I countered in Chapter 3.

Be that as it may, beyond this scepticism Plantinga proposes a nuanced position on revenge, which is worth exploring in more depth. He discusses the vigilantism of *Dirty Harry* (Don Siegler and Clint Eastwood, 1971), for example, as problematic because it legitimates 'discourses about guns and protection from criminals, guns and masculine power, guns and self-affirmation, and anger and retribution' (ibid. 165). This ties in nicely with a helpful test he introduces to help assess whether a portrayal in a screen story is ethically valuable or not, what I will label the harmful stereotype test (ibid. 160). It is easy to agree with Plantinga that *Dirty Harry* is problematic in its celebration of guns and masculinity, especially in an American context, because it plays up to a stereotype about masculinity in this culture. He postulates that due to the harmful effects of the revenge scenario, films should thus 'complicate revenge, question it, reveal its consequences' (ibid. 242). However, whereas the male avenger can be seen as a harmful stereotype in this cultural context, the revenge scenario can perhaps be more culturally challenging and progressive when the avenger is a woman because it breaks so radically with available gender scripts for women in general, and for rape survivors in particular.

Plantinga discusses the Western *True Grit* (Ethan Coen and Joel Coen, 2010) where the fourteen-year-old female protagonist Mattie is on a quest to bring her father's murderer Chaney to justice. Plantinga points out that this young female avenger is unconventional: she is portrayed as breaking with conventional femininity in the Western film as she is working outside the community, leaving her family behind and conforming to the code of the West instead (Plantinga 2018: 244). Indeed, he argues that this avenger 'defamiliarizes the revenge scenario without fully subverting the pleasures it offers' (ibid. 245). This is an intriguing idea in line with my discussion here. However, Plantinga seems to judge Mattie harshly for allowing her quest for justice to be sullied by anger and vengefulness: as her helper she chooses the marshal Cogburn, known to bring back his fugitives dead or alive, thus increasing the likelihood that Chaney will be killed rather than brought back to stand trial. She 'wants revenge as much as justice', writes Plantinga (ibid. 244). He explores how the film punishes Mattie the avenger, such as when she falls into a snake pit after shooting Chaney, from which she must be saved and which makes her lose an arm. Part of the film's exploration of the consequences of revenge in Plantinga's analysis is also the fact that we see Mattie as an ageing woman, alone and unmarried. However, this ending for Mattie might not focus on the bad consequences of revenge, as Plantinga suggests. The fact that Mattie never returns to conventional femininity might just as much serve to draw our attention to its constraints. In a feminist reading of the film, one might see Mattie as punished after seeking revenge for the death of her father very much because she is a girl. In Lisa Purse's terminology, this would be a containment strategy (Purse 2011). Would a son seeking justice for the murder of his father in a Western film be judged so harshly?[3] And the happiness or tragedy of her end-tale, remaining unmarried and independent, depends on the eyes of the beholder.

There are some interesting parallels in this film to a rape-revenge Western film discussed by Jacinda Read, *Hannie Caulder* (Burt Kennedy, 1971): Hannie too takes on a bounty hunter helper to get revenge, and in Read's analysis of this film, giving up on her revenge would be to accept the position as passive victim for Hannie, which is the only position society constructs for her. What is at stake in this female act of revenge in a Western film is women's relationship to society (Read 2000: 131–3; see also Cook 2005: 43ff). The revenge scenario is a way out of conventional femininity and the passive position constructed for women.

Thus, Plantinga also holds that revenge scenarios should not be off limits, and he does discuss some revenge films as ethically laudable, but only to the degree that they complicate revenge (ibid. 239, 242). Even in a theoretical

---

[3] See also Plantinga (1998), where he examines revenge in *Unforgiven* (Clint Eastwood, 1992), and Modleski's discussion of his analysis, where she points out that it is the vengeful desires of two sex-worker women that are portrayed as excessive in this film, and are devalued (Modleski 2010: 143–4).

context in which emotions are generally heralded as core to the ethics of screen stories, vindictive anger is not granted the same potential for ethical reflection and learning as are other emotions. There is an element of fear of ill effects in his discussion of revenge, and hence I discuss his account as the didactic argument. He reverts to reflexive techniques – so typical of the Brechtian-influenced theories he critiques as estrangement theories – and other ways to complicate or question revenge, such as by revealing the negative consequences of revenge within the narrative (ibid. 240). This nudges his discussion of revenge closer to the estrangement theories he is elsewhere critical of.

Against this view, I have explored how vindictive anger has important functions, such as for motivation and communication. It is beyond the scope of this book to develop a fully fledged account of emotions and ethical reflection, but I will flesh out a position here drawing on Plantinga's own work and my own work elsewhere. Films stirring up anger can have ethical and political potential in three ways. First, vindictive anger can be productive for ethical reflection by drawing our attention firmly to the causes of that anger, namely the horror of the violation that is rape, as explored in Chapter 4. This first function is tied in to the functions of anger explored there. In this view, feelings of anger are needed to trigger the relevant reflections.

Second, ethical reflection is often triggered if one is feeling conflicted, that is, when one has conflicting intuitions, as also argued by Plantinga (2018: 132), as well as by Joshua Greene (2013: 295). I discuss this elsewhere in relation to antihero series, where feeling conflicted about the antihero is discussed as a reality check triggering reflection (Vaage 2016: 20–6, 91–117). One is likely to feel conflicted about enjoying the avenger's violent punishment on-screen because of the disreputation of revenge, because it may go against most spectator's moral principles, yet is probably also coupled with a strong urge to find her revenge both pleasurable and rewarding to watch. This feeling of conflict can invite ethical reflection. Again strong, affective feelings are instrumental in triggering reflection.

Third, being invited to feel with the avenger's anger can have great potential for attitude change in relation to rape because of the motivating functions of emotions generally. As Plantinga puts it, '[e]motion is a great motivator; in many cases, it serves as a motivation for further critical thought and reflection' (Plantinga 2018: 153). This is a core idea in his engagement theory, explaining why one should not shy away from strong emotions in fiction film, as strongly felt emotions can motivate moral change.[4] One can thus say that there is potential for ethical reflection in strong emotions, such as vindictive anger triggered by watching revenge, and the stronger the emotion, the greater the motivation

---

[4] I also explore the potential of empathy for moral change further in Vaage (2023).

for moral change: we are more likely to change morally when we are made to truly feel something.

A critic might object that detachment is necessary for ethical reflection, and there is no such detachment when sucked into the maelstrom of vindictiveness. However, some kind of detachment will be offered by the fictional context: it is true that in real life, anger can carry us away and give rise to injustices, but when anger is triggered by a fiction film, it will be contained to a certain extent. And the angered spectator is in a sense already detached, as they know that they are only watching a film. This too is an important factor when considering how strong emotions in response to fiction film can trigger ethical reflection. In this sense, very strong emotional reactions can be said to have an in-built tendency for reflection – extreme emotions in the film-viewing experience might be where estrangement theory and engagement theory unexpectedly merge.

The Realist Argument against Rape-Revenge Film

Let us move on to another argument against representations of revenge scenarios in film. One assumption that is not clearly articulated in the literature on revenge in film, but that nevertheless seems to be at work, is the lack of realism in the rape-avenger's response to the trauma of rape. A related point is normative in nature: a rape survivor cannot and should not take violent revenge on the rapist in real life, so therefore a fiction film should not portray such acts either. Stories with a clear-cut socially realistic edge to them may be seen as preferable to the rape-revenge story, so stories that are sticking close to the realities facing rape survivors, such as portraying the aftermath of the trauma in realistic terms, the choice of whether to seek out medical assistance, whether or not to report it to the police, the experience of dealing with the police and the legal system, the reaction of partners, families and communities, post-traumatic stress syndrome, and the long path towards healing, and so on. The rape-revenge story takes a fantastical turn in the second half of the film: women who experience rape are not prone to take up a new role as warriors or action heroines. Indeed, I have not explored the research on actual responses to rape in depth in this book, such as research on trauma, exactly for this reason. What I do suggest is that the rape-revenge film explores dramatically this one emotion of anger that may play a part in the healing from rape, at least for some survivors, and that the exploration of this emotion can be productive for the general audience of women.

The rape itself in rape-revenge film is also often statistically untypical (for example, being kidnapped and attacked by groups of strangers in the woods), and stories portraying acquaintance rape rather than stranger rape, for example, can thus be said to be more grounded in realism. The tendency in some revisionist rape-revenge stories to explore the rapist's background is another way of making the exploration of rape more informed by realism: films may explore toxic masculinity, for example, or the rapist's own experiences of sexual abuse, or other such factors cultivating complex understanding of the causes of rape, which is surely a productive way forward as we, as a society, work to come to terms with rape culture and its root causes. Contrary to this, some rape-revenge film demonises the rapist in a Manichean, individualist world view devoid of systemic analysis, and this too can be said to remove the rape-revenge film from realities of rape and rape culture. Rape-revenge films that do offer some such analysis of the cultural causes of rape, beyond a metaphysically evil and deranged individual rapist, can be seen as informed by the realities of rape to a greater degree.

However, valuable as this realist counterargument is in its various manifestations, because of its focus on the political, legal, social and psychological realities of rape, I do not think this proves that rape-revenge film is by default wrong. Must there be only one correct way of representing rape in fiction, restricted to realism? I have discussed the rape-revenge film as having one root in horror film. So let us consider the realist argument in the horror genre context: claiming that rape-revenge stories are wrong or unethical because of a lack of realism would be akin to claiming that all horror films are wrong or unethical because real-life fear, terror and violence are not like this.

Yvonne Tasker points out that the action film has always been haunted by a realist paradigm, where critics and commentators tend to judge the films in terms of their truthfulness, and thereby dismiss them for their lack of realism. She observes that this was evident in the reception of *Thelma and Louise* (Ridley Scott, 1991), for example, which was dismissed by some as an unrealistic account of women's lives, and as such wrongly 'judged by the standards of feminist documentary film-making, rather than those of popular cinema' (Tasker 1993: 154). She rightly holds that the 'standards of truth against which popular films have been judged, standards which rarely admit the complexity of terms like fantasy, can also operate to silence the other stories to which they attempt to give a voice' (ibid. 8). Enforcing a strict paradigm of realism in fiction film would be a straightjacket in filmmaking, and fails to take films such as horror film, action film and rape-revenge film seriously. One needs to move beyond realism as an expectation, and away from truthfulness as the strict benchmark by which to evaluate such films, in order to understand their use of a fictional or fantasy setting to explore fears, desires and emotions in other ways, as argued in Chapter 3.

Moreover, the fear about the lack of realism is also tied to gender expectations. Purse observes how action films with women protagonists are questioned in critical reception to an even greater extent than action films with male protagonists: critics tend to question the female action hero's physical achievements as unrealistic, whereas the male action hero's ability to pull off the impossible has become naturalised (Purse 2011: 76). When women turn violent, a worry about the lack of realism quickly arises among critics. This worry is sometimes also tied to a concern that they are not being good role models. An underlying issue here might be a concern for the female spectator, thought to be impressionable and feeble, someone who needs to be protected more than the male spectator perhaps. As Sharon Willis puts it in her discussion of *Thelma and Louise*, 'men critics frequently expressed a certain fear and anxiety about feminist identifications with women as the subjects of violence and rage, while women critics, whether they defended or attacked the film, always seemed compelled to address the crude question of role models' (Willis 1993: 122). This is related to the idea of the moral purity of women as explored in my first chapter. The controversy surrounding rape-revenge film can be seen as related to gender expectations at two levels: the woman turns unacceptably violent on-screen, and perhaps it is particularly bad for women in the audience to watch women on-screen who are violent. A core cultural problem here is the view that women are either paragons of moral virtue, who would not be attracted to such nasty stories in the first place, or weak and helpless, impressionable and childlike, in need of protection from the most grotesque forms of fiction. Counter to this, one can argue that women actually make up a significant part of the horror film audience, and that female filmmakers explore horror and violence (see, for example, Creed 2022; Peirse 2020; Pisters 2020), including rape-revenge stories.

The exploitation argument against explicit portrayal of rape

Revenge is a prime motivator in many a story, but male characters who turn avengers are rarely raped.[5] Why the extreme humiliation of the female protagonist in rape-revenge film? Let us return to what I introduced initially as the exploitation argument, and the question of whether the portrayal of rape in these stories need be so graphic, and even more fundamentally, why the protagonist of rape-revenge film is raped at all. Is the graphic portrayal of rape in the rape-revenge film merely exploitative?

Fundamentally, what I have articulated as the exploitation argument is the worry that some viewers – perhaps particularly male viewers – will enjoy the

---

[5] There were early rape-revenge films with male rape victims, but Clover suggests that this victim experience was too 'messy and unwholesome' for the male spectator, and thus the rape-revenge film explored the victim position channelled through a female protagonist (Clover 1992: 18). See also Henry (2014: 109ff) for an insightful discussion of the shame facing male rape survivors, as explored in some recent rape-revenge films.

portrayal of rape in a perverse manner. I have not explored male spectators in this book, and I will stick to this focus on the female spectator and thus not address this worry at length here. I will point out that the representations of rape in the films I have concentrated on in this book are typically brutal, and firmly focused on her horror, so enjoyment is arguably not the response that these films will primarily invite. There are surely very problematic rape-revenge films, especially in the exploitation branch of this type of story, which invite a much more sinister response, and I do not defend these films.[6] Be that as it may, even when focusing on the female spectator, it is not a given that there is no perverse enjoyment of the rape, although I have assumed – and hold – that this is not the response that is primarily invited, nor the response typically experienced. There might be dark aspects of sexual fantasies, at least for some spectators, which I have brushed over here, and it is beyond the scope of this book to explore this further.[7] However, I would still hold that even if this were the case, engaging with representations of rape in this way would have the function of taking control in fantasy of something that is frightening in real life, and then still enjoy the ensuing revenge. So there might be complexities in watching rape which are relevant when considering the exploitation argument that I will not go fully into here.

Moving on to the representation of rape in film, some filmic techniques are more often discussed as the culprit in making the representation of rape more problematic, such as aligning the spectator with the rapist in subjective narration. Use of point-of-view shots from the rapist's perspective is often seen as one such exploitative technique, for example.[8] If the rape sequence is perceived as eroticising rape in any way, it will rightly be seen as exploitative.[9] Henry

---

[6] See also Heller-Nicholas (2021: 154–5) for a discussion of exploitative rape-revenge films made by women.

[7] For a discussion, see for example, Horeck's exploration of rape fantasies as a feminist taboo, and examination of some of the complexities of this topic in relation to feminist crime writing (Horeck 2004: 4, 119ff).

[8] See, for example, the comparison of the rape sequences in the Swedish adaptation of *The Girl with The Dragon Tattoo* (Niels Arden Oplev, 2009), a film which I also discuss in Chapter 2, and David Fincher's American adaptation or remake of the same film in 2011 by Philippa Gates (2013: 208–9), where she argues that in Fincher's version some of the identification with Lisbeth is lost. However, another complicating example is found in *Strange Days* (Kathryn Bigelow, 1995) where a rape sequence is shown from the rapist's point of view, who also forces his victim to experience the ongoing rape through his experiential point of view through virtual reality technology. Bigelow argued that the sequence was intended to be a critical interrogation of sadistic voyeurism of the male gaze; see Horeck for a discussion (2004: 107–9).

[9] See for example Heller-Nicholas's discussion of the undeniable 'intent of making rape sexually titillating' in *Thriller: A Cruel Picture* (Bo Arne Vibenius, 1973) (2011: 40).

offers an interesting comparison of the rape sequences in the original *Last House on the Left* (Wes Craven, 1972) and the recent remake with the same title (Dennis Iliadis, 2009). The rape sequences in the original include mutilation and dismemberment, and were deemed so violent that the BBFC refused classification of the film until 2002 on the condition that thirty-one seconds were cut. The remake, however, was passed at '18' because 'the focus on the girl's anguish and lack of sexualised nudity or graphic sexual detail means that the scene did not "eroticise or endorse sexual assault"' (BBCF cited in Henry 2014: 34). Henry disagrees with this latter assessment, and points out that while the remake dispenses with some of the worse acts of violence during the rape, the camerawork in the remake actually fails to portray her experience of horror:

> [t]he camera voyeuristically roves up and down her body, lingering on her naked flesh – it seems to be taking cues from pornography conventions as much as horror. The visuals are stylized and rhythmic and are accompanied by a porn soundtrack: Mari's cries and a slapping sound and no music. In short, I reacted with greater disgust at the graphic and affecting original, but with greater offence at the sanitized, aestheticized, and sexualised remake. (Henry 2014: 34)

The point Henry is making here, and also elsewhere in her book, is that showing the violence of rape explicitly, such as through wide shots and close-up shots of the woman's facial expression, can be a way of communicating clearly its horror, and attempts to offer a less graphic, and more stylised, representation of rape can actually be more problematic. Thus, establishing clear rules for which filmic techniques should be used to portray rape in a way that does not endorse sexual assault can be difficult.

Barbara Creed claims that part of what characterises Feminist New Wave films is a critique of the filmic language used to represent rape, i.e. these films do not represent rape visually (Creed 2022: 53). She discusses how *Promising Young Woman* (Emerald Fennell, 2020) avoids visual representation of rape altogether, and how in *Revenge* (Coralie Fargeat, 2017) conventional ways of depicting rape in rape-revenge film are subverted through showing only close-ups of Jen's face (and hand) pressed up against a window, and hearing her screams. Finally, she cites the director Jennifer Kent's claims about her own film *The Nightingale* (2018) that the gang rape is 'not a rape scene, it's a scene of someone's soul being destroyed' (Kent quoted in Creed 2022: 53). However, in *Revenge* we see Jen, wearing only a T-shirt and pink string underwear, as Stan is pressing her up against a window and touching her genitals and then her buttocks. The camera turns away only when Stan penetrates her, but it is inaccurate to say that the rape scene is not shown at all. Also, in *The*

Nightingale, although it certainly rings true to say that the gang rape of Clare is soul-destroying, it is still a gang rape taking place. And the director's claim that the scenes are 'really just close-ups of faces' is not accurate either (Kent quoted in ibid. 61): Kent is right to point out that we never see Clare naked, yet the rape she experiences is still depicted visually on-screen with medium shots of her body and the rapists' bodies during the rape. So, although I do agree with Creed that these films made by women filmmakers can be said to raise ethical questions about the representation of rape, and to make careful choices so as to block any kind of voyeuristic pleasure in the rape sequences, there is no total absence of explicit portrayal of rape in *Revenge* and *The Nightingale*.

Rape can also be represented indirectly in film, such as in *Women Talking* (Sarah Polley, 2022) where flashbacks reveal how the women who have been raped wake up to find blood on their bed sheets, vaginal bleeding and bruises on their bodies. The film thus avoids portraying rape, yet still communicates something about the violence of rape. One related convention is the shower scene, where the flowing of blood as the rape survivor cleans her traumatised body represents the violence of rape. This could fall in line with Creed's observation that women filmmakers negotiate representations of rape. However, one problem might be that rape is not always violent like this – there might not be bleeding and bruising.

I will concentrate on the strong claim that rape should never be portrayed on-screen. What is at stake here is whether the portrayal of rape is by necessity exploitative, even if it is portrayed in a way that firmly emphasises the victim's horror and trauma. This is sometimes voiced as the view that rape should never be used for entertainment purposes, or the worry that if rape is portrayed in a fiction film it is by definition used as a plot device. Strictly speaking, any element of the plot in a fiction can be said to be a plot device – none of it need be there, all of it is included in order to tell a story of some sort, for entertainment or education or whatever other purposes we consume fiction. However, presumably the critique that something is a mere plot device implies that an event is used in order to move the narrative forward in a film without exploring the ramifications of this event properly – so the event, let us say a rape, does not constitute the theme proper of the film. Then we might say that the rape is a mere plot device. It is related to the claim that the violence in a film is gratuitous, which also suggests that it is not necessary.

First, one may wonder whether this applies to rape more so than other moral transgressions and crimes commonly portrayed in fiction. Should fiction film portray murder for entertainment purposes? Torture? War? When voicing the worry that rape is a mere plot device, compare this to how commonly we see murder or physical violence in film without its consequences ever being explored properly and without it being the theme proper of the film. There are of course reasons why one might see rape as a special case. Even in extremely violent contexts, such as some of the American antihero television series and in video games, killing may be portrayed as acceptable in that the protagonist or avatar does kill other people, whereas rape is typically used to mark some characters as clear-cut villains, as discussed in the literature on film, television series and also video games (for example, Kjeldgaard-Christiansen 2020; Vaage 2016). Based on this it seems reasonable to claim that rape must be one of the human violations that spectators find the most unbearable to watch on-screen. So this can explain why one might then want to claim that it should not be portrayed at all. But in these discussions, it is usually presented as a puzzle for us: why is rape deemed so much more unacceptable in this fictional context when murder is not?

One thought here that has not been discussed in this literature, to my knowledge, is that perhaps the portrayal of rape is unbearable to watch because the response to rape in real life is so much more unsettled and muddled, as compared to the response to murder. A filmmaker can represent murder on-screen, and viewers and critics still seem to be able to rest assured that in real life, murder is wrong. Let us say the murder is really graphic, shown to us in close-ups, with the murder victim screaming in pain: the film might be deemed unsuitable for children, but there is still probably no moral outcry in the critical reception. However, take a rape-revenge film, in which a clearly villainous rapist rapes, and we as spectators are made to feel with the woman's experience of absolute terror, and parts of the audience will feel outraged by the portrayal of the crime. In real life, murder is typically seen as one of the gravest crimes a human being can commit, and as such one might assume that we would deem this highly unsuitable for entertainment purposes. However, in real life, there is little moral confusion about where to put the blame in murder cases: murder victims are rarely blamed for getting themselves killed. However, rape is different. I wonder whether rape-revenge film would have stirred up such a controversy if rape had been dealt with more effectively in our legal systems. Perhaps the intense discomfort one feels by witnessing this crime on-screen is tied to the muddled response to rape in real life. Rape is a blind spot in modern jurisdiction. Women are offered little legal protection against this crime. And here is a film that, provocatively, reminds the spectator what rape is.

It is also worth lingering on the observation that being aggressively vindictive is too culturally controversial for a woman unless there is something that whips the spectator into such strong emotions that any resistance to watching violent revenge evaporates. This might be a reason to portray rape explicitly: if we only see her revenge, but have not been put through the ordeal that elicited her vindictive anger, chances are that the female avenger will be perceived as villainous, and be a source of antipathy rather than sympathy and empathy.

Henry makes a similar point when discussing the conventional 'visible proof' of rape in rape-revenge film, without which the protagonist's revenge might seem less justified, perhaps resulting in the loss of sympathy with her (ibid. 73–4, 85–7).[10] In order to ensure that the spectator feels with the avenger rather than distancing herself from the avenger by seeing her as an antagonist, perhaps the emotional shock of watching the rape she endures is needed. It is an indication that a woman's violent behaviour has to be presented as being motivated by something as bad as rape.

Furthermore, in one way rape can be seen as the ultimate symbolic representation of the helpless, disempowered position that women are confined to in fiction film conventionally. The woman's role in fiction film has conventionally been one of vulnerability and passivity: she is the 'damsel in distress', the one who is threatened, who needs to be saved and protected. Female characters are typically represented as helpless to some extent, screaming in abject fear until a man comes to their rescue. They are portrayed as longed for and lusted after, objectified by the male characters and by the camera (Mulvey 1975). Rape pushes it all to the extreme. In her discussion of female action heroes, Tasker also makes the point that the traditional vulnerability of female characters is retained in rape-revenge film (Tasker 1993: 21). Elizabeth Hills argues that it is essential that the female action hero is both vulnerable and strong, both victim and her own rescuer, as it is when she is both in one and the same story that gender binaries are broken down in a productive manner (Hills 1999: 43). Had she only been strong and invincible, she might not have embodied vulnerability that enables the spectator to feel with her and for her. In extension of this, one can argue that if she is to take on the problematic that is a woman's vindictive anger, the spectator might need to understand what causes her fury in the first place.

The ethics of making us watch

The problem with rape is that there is a strong tendency to explain it away. As will be remembered from Chapter 1, Clover points out how easily a film will opt for an intellectual exit door in order to escape the horror of rape, and how storylines exploring the legal response, for example, are a way of pushing the raped women out of the picture and focusing on something else, such as the legal proceedings – and someone else, such as the lawyer acting on her behalf – all of which is more comfortable and less threatening. These can be seen as filmic ways of offering an exit door.

---

[10] See also Williams (2002), who makes a related point about the BBFC cuts of parts of the rape sequences in *I Spit on Your Grave*, asking whether this might tip the scales against the avenging protagonist's revenge.

Furthermore, in her philosophical exploration of her own rape experience, Susan Brison points out just how difficult it seemed for people around her to empathise with her as a rape survivor – how afraid people were to talk about it, or for her to talk about it (Brison 2002). Nancy Venable Raine also discusses the tendency for people around her not to want to hear her reflections on her own experience of rape, such as when reading an article about it to a group of women professionals at a luncheon and being told afterwards that 'no one wants to hear about such terrible things' (Raine 1999: 119). This exploration of the silence around rape gives Raine the book's title, *After Silence*, which she ties to a 'profound collective anxiety about rape that borders on cultural psychosis' that renders the experience of rape 'unspeakable' (ibid. 5–6). She ties this burden of silence to the deep feelings of shame that are typically induced in rape survivors about their own experience, and notes how she 'found it difficult not to feel ashamed when others reacted to me with embarrassment or discomfort. And this feeling of shame silenced me' (ibid. 131).

This unwillingness to focus on rape, and thus silencing, is also found in an empirical investigation of audience response to *Thelma and Louise*. Brenda Cooper found a stark gender difference when asking student respondents to write freely about the film and their reaction to it: female students gave the sexual assault of Thelma a prominent role in their summaries of the film, which they interpreted as being about women's lack of power and about sexism, whereas the majority of male respondents downplayed or trivialised the topic of sexism, and the sexual assault was 'virtually ignored by most men' (Cooper 1999: 29). One wonders what it takes to make all spectators pay attention.

As observed by Sarah Projansky, even in the critical and academic reception of *Thelma and Louise* the depiction of rape was by and large ignored, with only a few exceptions (Projansky 2001: 122–4, 144). She takes this film as one of her main case studies in a critical discussion of portrayals of rape in American media, which she argues are characterised by post-feminism. Post-feminism in Projansky's analysis is characterised by an emphasis on individual choice and pleasure in an era where feminism has allegedly become obsolete, and also a lack of attention to structural factors, all amounting to a problematic depoliticisation and dissociation of post-feminism from activism (ibid. 66ff). In addition to the critical examination of these post-feminist features of rape stories, one of her main points is that the sheer number of representations of rape in American media are problematic, and constitute a 'sustained cultural assault on women' (ibid. 95).

Tanya Horeck makes a similar point: she argues that whereas rape used to be silenced and ignored, deemed to be the most private of crimes, it has now become one of the most public crimes (Horeck 2004: vi). Horeck takes

The Accused (Jonathan Kaplan, 1988) as one of her main case studies, where the rape sequence was indeed widely discussed. Both Horeck and Projansky articulate this as a paradox: how can one increase the very same thing that one is trying to work against, that is, portray rape explicitly in order to work against rape (Projansky 2001: 19, 96), or encourage looking at rape in order to show how looking is damaging, as with the onlookers in the gang rape in *The Accused* (Horeck 2004: 97). Projansky points out that a related paradox is found in anti-war films or anti-racist films, for example, that may also portray war or racism, respectively (Projansky 2001: 96). Horeck and Projansky are right to point to this cultural dilemma. But one can also point to another paradox: if refusing to portray rape, would this not potentially also contribute to the silencing of rape, treating it as an event so shameful it is unspeakable and unwatchable? Ultimately, neither Horeck nor Projansky argues for a blanket ban on representations of rape. Rather, they both call for attention to the cultural significance of representation of rape across media, and offer careful analysis of the implications of these representations.

Furthermore, Projansky sees *Thelma and Louise* as an exception to this trend because it articulates a resistant relationship to conventional representations of sexual violence, and draws the viewer's attention to the links between rape and male control of the gaze in a feminist critique of sexually assaultive culture (ibid. 121ff, 232). This analysis is contextualised also by her suggestion that there might be feminist potential in the rape-revenge film with women avengers (ibid. 60). However, she also demonstrates that the feminist potential in *Thelma and Louise* was by and large ignored in the critical reception of the film, which tended to bypass the rape altogether and see the film as a celebration of female friendship and pleasure, in line with post-feminism. In Projansky's analysis, then, there can seemingly be feminist potential in some representations of rape, and her critical analysis of *Thelma and Louise* does not suggest that the main problem is the rape portrayed in the film, but rather that this rape, and the role it plays in the critical examination of rape culture in the film, was ignored in the heated public debate that followed.

Let us hone in on the effects of watching violence on-screen. In his discussion of graphic violence in television series, Peter Ellis points out that one effect of such portrayals is that it increases the saliency of the event, which may be narratively significant (Ellis 2020). He bases this argument on a study by Karyn Riddle, where she found that exposure to violence that is more graphic, or vivid, which is the notion she uses, captures the spectator's attention to a greater degree (Riddle 2014). She qualifies this by pointing out that if the violence is perceived as excessive, spectators may use methods to disengage (i.e. looking away or turning off), and that women are more likely than men to do so (ibid. 299–300). Nevertheless, her main point is that vivid violence does have distinct effects. Violence is more vivid the more it is concrete (for example, detailed, specific), the greater the proximity to the violence (for example, use of close-up shots), and the higher the sensory breadth in the portrayal (i.e. elicitation of various senses), and finally, the more depth of detail (i.e. higher quality representations in HD).[11] She demonstrates that vivid violence captures the spectator's attention effectively. It elicits stronger emotional reactions and feelings of presence, which in turn call for a higher degree of cognitive elaboration as spectators are processing the details of this portrayal. The detailed and vivid nature of the violence also makes the memory of the violence more accessible long term. In short, watching vivid violence greatly affects mental models, and makes mental models related to violence more accessible in memory. She also discusses how vivid violence can result in attitude change to a greater extent, if it is used in a context where the violence is related to central arguments. The main point in her study is that sanitised violence, which is by definition less vivid or graphic, would not have the same effects.

Returning to rape, then, which she does not discuss explicitly, the question is whether more sanitised depictions of rape could potentially be easier to ignore, explain away or forget. Representing rape in its horror graphically could capture the spectator's attention more effectively, eliciting stronger emotions, calling for more cognitive elaboration and making the memory of the horrific event more accessible in memory. This aspect of Riddle's study is related to the point Plantinga makes about emotion as a motivator for change. In his discussion of how ethical thinking can be elicited through immersion in a story and the emotions it stirs up, Plantinga suggests that some particular emotional states might be more prone to challenge the spectator in a way that triggers reflection (Plantinga 2018: 132). Emotional shock is one such state. Watching something that is shocking can be disorientating, and call for intense cognitive work on the spectator's part to make sense of what it is they see, and why it is part of the story. Plantinga's example is a frame shifter, or twist ending, but arguably truly emotionally shocking sequences such as extreme violence and rape might serve a similar function.

However, in the public discourse on representations of rape it sometimes seems to be assumed that it is by definition more ethically and politically laudable not to portray rape vividly on-screen. If a character in a story is raped, it is better not to show it, the reasoning goes. The camera turns away respectfully, leaving the character to go through this traumatising experience alone. We may, or may not, witness her trauma afterwards. However, I have

---

[11] She also includes another criterion – the more relevant the emotional stimuli are for the spectator – but as this complex question seems to move beyond filmic representations strictly speaking, to an assessment of emotional resonance subjectively, I do not include it here.

pointed to the tendency to explain the horrors of rape away or ignore them, the unwillingness to know, rape as a blind spot in our jurisdiction, all of which point to reluctance to see this crime for what it is. Thus one can ask what or whom is being protected when the camera turns away from the rape itself. For some feminist scholars, the danger of portraying rape in a titillating way is one sound worry behind the resistance towards visualisation of rape, and I will turn to one such account shortly. However, I wonder whether there is a less noble reason at work in the preference for sanitised portrayals of rape in the general public, or the blanket ban on portrayals of rape as voiced by some critics and viewers, and that is the average spectator's unwillingness and discomfort by being made to witness this crime: the more vivid it is, the harder it is for the spectator to ignore. In short, there is a danger that by not portraying it vividly, the victim's pain is not communicated as effectively. And grasping her pain is a central feature of the intended affective structure of some rape-revenge films. The rape-revenge film can perhaps effect change because its vivid violence might change mental models in such an argumentative context.

So this is one cluster of arguments in defence of vivid representation of rape in some rape-revenge films, based on the idea that eliciting the horror of rape can be important. Another argument is that not portraying the rape at all may activate hesitation or doubt about it, as is so often the case in real life: perhaps she is making it up, perhaps she misremembers, perhaps she is not trustworthy and so on. The rape survivor's confrontation of her rapist in M.F.A (Nathalia Leite, 2017) might serve as an interesting example here. In this film we follow the fine-art student Noelle, who is raped by a fellow student, Luke, at a party he invites her to in his flat. This is one of those acquaintance rapes committed by a seemingly charming young man, articulate and handsome, a popular guy, that might be deemed a grey zone of difficult boundaries and hazy consent at parties where alcohol is involved, and where she willingly comes with him to his room and kisses him at first – unless, that is, we witness the whole scene and see how he turns on her, pushes her forcibly down on the bed in spite of her protests, keeps pinning her down and hisses at her to stay still. This is not what consensual sex looks like. However, when Noelle confronts Luke in daylight later, he is portrayed as thoroughly perplexed by her perception that it was rape (Figure 7.1). He finds the idea ridiculous and funny, and accuses her of not owning the fact that they had casual sex. I wonder how many in the audience might find him convincing had we not seen the rape. In rape-revenge film, this exit door too is closed, as we cannot but believe it because we saw it. There can thus be epistemological value in explicit portrayal: it gives the spectator essential first-hand access and knowledge.

It is interesting here to return to the empirical study of British women watching *The Accused*, where the protagonist Sarah Tobias is enjoying a night out in a bar, drinking, dancing and flirting, before she is gang-raped

Figure 7.1 Luke finds Noelle's accusation of rape ludicrous (*M.F.A.*, 2017).

by several men in the bar while many others are watching. We only see a portrayal of the actual rape sequence fairly late in the film as a male witness's flashback memory of the event. Philip Schlesinger and his colleagues point out that it is 'the long rape scene itself that evoked the most profound feelings of anger, outrage and distress' in their respondents (Schlesinger et al. 1992: 150). Watching the rape sequence is described as being 'numbingly disorientating' for some of these women (ibid. 151). I agree with these researchers that this is unsurprising – watching graphic portrayals of rape is deeply disturbing. In the structured group discussions used by Schlesinger and his colleagues, some of the worries I have discussed here emerged, such as the view that the film might be exploiting sexual violence. A substantial minority of their respondents did have reservations about the rape sequence, arguing for example that the film could have achieved a similar impact without such explicit and graphic depiction of rape. Some respondents were concerned about the potential sexual pleasure watching this sequence might offer male spectators, and the potential for copycat behaviour – in short, worries what men might make of the film. However, notably Schlesinger and his colleagues found that in spite of the strong negative emotions universally elicited by watching the rape sequence, the majority of their respondents still felt that the explicit portrayal of rape should be included in the film, justified on 'the basis of its impact, the horror of which could be argued to have a beneficial effect on the audience' (ibid.). A reflection made by one respondent, anonymised as an English Asian woman, might serve to illustrate this further. She described how, when she watched *The Accused* for the first time, she kept thinking:

'What actually happened in that club? Is she telling the truth? Was she really giving him the come on?' Yeah ... I was thinking, 'What else went on that made that happen?' But until I actually saw the rape scene, and I thought, 'Oh God, that was out of order! Nothing she did justified that the rape's happening to her.' So to me it was important to have the rape scene in there, to stop me giving her any blame, as the victim. (Ibid. 144)

Explicit portrayal of rape could arguably be important to block the tendency to blame the rape victim, or to explain away the horrors of rape.

One theorist who might be critical of this line of argument is Alison Young, who holds that we should refuse the invitation offered by some of these films to look at rape, in other words, that it is ethically problematic to portray rape graphically on-screen, in her valuable exploration of what she labels 'crime-images' in fiction film (she explores rape, torture, homicide and terrorism). She makes several arguments for why we should be sceptical of explicit portrayals of rape in her analysis of the Dirty Harry film *Sudden Impact* (Clint Eastwood, 1983). In this film Dirty Harry discovers that a series of murders he is investigating were committed by a woman going after a group of men who raped her and her sister. Young reiterates how in the revenge sequence 'one of the rapists says to her, "It wasn't that bad, was it? Not bad enough to kill me for?" The spectator must agree with the victim that the rape was indeed *that bad*' (Young 2010: 45, emphasis original). Young argues that this and other rape-revenge films rely on a harmful rape myth that persists in the legal system, namely what rape looks like: an unknown assailant using additional violence.

Young's more central argument relates to the ethical responsibilities inherent in watching rape. She draws a parallel between the spectator of fiction film and characters in fiction film who merely watch without interfering or helping the rape victim, such as Joyce, a man who witnesses the rape of Sarah in *The Accused* but does not help her, and an unnamed character who walks in on the rape of Alex in *Irreversible* (Gaspar Noé, 2002) but turns away and leaves. Young argues that 'such is the implication of vision in violence in the rape-revenge genre that the spectator's *not* turning away during the rape scene also constitutes an indifference to her graphically represented suffering' (Young 2010: 65, emphasis original). An assumption is made that a witness to rape in the real world, and the spectator of fiction film watching a rape, carry the same or similar moral obligations, and not turning away would constitute indifference. Young thus criticises the assumption that 'we can "just look", without being implicated within it' (ibid. 69). She argues that the inclusion of rape sequences should therefore always be questioned. This is Young's second argument against explicit portrayals of rape. But why would this be so? Watching does not mean that one is indifferent, and turning away does not mean that one empathises and cares more. Indeed, the spectator is in an entirely different position from the witness in the storyworld, and arguments need to be made for why the ethical implications of watching from our position outside of the storyworld in any way resembles the ethical implications for a bystander watching a rape in the storyworld.

Young presents a third argument in her discussion of *Kill Bill: Volume 1* (Quentin Tarantino, 2003), where the repeated rape of protagonist The Bride when she lies comatose in hospital is not explicitly portrayed, but where the film manages to communicate her experience with dread and horror no less. She compares this to the problematic flashback used in *The Accused* in which there is explicit portrayal of Sarah being raped: Young rightly explores this flashback as problematic because it is Joyce, the male witness's, memories which are used to validate Sarah's story. This male witness thus gets to show the spectator what is objectively true in this story. Young argues that

> [d]espite claims made for the pedagogic benefits arising from the depiction of rape, films such as *The Accused* do worse than take insufficient care in their representation of the event – they perpetuate the notion that rape must be seen before it can be condemned. In this notion resides the assumption that a woman's words, and a woman's memories of sexual injury, cannot be trusted or taken for granted: both the spectator and the law are alike in requiring corroboration of her claim. (Ibid. 70)

However, in relation to *The Accused* especially – and as pointed out by Young – what is problematic here is that a male witness is needed to convey objective truth. On the one hand, Young is right to point to the pervasive problem here of credibility, and how difficult it is for a woman to be believed without someone else having witnessed the rape, and how the rape-revenge film in its explicit portrayal of rape can be said to reflect this. On the other hand, I have argued that any suggestion that the woman's claim cannot be trusted will indeed offer the spectator an exit door – as it offers judges, jurors and others an exit door in real life. The explicit portrayal of rape should not be seen as an endorsement of the harmful myth that the victim is unbelievable unless there are witnesses, but rather as a filmic strategy to prevent the spectator from reverting to such myths. Again, there is a relevant difference between witnesses in the storyworld and the spectator as a witness to the fiction film: the harmful myth is that witnesses to the crime are needed, but the spectator serves no such role in relation to the storyworld, and as such is not used to corroborate or validate her story in that world.

The last argument that Young presents seems intended to tackle the claim that portrayals of rape are somehow informative or educational by pointing to the affective impact:

> we watch rape scenes from behind our fingers or with closed eyes, or when we shift uncomfortably in our seats as we endure another protracted rape scene, or when scenes live on in the memory long after their viewing. [...]
>
> As a spectator, I have always felt implicated in these crime-images: in their construction, these scenes address me as a woman whose body vision and violence could meet. [...]
>
> In response, then, to the claim that inclusion of a rape scene permits the education of the audience, I would ask: at what cost? (Ibid. 72)

Young's description of embodied responses to watching rape resonates with me, as it will with many female spectators, I am sure. I too can think of examples where the experience of watching rape, and empathising with the woman who is being raped, was felt so acutely that it stayed with me for months and years. Watching rape can clearly be deeply disturbing, and Young is right to question the cost of portraying rape on-screen. The affective cost for the spectator can be high.

However, to reiterate my position, I am not sure this in itself is an argument for why rape should not be portrayed in film, and should not be watched. It is, however, an argument for why explicit portrayals of rape should be used with great caution. I want to argue that graphic portrayals of rape can be warranted, but such portrayals will feel exploitative if the spectator does not perceive the rape as essential to the overarching theme, topic or argument in the film, which can be affective in nature. Central here is that the focus is firmly on the woman who is raped and her experience. This can be linked back to my discussion of the spectator's anger in Chapter 4: ideally, the spectator of rape-revenge film should be angered in the right way, which I want to argue is to feel empathic anger as a result of feeling with the protagonist, and feeling anger at rape, as a violation, beyond fiction. However, if the portrayal of rape does not work in this way, one might be more prone to feel angry with the filmmaker for using rape for other purposes, which I want to argue is not the kind of anger I am discussing here, but rather an indication that the portrayal of rape does feel exploitative. There is probably going to be a huge variation among spectators when it comes to which filmic portrayals of rape stir up what kind of anger. In this book I have discussed films in which I would argue some explicit portrayals of rape are warranted, such as in *The Nightingale*, although I have also argued that the difference between depictions of the experience of rape by the White woman, and the Indigenous Australian woman, is problematic in this film. *Promising Young Woman* leaves out explicit portrayals of rape, but in my analysis this film is no more praiseworthy for that reason alone. I can also easily think of examples where I found the graphic portrayal of rape problematic, and I will go on to look at one such example shortly. If wanting to discuss further when explicit portrayals of rape are legitimate, a discussion of the argumentative context in the film is the way to go.

By suggesting that it depends on narrative and argumentative context, I also implicitly deny the idea that there is – or ever will be – a filmic technique that would ensure that rape is portrayed ethically. This idea is discussed by others as ethical formalism, i.e. the view that 'specific filmic forms and styles have inherent, universal ethical implications' as explained by Plantinga, a view that he also dismisses (Plantinga 2018: 119). He points out that formal storytelling strategies cannot be isolated from the function they fulfil in the story, and that filmic techniques must therefore always be considered as part of the propositional content and rhetorical purpose they serve in the film (ibid. 120). In line with this, I want to deny that it is automatically ethically better not to portray rape, as in more politically sound, or progressive, or less exploitative. I dismiss this idea, leaving us with the difficult conclusion that it depends on narrative context, or on whether or not there is such a thing as an argument in the film that the vivid portrayals of rape can be said to enhance.

The explicit rape sequence and argumentative context: *Irreversible* and *Holiday*

I cannot fully settle what counts as a valid argumentative context that would legitimate explicit portrayal of rape. However, a promising line for further investigation would be to tie it to discussions in feminist film theory about what counts as a feminist film, and postulate that if a film can be said to offer a feminist perspective on rape, then portrayal of rape might be legitimate. However, what counts as a feminist film has proven to be a difficult question too, and a woman filmmaker does of course not automatically bring a feminist perspective. Christina Lane's examination of what she labels Feminist Hollywood films offers a helpful overview (Lane 2000). She explores films that privilege a woman's perspective through various filmic techniques, thus offering 'an economy of gazes controlled by female protagonists' in stories 'governed by a narrative trajectory based, at least in part, on female agency' (ibid. 17). This could be said to be one main feature of what might be considered a feminist film: a woman's perspective and agency is central to the story. Lane is careful to point out that this does not mean that identification with the woman is somehow easily secured or determined: rather, she explores how feminist films in Hollywood are influenced by counter-cinematic techniques, complicating identification and the spectator position. The notion counter-cinema is closely related to the estrangement aesthetics explored earlier, and could be said to have two strands, one of which is a Brechtian call for alienation, as articulated in Peter Wollen and Laura Mulvey's call for counter-cinema breaking with realism, identification and denial of the pleasures offered by mainstream films

(Mulvey 1975; Wollen 1982). However, in feminist film theory, just as influential is Claire Johnston's notion of women's counter-cinema, which she argues can be found in Hollywood films made by Dorothy Arzner and Ida Lupino, for example (Johnston 1999). In these films dominant myths about gender are distorted from within dominant filmic codes, thus not breaking down conventional engagement completely but still interrogating dominant ideology.

Furthermore, drawing on Teresa de Lauretis as well as Johnston, Lane shows that a promising strategy for defining a feminist film is to focus on what might be labelled a feminist address. Feminist address is found in films that take gendered spectatorship as a starting point, and that can be said to engage in a 're-writing of our culture's "master narratives"' (de Lauretis quoted in Lane 2000: 23). Central here is the idea that the film involves revision, inviting the spectator to see and notice (gender) difference: 'feminist counter cinema appropriates dominant codes in order to attend to female subjectivities and modes of seeing – female spectacle becomes female point of view' (Lane 2000: 24). Thus, one can rephrase this as the following added criterion for a feminist film: female perspective and agency is used in order to challenge dominant filmic codes in relation to the portrayal of women on-screen, and dominant narratives culturally about women. What exactly this might look like, or mean, in practice, might by necessity be contentious, by the mere fact that female perspectives, and feminist perspectives, will differ and be a source of disagreement and ongoing negotiation. Lane agrees with Christine Gledhill's remark that it is ultimately feminist criticism that can draw the film into a 'feminist orbit' by tapping into this cultural energy (Gledhill cited in Lane 2000: 26).

My analysis of rape-revenge film made by women directors has arguably aimed to do exactly this – teasing out how their exploration of a woman rape survivor's anger resonates with feminist film theory, feminist activism and feminist philosophy. The extent to which a rape-revenge film can be seen as feminist depends on whether it can be said to be firmly focused on the woman's perspective, allowing her agency to shape the narrative, and also whether or not the portrayal of her experience can be said to challenge dominant filmic and cultural norms about women. The feminist potential in some rape-revenge films could thus be the unrelenting focus on her vindictive anger, allowing this response to fuel the entire narrative. Such a portrayal does challenge dominant filmic norms, where women are prone to be victims but not aggressors.

Tania Modleski offers a related way to see explore the exploitative fringes of what might be considered women's cinema in her discussion of counter-phobic women's cinema (Modleski 2007), as discussed in Chapter 4. This relates to Schubart's claims, explored in the first chapter here, on women using horror to master their fears, which is arguably the kind of engagement Modleski is describing. A counter-phobic engagement is to refuse to feel terrorised by the representation of female victimisation. Modleski adds an important point to the literature about women's counter-cinema, in pointing to the ways a film can work counter-cinematically for women exactly by channelling fears about objectification and violation. To the extent that some rape-revenge films made by women should be considered examples of women's cinema and as counter-cinema, they may be counter-phobically so.

Again, I want to emphasise the importance of the revenge sequences when assessing the feminist potential of some rape-revenge films. It is of central importance that the focus remains firmly on the rape survivor's perspective in response to rape. It is her response that gives her agency, moving her out of the stagnate position as victimised woman so often quickly left behind in the narrative as others – mainly men – take centre stage. This is how we typically see the rape survivor in most crime stories: a woman is traumatised and hurt, and then quickly whisked off-screen as the male detective takes charge (see, for example, Cucklanz 2000). The revenge sequences in rape-revenge film are important as justice sequences, articulating what is at stake for whom (cf. Raney and Bryant 2002: 404; see Chapter 2 in the present study). My defence here of explicit portrayal of rape in some films can therefore not be used to legitimate the widespread portrayal of rape in crime fiction, for example, without careful analysis of whose perspective and whose agency the portrayal serves, and whether the portrayal can be said to do counter-cultural work – challenging dominant codes or narratives. I have explored how some rape-revenge films can be said to explore some such dominant myths about rape, confronting the tendency for victim-blaming, for example, or explaining away the horror of rape.

I want to end this chapter by outlining an analysis of two rape-revenge films, both with explicit rape sequences, in order to argue that there is a relevant feminist argumentative context to legitimate the explicit portrayal in *Holiday* (Isabella Eklöf, 2018), but not in *Irreversible* (Gaspar Noé, 2002). This is not to say that *Irreversible* does not have other values or functions: others have analysed the film as an analysis of time (Brinkema 2005; Brottman and Sterritt 2004), or as a mere exploration of the act of looking at images so painful that they verge on the unwatchable (Grønstad 2011: 54). I will bracket any such considerations here only to focus on the film through a feminist lens.

The rape sequences in *Irreversible* and *Holiday* are similar in style, but also mirror inversions of one another: in *Irreversible*, it is a stranger rape happening outdoors in an urban space, in the red darkness of an underpass at night-time, whereas in *Holiday* it is a partner rape in the bright daytime whiteness of the living room in a new-built coastal villa. However, in both cases the rape is filmed in one long unrelenting take without editing. In *Irreversible* the camera is placed on the floor just over Alex's face as she is raped in the underpass, and in *Holiday* it is placed further away, showing the entire living room where Sascha is raped. In both cases a person walks in on the rape halfway through, only to turn around and disappear as they see what is going on. It is the long take and the unhelpful witness that makes the rape sequence in *Holiday* appear to cite, and perhaps even comment on, the rape sequence in *Irreversible*. I will focus on the extent to which the films focus on Alex's and Sascha's respective perspectives, on their agency, and on whether or not the films can be said to subvert dominant filmic and cultural forms.

The infamous rape sequence in *Irreversible* takes place around halfway through the film, which is told in thirteen sequences in reverse: first we see Alex's enraged partner Marcus, and her ex-boyfriend Pierre, frantically search through the gay SM sex club The Rectum for a man called el Tenia in chaotic sequences ending with Pierre bashing a man's head in with a fire extinguisher to prevent Marcus from being raped by him. We then see the sequences leading them there, and the event that caused Marcus's violent rage: Alex is raped and beaten unconscious. We then learn how she left a party the three were at because she got angry with Marcus, and see how Alex and Marcus's day unfolded before this, with the two of them waking up in bed after an afternoon snooze, the film ending with Alex enjoying a summer day in the park. The first forty minutes of the film aligns the spectator with Marcus and Pierre, and it is Marcus's rage that fuels the storytelling: this is in many ways a masterful example of subjective narration where the style is completely infused by his state of mind (cf. Branigan 1984: 132ff). Circling, restless, disorienting and almost nauseating camerawork, disturbing background sound,[12] and rapid editing communicates clearly how he is caught up in the rush of bloodlust, not thinking clearly but 'seeing red', as the expression goes, emphasised also by the red colour tint in the sex club, portrayed as a Hellish Inferno as Marcus is chasing what he has been told is the man who raped Alex. Marcus is clearly allowed to do the storytelling here, the camera following him in tight alignment, and the style also working as a projection of his rage. Film technique and style is used skilfully to induce embodied empathy (cf. Vaage 2010).

The way the film works very hard to immerse the spectator fully in his state of mind contrasts with the portrayal of Alex, who only appears halfway through the film. The first we see of her is her bloodied face from Marcus's point of view as she is wheeled into an ambulance. She is unconscious, and this is where she leaves the story: *Irreversible* is the story about Marcus's response, not hers. She is half beaten to death. This silencing of her is found also in the style of the rape sequence, at least if comparing it to the way the film worked so hard to give access to Marcus's rage through filmic techniques and style: Alex is utterly terrified when she is suddenly attacked by a stranger in the underpass, but the camera calmly observes, with no editing, movement, or non-diegetic sounds to

---

[12] Caroline Eastwood explains how low frequency drone sound is used in club sequences, causing low-level effects of anxiety and discomfort (Eastwood, in progress).

Figure 7.2 Alex is terrified when a stranger turns his anger towards her in an underpass (*Irreversible*, 2002).

try to convey her state of mind (Figure 7.2). The anal rape takes seven minutes, and the camera only leaps up, so to say, and brings us closer when the rapist starts slamming her head against the floor, again stirred up only by a man's rage. The rape brings about a feeling of bearing witness, but does not use filmic techniques to try to portray Alex's state of mind, except perhaps the feeling of being completely entrapped, in the sudden stillness of the camera, almost as if lame and unable to move, as she is pinned down on the floor. Her helplessness is emphasised when a person comes into the underpass, sees what is happening, and simply turns to walk away without doing anything.

By and large the film is arguably characterised by lack of access to Alex. Only at the party does the camera part ways with Marcus and start following her, and in most of the following sequences we are aligned not only with her but also Marcus and Pierre, as the three travel on the metro, and at home, where Alex is with Pierre. Only at the very end of the film do we see her alone, and learn something only she knows that evening; that she is pregnant. In the conversations she is having with both Marcus and Pierre the focus tends to be on their interrogation of her sexuality: on the metro, Pierre keeps questioning her about her orgasms. In the bedroom with Marcus, he jokes that he wants to have anal sex with her and hovers over her. The one sequence that perhaps most clearly gives access to her state of mind is the ending, where a warm glow in the room and the calm quietness as she is sitting on the sofa smiling does communicate her happiness at being pregnant. However, this is not a film where Alex's perspective is allowed to take centre stage: the film aligns the spectator with her to a limited extent, does not use style to give access to her state of mind as extensively as to Marcus's, and the narrative trajectory in the film is not governed by her agency, but by Marcus's.

Indeed, *Irreversible* is arguably all about masculinity, or to be more specific, about straight, White masculinity. It is about Marcus's response to the rape of his girlfriend. Furthermore, his response is not one of concern for Alex and her well-being. He does not go to the hospital with her, but on a revenge mission. The film's portrayal of this can be said to be a study of misdirected anger, where his rage finds expression in racism, transphobia and homophobia. Interestingly, it is two minority ethnic men that first plant the idea of seeking revenge in Marcus's mind: as he is standing in shock after Alex is taken away in the ambulance, they suggest to him that the manly thing to do is to seek revenge, and they can help him find the rapist. This takes Marcus, and his reluctant partner-in-crime Pierre, on a search for a man with a notably foreign name, Guillermo Nunez. When Nuez turns out to be a trans woman sex worker named Concha, an increasingly agitated Marcus starts taking his anger out on her. This is where he picks up the lead on a man called el Tenia, who is said to be at the gay club The Rectum, taking Marcus and Pierre into the chaotic search through its SM sex dungeons in what is probably, for some straight men, unpleasant images of gay sex. The sex club is portrayed as deranged, with men offering their bare arses to Marcus, with a man trying to rape Marcus, and with spectators standing by, smiling gleefully and egging Pierre on when he saves Marcus from anal rape by hitting the attacker. This is where Marcus's anger is directed – at gay men. It is as if it is suggested that the root cause of the rapist le Tenia's cruelty is somehow found here.

Furthermore, ethnic minority men plant the destructive idea about manliness in Marcus's head. And what sets off the rape of Alex in the first place is a quarrel between Nunez, the trans sex worker with a Spanish name, and her pimp le Tenia: Alex walks in on it in that underpass, and when the pimp turns to Alex instead, Nunez simply runs away, making no effort to help Alex. The revenge sequences stir up a White, straight Frenchman's fears: the fear that one's girlfriend is raped, xenophobia, racism, transphobia and homophobia. This film explores these fears from a masculine point of view. Adding Marcus and Pierre's objectification of Alex into the mix makes it a study of how masculinity fails to understand her perspective, seeing it only from the outside, almost making them complicit – as signalled in the ways the rape sequence is subtly referenced in other sequences, such as Marcus holding his hand over Alex's mouth when they wake up and she wants to talk and he wants to keep slumbering, mirroring how the rapist will later clamp her mouth to prevent her from screaming, or his remark about wanting anal sex, which she brushes off as unromantic. There is thus a lot to be said about this film as a critical study of masculinity, but this is not my aim here. My point is that there is limited access to and focus on Alex and her agency. The film can be said to rework conventions in rape-revenge films in interesting ways, by telling the story in reverse for example, but it is problematic in its focus on a male response to a stranger rape, somehow latching this onto fears of the racial and sexual Other and displacing blame here, doing little to counter myths about rape, or to rework the dominant portrayal of woman as passive victim.

This film resonates in complex ways with *Holiday*, which does align us closely with its female protagonist, yet keeps her state of mind and her motivation opaque in line with art film conventions (cf. Bordwell 1979). The film follows Sascha as she arrives in a holiday resort abroad with money from Denmark for her drug dealer Danish boyfriend Michael, who is ruling his drug empire from a coastal villa populated by a group of subordinate men and their girlfriends. This film too can be said to be a study of toxic White masculinity, represented by Michael. As the film unfolds Sascha and Michael's relationship turns – or is revealed to be – abusive, as is Michael's relationship to his henchmen. Sascha is portrayed as being in danger throughout the film, starting with her being slapped by one of Michael's henchmen when he picks her up to drive her to the villa initially. This is the argumentative context in the film: how this woman is caught up in an abusive relationship.

Michael's abuse of Sascha comes to light in three sequences. The first is when he spikes her drink one evening and is portrayed as trying out various ways of positioning her unconscious body on the bed, intermittently touching his crotch as if to check whether he is now sufficiently turned on. He spreads her legs, he pushes her feet down and places her hands behind her back, and watches the reflection of himself over her limp body in the window reflection. Then there is a cut, so we do not see what happens next. What it does take to turn him on is portrayed in a later sequence following a fit of violent rage against one of his henchmen: the young man is accused of potentially leading the police to the property, and he is taken into the basement for a beating by the group of men, led by Michael. Sascha is ushered indoors to the living room, where she watches TV with two resident children, turning the volume up to mask the screaming from the basement. The next sequence shows Michael sitting on the sofa after the beating, Sascha trying to comfort him, her hunched posture revealing her anxious subordination. She urges him not to be sad. He gently pushes her down on the sofa, but then chokes her. She protests, telling him it hurts and to stop, and tries to get away. This turns him on. He slowly takes off his wristwatch (Figure 7.3). He goes on to rape her vaginally and then orally on the living room floor, hitting her when she bites his fingers, and telling her to go ahead and scream. She is whimpering, choking on his penis. One of Michael's henchmen comes down the stairs from the first floor but turns to go back up when he sees what is happening.

After this rape, we see Sascha's behaviour change only subtly: she is still the willingly smiling, softly complying partner, but increasingly she is anxious around Michael, as the abuse picks up. This is explored through her relationship with another vacationer in the resort, a Dutch man named Tomas, whom

Figure 7.3 Michael carefully removes his wristwatch before raping his girlfriend Sascha (*Holiday*, 2018).

Sascha meets in a queue in an ice-cream store and has a fling with. Michael finds out and is jealous, starts following her and checking her phone in increasingly controlling behaviour, and invites Tomas to the villa to confront him. Sascha is clearly anxious in this awkward situation, hesitantly trying to please Michael. The third abusive sequence takes place when Michael orders her to come over to the sofa where he and Tomas are sitting, tells her to take off her underwear, and fingers her, trying to make Tomas smell his fingers afterwards. Sascha endures this almost expressionlessly, as if emotions have been drained away from her, showing shock and sadness only when Michael slaps her after Tomas has stormed out, and she starts crying.

Sascha is portrayed as lonely and isolated in this environment, the tacky beach resort restaurants and the nouveau riche new-built villa. We sometimes see her observe Michael from afar in enigmatic close-up shots, cut off from him and the others, when the spectator is left to try to imagine what is going through her mind (cf. Vaage 2010). She is portrayed as seduced by Michael and the rich lifestyle he offers, pleased when he buys her expensive jewellery, and scrutinising her mirror image repeatedly, as if gauging who she is, or whether she is attractive. She willingly laughs when interacting both with Michael and Tomas, fulfilling the role of bubbly and charming young woman. But her agency is most prominently explored in relation to Tomas. She seeks him out and has an affair with him, seemingly more relaxed with him than with Michael. Tomas is also portrayed as having more human warmth than is Michael, and represents another type of masculinity: in one sequence in his boat, where Michael has followed Sascha and brutishly joins in, Tomas talks about breaking away from a career and from hate, seeking out other pleasures before losing his soul – which is ridiculed by Michael. The interaction between Sascha and Tomas that we see is more playful, taking place in more open environments such as on the beach, and on the deck of his boat. Arguably Tomas represents something different for Sascha, a promise of another kind of relationship with a more thoughtful man perhaps, and a way out of the cold, soulless spaces dominated by Michael.

Intriguingly, Tomas can fulfil what Projansky discusses as the New Man in post-feminist rape stories: this is a man who is more feminist than the women around him, and takes on the role as teacher or mentor to educate them, and who not only saves the woman in peril but also secures a heteronormative resolution to the story when the two end up as a couple.[13] There is a growing expectation that Tomas might be this kind of man, but the film resists such a problematic solution as a fix to the destructive psychology of abuse.

This becomes clear in the revenge sequence in the film, which breaks with rape-revenge conventions. Sascha does take revenge on Michael. Rather, she kills Tomas in a fit of rage. In some ways this is again misdirected anger, but in other ways it is not. The scene takes place when she seeks him out on his boat after the humiliating dinner in the house with Michael. Sascha comes to apologise. Tomas asks her to clarify what is going on, and whether she is being abused or not. This, I think, is the central question that suddenly stirs up a lot of emotion for Sascha, although she hastily denies abuse. Her reaction is fuelled by a lengthy reprimand he shouts at her after falling down the stairs in the boat and hurting himself, yelling at her that she is crazy and playing wicked games. This is when Sascha snaps, picks up a glass blender from the kitchen top, and hits his head several times with it until he dies. This is the one sequence where we see Sascha act on her own emotions the most clearly, and she is angry. It is certainly open for interpretation, but my take on it is that what is unbearable to her is to have this man blame her so harshly.

As is explored so carefully in the first season of the TV series *Big Little Lies* (David E. Kelley, 2017), it is difficult for a woman to come to terms with the abuse she is facing, and to understand it as such. In this series, careful use of flashback sequences is used to slowly reveal that Celeste does not have a passionate relationship with her husband Perry, as she first claims – he is violently abusing her. The spectator is given access to this only as Celeste is painfully coming to terms with the abuse, thus adjusting her own perceptions and memories of their marriage. It is a long process, and it takes much more than a single question from a bystander.

In *Holiday*, Sascha is not yet there. She is struggling to understand the unfolding relationship with Michael, but having this seemingly nice guy Tomas blame it all on her makes her arguably realise, at least momentarily, that what he is saying is wrong, and she responds with anger. It is a glimpse of a

---

[13] Projansky discusses Hal in *Thelma and Louise* as such a figure (Projansky 2001: 136, see also 84–6).

self-maintaining, genuine emotion in a situation in which she is lost. Of course, Tomas does not deserve to die for his lack of insight into the psychology of abuse, but lack of insight it is. As a post-feminist New Man, his sympathetic attitude is only skin-deep. The next sequence we see, Sascha turns up at a police station, but she hesitates and leaves without telling the three male police officers, probably assuming it is going to be a tough call to make them understand. Instead she returns to Michael. His crew gets rid of Tomas's dead body. The last image in the film shows her on Michael's new boat, turning smilingly to the camera, back in her old, cheery persona, and presumably increasingly entrapped in it. It is a chillingly unmotivated 'happy ending' (see Vaage 2022: 170).

The argumentative context in this film is about abusive relationships, and how a woman who finds herself in one may be less prone to suddenly act out against her abusive partner, as the avenger in the rape-revenge film takes revenge on her rapist, and more likely to really struggle even to recognise the abuse, and not least of all to leave. It shows an abusive relationship forming, and how Sascha is unable to act. The focus is on her perspective, even though the lack of explicit access to her thoughts and feeling necessitates imaginative empathy to understand her: the film can be said to call for understanding of the psychology of abuse. Look at this woman, seemingly shallow and focused only on material comforts, and try to understand her situation and the pain that she herself is trying to suppress. The revenge sequence does articulate something genuine about her state of mind, and it is her sudden expression of anger that is informative. The film is governed by her agency, as she is trying to negotiate or escape the situation with Michael through the relationship with Tomas. The film is arguably pleading with us to try to understand the young party-girl, and extend our sympathies also to her. She is living the White post-feminist dream of luxury and individual choice, and this film certainly resonates with the post-feminist ideology that Projansky examines in her corpus in this regard, but the dream is poisoned by abuse, which is the feminist edge to this film.

Thus I want to argue that the explicit rape sequence in *Holiday* is not exploitative, but does serve a function: this is where the abuse takes place, and this is what rape in a close relationship – so often ignored in public scrutiny of rape – looks like. Had the ugliness of the rape been left out, it might have been trivialised, as Sascha is too numb or dissociated to have much of a reaction to it. The emotional shock of seeing its ugliness is important. Partner rape in the glossy private setting of a villa breaks with conventions for portraying rape, and highlights the myth about the prevalence of stranger rape. This is the much more statistically typical scenario. The rape sequence feeds into an argument about the psychology of abuse, revealed also in the revenge sequence, where Sascha's anger is one rare expression of the pain she is experiencing. This film remains focused on Sascha's perspective, and allows her agency to form the narrative, hesitant as it is as she is struggling to maintain a strong sense of self and to recognise the abuse for what it is. Comparably, *Irreversible* does not allow Alex to take centre stage. Indeed, the main bulk of the film is organised around Marcus, and as he is not present when she is raped, one wonders why the spectator must be. Furthermore, the revenge sequence does not articulate a feminist perspective on rape that would thereby warrant its portrayal. Strangely, as the rape sequence takes up so much time, and is so unbearable to watch, this story does not really seem to be about a woman's experience of rape at all.

CONCLUSION: THE RAPE-REVENGE CONVENTION IN COMPLEX CONTEXTS

Rape and the response to rape continue to be a recurring and difficult topic in the public discourse. The revelations of a misogynistic culture in the Metropolitan Police have evoked strong emotions in the public debate in the UK over the last few years, with several police officers sentenced for crimes against women in the wake of the media coverage of the rape and death of Sarah Everard by the hand of a police officer during one of the pandemic lockdowns. Yet White middle-class women continue to stir up more media attention than women of colour: C. A. York sums up reports from family and relatives that the police delayed the investigation of the disappearance of women of colour, such as Nicole Smallman, Bibaa Henry and Bennylyn Burke, around the same time as Everard's kidnapping, in cases that were much less publicised in the media (York 2022: 18–19). Furthermore, when exploring their identities as boys and men, and how to relate to girls and women, young boys and men in Britain and elsewhere negotiate views such as those of the social media influencer Andrew Tate, known for claiming that 'women are partly responsible for being raped and that they "belong" to men' (Weale 2023). In short, the response to rape is no more settled now than when I started working on this book – perhaps even less so.

In stark contrast to witnessing how difficult it is for rape survivors to find justice in real life, it can be an intuitively gratifying feature of a fictional film or television series to see a humiliated woman take revenge for herself. It is a more personal, affective way to explore the response to rape. Fiction offers a way to explore crime such as rape from a deeply personal point of view, peeling away the bureaucratic complications of the law and exploring the crime, and the response to it, affectively and reflectively through eliciting empathy with the rape survivor's anger. Ideas about the function of fiction in relation to the law and justice have surfaced at various points in this study, such as the view that revenge in vigilante film is posing questions about what is just in a clearer, more affective way than films exploring the response in the legal system. The portrayal of revenge in rape-revenge film should therefore not be dismissed as in opposition to justice, but should rather be acknowledged as an affective exploration of what feels just. As explored in Chapters 4 and 7, strong emotions can elicit moral change. And anger is an emotion with an especially strong motivating function.

As argued in this book, the rape survivor's revenge can be a way of firmly placing the responsibility for rape with the rapist, and communicating clearly the horror of its violation. But in real life it should not be the response to rape, and it is confined to the imagination, as is Arabella's revenge in *I May Destroy You* (Michaela Coel, 2020), for example. Nevertheless, the fact that creator Michaela Coel includes rape-revenge storylines in her complex exploration of sexual assault and consent in *I May Destroy You* highlights a trend of female creators and filmmakers who explore this convention. We saw how creator Jenji Kohan did so in her story about Pennsatucky in *Orange Is the New Black* (Jenji Kohan, 2013–19), which I explored in Chapter 1, and in the rape-revenge films made by women that I have explored in this book. I want to sum up some tendencies in these films here.

In her book on horror films made by women filmmakers, Patricia Pisters suggests that explicit portrayals of rape may be less prominent in films made by women (Pisters 2020: 194). Barbara Creed makes a related observation in her discussion of *Revenge* (Coralie Fargeat, 2017), *The Nightingale* (Jennifer Kent, 2018) and *Promising Young Woman* (Emerald Fennell, 2020) as Feminist New Wave rape-revolt films, arguing that they break with conventional approaches to representations of rape (2022: 53–4). Yet, in the films and television series I have explored, there are explicit, graphic and violent representations of rape in several rape-revenge films made by women, such as *Baise-moi* (Virginie Despentes and Coralie Trin Thi, 2000), *The Nightingale*, *M.F.A* (Natalia Leite, 2017) and *Holiday* (Isabella Eklöf, 2018), and in both television series just mentioned there are explicit portrayals of rape too. Nevertheless, Creed's point about women filmmakers raising ethical questions about the representations of rape and challenging conventions arguably apply. Sometimes graphic portrayals are broken up in a series of defamiliarising close-up shots, such as in *Violation* (Dusty Mancinelli and Madeleine Sims-Fewer, 2020), for example, or partly left out, such as in *Revenge* where Jen is ultimately left alone to go through the ordeal.

In *Promising Young Woman* we simply watch Cassie's facial expression as she watches a recording of the rape. There is thus considerable variation in the portrayal of rape in these films, but some of them do include graphic portrayals.

One tendency that is clear in these films, is the move away from the portrayal of stranger rape, which Alison Young discusses as one of the harmful rape myths maintained by the early phase of rape-revenge films (Young 2010: 44–5). In contemporary films made by women, the rapist is more likely to be someone the protagonist knows, such her boyfriend's friend (*Revenge*), the lieutenant in charge in an Australian penal colony (*The Nightingale*), her fellow-student and host at a party (*M.F.A*), her sister's boyfriend (*Violation*), her fellow students (*Promising Young Woman*) or her boyfriend (*Holiday*). Adding to this emphasis on rape in relationships, there is problematisation of the seeming good guy that the protagonist is dating (*Blue Steel*, Kathryn Bigelow, 1990; *Promising Young Woman*), who fails her or even represents a threat to her. Relatedly, several films draw attention to the danger posed by men the protagonist should be able to trust, such as male authorities (*Twilight Portrait*, Angelina Nikonova, 2011; *Women Talking*, Sarah Polley, 2022). In several films this serves as part of a critique of the systemic nature of violence against women.

The rapist is more likely to be portrayed as a powerful and/or successful man, and less likely to be portrayed as lower class, as was more of a tendency in early rape-revenge film (Clover 1992). These contemporary rape-revenge films can thus be said to actively rework the myths about rapists as predominantly lower class and ethnic Other. As discussed in Chapter 5, Angela Y. Davis points out how, historically, White rapists typically walked free, enjoying anonymised protection by the law, whereas the rape charge was aimed indiscriminately at Black men (Davis 1981: 155). An important point she makes is thus how the myth of the Black rapist diverts attention away from the many actual rapists historically who have never faced prosecution (ibid. 179). Indeed, in the selection of rape-revenge films made by women that I have explored, the rapist is more likely to be one of these powerful White men who has enjoyed anonymised protection by the law historically.

This could also be tied to the thorny question of explicit portrayal of rape: as discussed in Chapter 7, there has been a tendency to celebrate films that respectfully turn away to leave a woman go through the trauma of rape without representing it explicitly, but in that chapter I asked who the film is thus protecting. Perhaps film has thus protected the powerful. Portraying the rape can be a way to retrieve the rapist from this anonymity, and serve as recognition that rape culture is not found at the margins of society but at its centre: some of these rapists are indeed what society would generally perceive as promising young men, others are men in positions of power.

There is also more of a tendency in these contemporary rape-revenge films to complicate revenge, in continuation of the cycle of revisionist rape-revenge films explored by Claire Henry (2014). Revenge is complicated through realistic portrayal of its human implications in *Violation* and *Monster* (Patty Jenkins, 2003), for example, taking the pleasure out of it when the avenger reacts with bodily dread and repulsion when mutilating another human being, or when the revenge is part of a defensive response of intense fear in post-traumatic stress. Revenge can be partially replaced or complemented by verbal confrontation rather than torture and killing, such as in *The Nightingale*. Such negotiation of rape-revenge conventions is also clear in both *I May Destroy You* and *Orange Is the New Black*, where rape-revenge storylines are used to portray one step the rape survivor takes on the way towards healing, but where revenge is ultimately rejected.

These are the tendencies that I want to highlight in this – admittedly small – selection of contemporary rape-revenge films made by women. However, it is interesting that there is such a trend emerging, suggesting that Creed was right in her original observation (Creed 1993: 155–6): if more women make (horror) film, one can expect more explorations of the problematic that is rape, for the reason that this is something that affects many women, and that many women fear.

An even more fundamental reason that rape-revenge conventions might interest women filmmakers is that they offer an opportunity to explore a woman's anger. One final case I want to bring in here is *Red Road* (Andrea Arnold, 2006), which might at first seem like an odd choice to end this book as it is not a rape-revenge film. This film is about the protagonist Jackie who works in the Glasgow surveillance team in co-operation with the police to pick up on crime on the city streets through a network of CCTV cameras. Through her work she spots a man who seems to stir up something in her, and whom she starts stalking through the CCTV cameras and then pursuing in real life (Figure 8.1). Jackie seems to be a woman on a revenge mission, but skilfully, the narration is holding one bit of essential information back, namely what the man, Clyde, has done. A series of subtle clues that will ultimately be revealed as misleading seems to encourage the spectator to hypothesise – or less reflectively, get a sense – that sexual abuse might be involved. Jackie first picks up on Clyde on CCTV as he is running after a woman in a deserted area behind buildings, making Jackie pay attention as it looks like his intentions are far from good – but the two then have consensual sex. And it is when Clyde turns around that Jackie seems to recognise him. Nevertheless, the first impression we get of Clyde is that he might be a rapist, and first impressions are of course stubborn.

Other cues that corroborate this are related to disgust: Jackie has ventured into a local café where Clyde hangs out, and as he is finishing his meal he demonstratively licks his plate only to be told off by the waitress who calls him

Figure 8.1 Jackie is drawn to Clyde but also disgusted by him (*Red Road*, 2006).

an animal. When Jackie picks up the courage to approach him at a party in his flat on the Red Road estates, her visceral reaction is one of nausea and she has to flee the scene to throw up. And notably, later Jackie has consensual sex with him but immediately afterwards she goes to the bathroom to stage it as rape: she smears his semen from the condom they used onto herself, and hits herself with a rock in order to claim that violence was used.

Pisters argues in her analysis of this film that it makes use of a distinct form of suspense where a slow build-up of mixed bodily feelings such as disgust generate tension in what she labels the neurothriller (Pisters 2014). I want to argue that the convention being evoked here is rape-revenge film. It is revealed in the first part of the film that Jackie's daughter has died, so it is unclear whose abuse is being avenged – whether it is Jackie's or the daughter's, or both. Only at the end of the film are these hypotheses revealed as wrong, as it turns out that Clyde was guilty of killing the daughter by accident when driving while intoxicated, and crashing into a bus shed where she happened to be standing. So this is not a rape-revenge film.

However, rape-revenge conventions are used for a specific purpose in this film, namely to explore a difficult and perhaps under-communicated part of grief – Jackie's vindictive anger. Jackie is portrayed as having withdrawn from everyone and everything after the death of her daughter, in a state of incapacitating grief. Her final confrontation with Clyde is portrayed as cathartic: working through her anger enables her to reconnect to all her feelings, and to people around her, and by extension, to the world. Anger is the final bit of mourning that she needs to go through, and rape-revenge conventions are used to explore it. It could be read as revisionist in that it ultimately complicates revenge as Jackie does withdraw her rape accusation, and finally merely confronts Clyde verbally. Jackie's revenge mission is portrayed as destructive in one sense. However, it would be wrong to conclude that revenge is therefore simply rejected – rather, revenge is used to explore anger, even if her revenge mission is ultimately abandoned. Just as in *I May Destroy You*, revenge plays a role, though it is not portrayed as the final answer.

This is one of the reasons I think women filmmakers might be drawn to the rape-revenge convention. The rape-revenge film does not only explore a crime that many women fear, as pointed out by Creed, but it explores a response to it – anger – that is culturally difficult. One root of this convention is found at the illicit fringes of film culture, in the dark corners of exploitation film, but the convention has found its way into a wide variety of film genres, modes and cultures, as explored by Alexandra Heller-Nicholas (2021), and even in films that can arguably be considered as part of a feminist orbit. One reason, I suggest, is the potential in the convention to explore the difficult emotion that is women's anger.

With roots in exploitation film, many rape-revenge films can be said to capitalise on the illicit, and therefore sensational, aspect of rape and of women's anger and aggression, and often for all the wrong reasons. However, as mentioned in the first chapter, some feminist film theorists seemed to be on the verge of finding something progressive in the rape-revenge film. Clover, for example, writes that feminist critics with whom she discussed rape-revenge films hated themselves more for having seen regular mainstream fare such as *Dirty Harry* (Don Siegler and Clint Eastwood, 1971), *First Blood* (Ted Kotcheff, 1982) and Hitchcock's *Frenzy* (1972) 'than *I Spit on Your Grave* [Meir Zarchi, 1978], which for all its disturbing qualities at least problematizes the issue of male (sexual) violence' (Clover 1992: 115). Creed writes how although her exploration of the portrayal of the monstrous-feminine in horror film, including rape-revenge film, was intended to reveal these films as a misogynistic construct of patriarchal society intended for a male viewer, 'feminist viewers often found [the female protagonist] empowering' (Creed 2022: 4). Indeed, writing about contemporary rape-revenge films as part of Feminist New Wave Cinema, Creed observes that 'since then her oppositional stance as represented by feminist directors has transformed into one of revolt' (ibid.).

In this book, my exploration has repeatedly led me to the origin of the female avenger in various manifestations of exploitation film – in Blaxploitation films, exploitation rape-revenge films and women-in-prison films. Several film scholars have pointed to the complex relationship between exploitation film and politics, for example its relationship to feminism (Cook 1976; Modleski 2007), and how the women-in-prison films explore lesbian pleasures in complex ways (Ciasullo 2008; Mayne 2000; Walters 2001), and between Blaxploitation film and the civil rights movement (Dunn 2008; Mask 2009). The rape-revenge film has been seen as a way for popular culture to explore feminism (Clover 1992; Henry 2014; Read 2000). Low-status genres can be lifted to higher status when filmmakers use their potential to explore something more serious (cf. Bordwell 2006). Such a process is arguably at work with these contemporary rape-revenge films, through which some women filmmakers draw out the political potential in this type of film.

So, a more politically minded filmmaker can draw out the political potential in the rape-revenge convention, as Creed has argued that some women filmmakers have done in what she discusses as Feminist New Wave rape-revolt films. Although all rape-revenge films are far from progressive, perhaps some of them might be, for this reason: the female avenger is all about emotion, she is all about anger, and psychologically, politically and culturally, there is much potential in this emotion. A well-made rape-revenge film can create a new imaginary premised on a greater salience of anger in women's lives. Anger permits women to see rape, survivors and perpetrators differently, and may contribute to a change in the individual and collective response to rape stories, without misattribution of blame onto the rape survivor: this is what the female avenger teaches us.

BIBLIOGRAPHY

Aaron, Michele (2007) *Spectatorship: The Power of Looking On*. London: Wallflower.
Abley, Sean (2021) 'Problematic Films: in defence of I SPIT ON YOUR GRAVE'. *Fangoria*, available at <https://www.fangoria.com/original/problematic-films-in-defense-of-i-spit-on-your-grave/> (last accessed 12 January 2023).
Agger, Gunhild (2016) 'Nordic Noir – location, identity and emotion'. In *Emotions in Contemporary TV Series*. Ed. Alberto N. García. London: Palgrave Macmillan, 134–52.
Aitkenhead, Decca (2004) 'The Gift of a Killer', *The Guardian*, available at <https://www.theguardian.com/film/2004/mar/27/features.weekend1> (last accessed 6 August 2023).
Alexander, Camille S. (2019) 'Forget Mammy!: Blaxploitation's Deconstruction of the Classic Film Trope with Black Feminism, Black Power, and "Bad" Voodoo Mamas'. *Journal of Popular Culture* 52(4): 839–61.
Andrews, David (2012) 'The Rape-Revenge Film: Biocultural Implications'. *Jump Cut* 54 (Fall).
Appiah, Kwame Anthony (2010) *The Honor Code: How Moral Revolutions Happen*. New York: W. W. Norton & Company.
Appiah, Kwame Anthony (2020) 'The Case for Capitalizing the B in Black'. *The Atlantic*, available at <https://www.theatlantic.com/ideas/archive/2020/06/time-to-capitalize-blackand-white/613159/> (last accessed 21 July 2023).
Arvas, Paula and Andrew Nestingen (2011) 'Introduction: Contemporary Scandinavian Crime Fiction'. In *Scandinavian Crime Fiction*. Ed. Andrew Nestingen and Paula Arvas. Cardiff: University of Wales Press, 1–17.
Bacon, Henry (2015) *The Fascination of Film Violence*. Basingstoke: Palgrave Macmillan.
Baker, Martin (2011) 'Watching Rape, Enjoying Watching Rape ...: How Does a Study of Audience Cha(lle)nge Mainstream Film Studies Approaches?' In *The New*

Extremism in Cinema. From France to Europe. Ed. Tanya Horeck and Tina Kendall. Edinburgh: Edinburgh University Press, 105–16.

Barash, David P. and Judith Eve Lipton (2011) *Payback. Why We Retaliate, Redirect Aggression, and Take Revenge*. New York: Oxford University Press.

Barr, Marleen S. (1993) *Lost in Space: Probing Feminist Science Fiction and Beyond*. Chapel Hill: University of North Carolina Press.

Bastién, Angelica Jade (2021) 'Emerald Fennell Explains Herself: Her Icy Film *Promising Young Woman* Set Off a Fascinating Conversation about What We Expect from Rape-Revenge Stories'. *Vulture*, available at <https://www.vulture.com/2021/01/promising-young-woman-ending-emerald-fennell-explains.html> (last accessed 27 December 2021).

Benson-Allott, Caetlin (2020) 'How *I May Destroy You* Reinvents Rape Television'. *Film Quarterly* 74(2): 100–5.

Bergman, Kerstin (2012) 'Lisbeth Salander and Her Swedish Crime Fiction "Sisters": Stieg Larsson's Hero in a Genre Context'. In *Men Who Hate Women and Women Who Kick Their Asses: Stieg Larsson's Millennium Trilogy in Feminist Perspective*. Ed. Donna King and Carrie Lee Smith. Nashville: Vanderbilt University Press, 135–44.

Blanchet, Robert and Margrethe Bruun Vaage (2012) 'Don, Peggy and Other Fictional Friends? Engaging With Characters in Television Series'. *Projections* 6(2): 18–41.

Bordwell, David (1979) 'The Art Cinema as a Mode of Film Practice'. *Film Criticism* 4(1): 56–64.

Bordwell, David (1996) 'Contemporary Film Studies and the Vicissitudes of Grand Theory'. In *Post-Theory: Reconstructing Film Studies*. Ed. David Bordwell and Noël Carroll. Madison: University of Wisconsin Press, 3–36.

Bordwell, David (2006) *The Way Hollywood Tells It. Story and Style in Modern Movies*. Berkeley: University of California Press.

Branigan, Edward (1984) *Point of View in the Cinema. A Theory of Narration and Subjectivity in Classical Film*. Berlin: Mouton Publishers.

Brinkema, Eugenie (2005) 'Rape and the Rectum: Bersani, Deleuze, Noé'. *Camera Obscura* 58, 20(1): 33–57.

Brison, Susan J. (2002) *Aftermath. Violence and the Remaking of a Self*. Princeton: Princeton University Press.

Brottman, Mikita and David Sterritt (2004) 'Irréversible'. *Film Quarterly* 57(2): 37–42.

Brown, Jeffrey A. (2011) *Dangerous Curves: Action Heroines, Gender, Fetishism, and Popular Culture*. Jackson: University Press of Mississippi.

Brown, Jeffrey A. (2015) *Beyond Bombshells. The New Action Heroine in Popular Culture*. Jackson: University Press of Mississippi.

Brownmiller, Susan (1975) *Against Our Will: Men, Women and Rape*. London: Secker and Warburg.

Brunsdon, Charlotte (2000) 'Not Having It All: Women and Film in the 1990s'. In *British Cinema of the 90s*. Ed. Robert Murphy. London: BFI, 167–77.

Butler, Judith [1990] (2007) *Gender Trouble. Feminism and the Subversion of Identity*. New York: Routledge.

Carli, Linda L. (1999) 'Cognitive Reconstruction, Hindsight, And Reactions To Victims And Perpetrators'. *Personality and Social Psychology Bulletin* 25(8): 966–79.

Carlsmith, Kevin M., Timothy D. Wilson and Daniel T. Gilbert (2008) 'The Paradoxical Consequences of Revenge'. *Journal of Personality and Social Psychology* 95(6): 1316–24.

Carroll, Noël (1996) 'Prospects for Film Theory: A Personal Assessment'. In *Post-Theory: Reconstructing Film Studies*. Ed. David Bordwell and Noël Carroll. Madison: University of Wisconsin Press, 37–68.

Carroll, Noël (1997) 'Fiction, Non-fiction, and the Film of Presumptive Assertion. A Conceptual Analysis'. In *Film Theory and Philosophy*. Ed. Richard Allen and Murray Smith. New York: Oxford, 173–202.
Carroll, Noël (2008) *The Philosophy of Motion Pictures*. Malden, MA: Blackwell.
Chemaly, Soraya (2016) 'Slut-Shaming and the Sex Police: Social Media, Sex, and Free Speech'. In *Gender, Sex and Politics: In the Streets and Between the Sheets in the 21st Century*. Ed. Shira Tarrant. New York: Routledge, 125–40.
Chemaly, Soraya (2018) *Rage Becomes Her. The Power of Women's Anger*. London: Simon and Schuster.
Cherry, Myisha (2018) 'The Errors and Limitations of Our "Anger-Evaluating" Ways'. In *The Moral Psychology of Anger*. Ed. Myisha Cherry and Owen Flanagan. London: Rowman and Littlefield, 49–65.
Cherry, Myisha (2021) *The Case for Rage. Why Anger Is Essential to Anti-Racist Struggle*. New York: Oxford University Press.
Ciasullo, Ann (2008) 'Containing "Deviant" Desire: Lesbianism, Heterosexuality, and the Women-in-Prison Narrative'. *The Journal of Popular Culture* 41(2): 195–223.
Clover, Carol (1992) *Men, Women and Chain Saws: Gender in the Modern Horror Film*. Princeton: Princeton University Press.
Cook, Pam (1976) '"Exploitation" Films and Feminism'. *Screen* 17(2): 122–7.
Cook, Pam (2005) *Screening the Past: Memory and Nostalgia in Cinema*. Abingdon: Routledge.
Cooke, Lucy (2022) *Bitch. A Revolutionary Guide to Sex, Evolution and the Female Animal*. London: Penguin.
Cooper, Brenda (1999) 'The Relevancy and Gender Identity in Spectators' Interpretations of *Thelma and Louise*'. *Critical Studies in Media Communication* 16(1): 20–41.
Cooper, Brittney (2018) *Eloquent Rage: A Black Feminist Discovers Her Superpower*. New York: St Martin's Press.
Covey, Russell D. (2001) 'Revenge explained – and justified? A Review of Peter French's *The Virtues of Vengeance*'. Findlaw.com, available at <https://supreme.findlaw.com/legal-commentary/a-review-of-peter-frenchs-the-virtues-of-vengeance.html> (last accessed 13 September 2021).
Creed, Barbara (1993) *The Monstrous-Feminine: Film, Feminism, Psychoanalysis*. London: Routledge.
Creed, Barbara (2022) *Return of the Monstrous-Feminine. Feminist New Wave Cinema*. London: Routledge.
Cuklanz, Lisa M. (2000) *Rape on Prime Time. Television, Masculinity, and Sexual Violence*. Philadelphia: University of Pennsylvania Press.
Currie, Gregory (1990) *The Nature of Fiction*. Cambridge: Cambridge University Press.
Dadlez, Eva, William L. Andrews, Courtney Lewis and Marissa Stroud (2009) 'Rape, Evolution, and Pseudoscience: Natural Selection in the Academy'. *Journal of Social Philosophy* 40(1): 75–96.
Daniels, Jessie (2012) 'Feminist Bloggers Kick Larsson's Ass. Reading Resistance Online'. In *Men Who Hate Women and Women Who Kick Their Asses. Stieg Larsson's Millennium Trilogy in Feminist Perspective*. Ed. Donna King and Carrie Lee Smith. Nashville: Vanderbilt University Press, 181–92.
Davis, Angela Y. (1981) *Women, Race and Class*. London: Penguin Random House.
Despentes, Virginie (2020) *King Kong Theory*. London: Fitzcarraldo Press.
Diawara, Manthia (1988) 'Black Spectatorship: Problems of Identification and Resistance'. *Screen* 29(4): 66–79.
Doane, Mary Ann (1982) 'Film and the Masquerade: Theorising the Female Spectator'. *Screen* 23(3–4): 74–88.

Dunn, Stephane (2008) *'Baad Bitches' and Sassy Supermamas: Black Power Action Films*. Urbana and Chicago: University of Illinois Press.

Eadeh, Fade R., Stephanie A. Peak and Alan J. Lambert (2017) 'The Bittersweet Taste of Revenge: On the Negative and Positive Consequences of Retaliation'. *Journal of Experimental Social Psychology* 68: 27–39.

Eastwood, Caroline (in progress) *Feeling Sound: Cinematic sound, subjective narration and embodiment*. University of Kent: PhD thesis.

Edwards, Marlo (2004) 'The Blonde with the Guns: *Barb Wire* and the "Implausible" Female Action Hero'. *Journal of Popular Film and Television* 32(1): 39–47.

Ellis, Peter (2020) *Memorable and Ambiguous: The Dramaturgy of Violence in Complex Serial Drama*. Flinders University: PhD diss.

Elster, Jon (1990) 'Norms of Revenge'. *Ethics* 100(4): 862–85.

Fine, Cordelia (2017) *Testosterone Rex. Unmaking the Myths of Our Gendered Minds*. London: Icon.

Flanagan, Owen (2017) *The Geography of Morals. Varieties of Moral Possibility*. New York: Oxford University Press.

Flanagan, Owen (2018) 'Introduction: The Moral Psychology of Anger'. In *The Moral Psychology of Anger*. Ed. Myisha Cherry and Owen Flanagan. London: Rowman and Littlefield, vii–xxxi.

Flesch, William (2007) *Comeuppance: Costly Signaling, Altruistic Punishment, and Other Biological Components of Fiction*. Cambridge, MA: Harvard University Press.

Flory, Dan (2005) 'Race, Rationality, and Melodrama: Aesthetic Response and the Case of Oscar Micheaux'. *The Journal of Aesthetics and Art Criticism* 63(4): 327–38.

Flory, Dan (2016) 'Racialized Disgust and Embodied Cognition in Film'. *Projections* 10(2): 1–24.

Flory, Dan (2019) 'Racialized Disgust and Character in Film'. In *Screening Characters. Theories of Character in Film, Television, and Interactive Media*. Ed. Aaron Taylor and Johannes Riis. New York: Routledge, 110–26.

Flory, Dan (2021) 'Racialized Disgust, Embodied Affect, and the Portrayal of Native Americans in Classic Hollywood Westerns'. *The Journal of Aesthetics and Art Criticism* 79(4): 465–78.

Flory, Dan (2023a) 'Disgust, Race, and Carroll's Theory of Solidarity'. *Film and Philosophy* 27: 1–27.

Flory, Dan (2023b) 'Racialized Disgust and the Depiction of Native Americans in the Ranown Cycle Westerns'. *Film and Philosophy*, online first: <https://doi.org/10.5840/filmphil20238723>.

Fister, Barbara (2013) 'The Millennium Trilogy and the American Serial Killer Narrative: Investigating Protagonists of Men Who Write Women'. In *Rape in Stieg Larsson's Millennium Trilogy and Beyond: Contemporary Scandinavian and Anglophone Crime Fiction*. Ed. Berit Åström, Katarina Gregersdotter and Tanya Horeck. Basingstoke: Palgrave Macmillan, 34–50.

Freeland, Cynthia A. (1996) 'Feminist Frameworks for Horror Films'. In *Post-theory: Reconstructing Film Studies*. Ed. David Bordwell and Noël Carroll. Madison: The University of Wisconsin Press, 195–218.

French, Peter A. (2001) *The Virtues of Vengeance*. Lawrence: The University Press of Kansas.

Frijda, Nico H. (1986) *The Emotions*. Cambridge: Cambridge University Press.

Frijda, Nico. H. (1994) 'The Lex Talionis: On Vengeance'. In *Emotions. Essays on Emotion Theory*. Ed. Stephanie H. M. Van Goozen, Nanne E. Van de Poll and Joseph A. Sergeant. New York: Psychology Press, 263–89.

Frye, Marilyn (1983) *The Politics of Reality. Essays in Feminist Theory*. Berkeley, CA: Crossing Press.

Gaines, Jane (1988) 'White Privilege and Looking Relations: Race and Gender in Feminist Film Theory'. *Screen* 29(4): 12–27.
Gates, Philippa (2013) '"Hidden in the Snow": Female Violence against the Men Who Hate Women in the Millennium Adaptations'. In *Rape in Stieg Larsson's Millennium Trilogy and Beyond: Contemporary Scandinavian and Anglophone Crime Fiction*. Ed. Berit Åström, Katarina Gregersdotter and Tanya Horeck. Basingstoke: Palgrave Macmillan, 193–213.
Gilpatric, Katy (2010) 'Violent Female Action Characters in Contemporary American Cinema'. *Sex Roles* 62(11–12): 734–46.
Gjelsvik, Anne (2016) 'Unspeakable Acts of (sexual) Terror as/in Quality Television'. In *Women of Ice and Fire. Gender, Game of Thrones, and Multiple Media Engagements*. Ed. Anne Gjelsvik and Rikke Schubart. New York: Bloomsbury, 57–78.
Greene, Joshua (2013) *Moral Tribes: Emotion, Reason, and the Gap between Us and Them*. New York: Penguin.
Griggers, Cathy (1993) 'Thelma and Louise and the Cultural Generation of the New Butch-Femme'. In *Film Theory Goes to the Movies*. Ed. Jim Collins, Hilary Radner and Ava Preacher Collins. New York: Routledge, 129–41.
Grønstad, Asbjørn (2011) *Screening the Unwatchable: Spaces of Negotiation in Post-Millennial Art Cinema*. Basingstoke: Palgrave Macmillan.
Guerrero, Ed (1993) *Framing Blackness: The African American Image in Film*. Philadelphia: Temple University Press.
Haidt, Jonathan (2012) *The Righteous Mind: Why Good People Are Divided by Politics and Religion*. London: Allen Lane.
Halberstam, Jack (1993) 'Imagined Violence/Queer Violence: Representation, Rage, and Resistance'. *Social Text* 37: 187–201.
Halberstam, Jack (1998) *Female Masculinity*. Durham, NC: Duke University Press.
Hallam, Julia and Margaret Marshment (2000) *Realism and Popular Cinema*. Manchester: Manchester University Press.
Hanich, Julian (2018) *The Audience Effect. On the Collective Cinema Experience*. Edinburgh: Edinburgh University Press.
Hansen, Miriam (1986) 'Pleasure, Ambivalence, Identification: Valentino and Female Spectatorship'. *Cinema Journal* 25(4): 6–32.
Heller-Nicholas, Alexandra (2011) *Rape-Revenge Films: A Critical Study*. Jefferson, NC: McFarland.
Heller-Nicholas, Alexandra (2017) *Ms. 45*. London: Wallflower Press.
Heller-Nicholas, Alexandra (2021) *Rape-Revenge Films: A Critical Study*, 2nd edition. Jefferson, NC: McFarland.
Henberg, Marvin (1990) *Retribution. Evil for Evil in Ethics, Law, and Literature*. Philadelphia: Temple University Press.
Henry, Claire (2013) '*The Girl with the Dragon Tattoo*: Rape, Revenge, and Victimhood in Cinematic Translation'. In *Rape in Stieg Larsson's Millennium Trilogy and Beyond: Contemporary Scandinavian and Anglophone Crime Fiction*. Ed. Berit Åström, Katarina Gregersdotter and Tanya Horeck. Basingstoke: Palgrave Macmillan, 175–92.
Henry, Claire (2014) *Revisionist Rape-Revenge: Redefining a Film Genre*. New York: Palgrave Macmillan.
Hill, Annette (2001) '"Looks Like It Hurts": Women's Responses to Shocking Entertainment'. In *Ill Effects. The Media/Violence Debate*, 2nd edition. Ed. Martin Baker and Julian Petley. London: Routledge, 135–49.
Hills, Elizabeth (1999) 'From "Figurative Males" to Action Heroines: Further Thoughts on Active Women in the Cinema'. *Screen* 40(1): 38–50.
hooks, bell (1996) 'The Oppositional Gaze: Black Female Spectators'. In *Reel to Real: Race, Sex and Class at the Movies*. New York: Routledge, 253–74.

Horeck, Tanya (2004) *Public Rape. Representing Violation in Fiction and Film*. London: Routledge.
Huebner, Bryce (2018) 'Anger and Patience'. In *The Moral Psychology of Anger*. Ed. Myisha Cherry and Owen Flanagan. London: Rowman and Littlefield, 89–104.
Jacoby, Susan (1983) *Wild Justice. The Evolution of Revenge*. New York: Harper and Row.
James, Erwin (2014) 'Prison Is Not for Punishment in Sweden: We Get People into Better Shape'. *The Guardian*, available at <www.theguardian.com/society/2014/nov/26/prison-sweden-not-punishment-nils-oberg> (last accessed 27 December 2021).
Jeffers McDonald, Tamar (2010) *Hollywood Catwalk: Exploring Costume and Transformation in American Film*. London: I. B. Tauris.
Johnston, Claire (1999) 'Women's Cinema as Counter-Cinema'. In *Feminist Film Theory. A Reader*. Ed. Sue Thornham. Edinburgh: Edinburgh University Press, 31–40.
Kamm, Frances A. (2019) 'The Gothic in Space. Genre, Motherhood, and *Aliens* (1986)'. In *Gothic Heroines on Screen. Representation, Interpretation, and Feminist Enquiry*. Ed. Tamar Jeffers McDonald and Frances A. Kamm. London: Routledge, 99–114.
Kauppinen, Antti (2018) 'Valuing Anger'. In *The Moral Psychology of Anger*. Ed. Myisha Cherry and Owen Flanagan. London: Rowman and Littlefield, 31–48.
Kay, Jilly Boyce (2019) 'Introduction: Anger, Media, and Feminism: the Gender Politics of Mediated Rage'. *Feminist Media Studies* 19(4): 591–615.
Kay, Jilly Boyce and Sarah Banet-Weiser (2019) 'Feminist Anger and Feminist Respair'. *Feminist Media Studies* 19(4): 603–9.
Kennedy, Helena (2018) *Eve Was Shamed. How British Justice Is Failing Women*. London: Chatto and Windus.
King, Donna, and Carrie Lee Smith, eds (2012) *Men Who Hate Women and Women Who Kick Their Asses: Stieg Larsson's Millennium Trilogy in Feminist Perspective*. Nashville: Vanderbilt University Press.
Kjeldgaard-Christiansen, Jens (2016) 'Evil origins: A Darwinian Genealogy of the Pocultural Villain'. *Evolutionary Behavioral Sciences* 10(2): 109–22.
Kjeldgaard-Christiansen, Jens (2019) 'A Structure of Antipathy: Constructing the Villain in Narrative Film'. *Projections* 13(1): 67–90.
Kjeldgaard-Christiansen, Jens (2020) 'Splintering the Gamer's Dilemma: Moral Intuitions, Motivational Assumptions, and Action Prototypes'. *Ethics and Information Technology* 22: 93–102.
Kjeldgaard-Christiansen, Jens, Anne Fiskaali, Henrik Høgh-Olesen, John A. Johnson, Murray Smith, Mathias Clasen (2021) 'Do Dark Personalities Prefer Dark Characters? A Personality Psychological Approach to Positive Engagement with Fictional Villainy'. *Poetics* 85: 101511.
Klinger, Barbara (1984) 'Cinema/Ideology/Criticism Revisited: The Progressive Text'. *Screen* 25(1): 30–44.
Lane, Christina (2000) *Feminist Hollywood: From* Born in Flames *to* Point Break. Detroit: Wayne State University Press.
Larsson, Mariah (2016) 'Adapting Sex: Cultural Conceptions of Sexuality in Words and Images'. In *Women of Ice and Fire. Gender, Game of Thrones, and Multiple Media Engagements*. Ed. Anne Gjelsvik and Rikke Schubart. New York: Bloomsbury, 17–38.
Larsson, Stieg (2015) *The Girl Who Kicked the Hornet's Nest*. Trans. Reg Keeland. London: MacLehose.
Leboeuf, Céline (2018) 'Anger as a Political Emotion: A Phenomenological Perspective'.

In *The Moral Psychology of Anger*. Ed. Myisha Cherry and Owen Flanagan. London: Rowman and Littlefield, 15–30.
Leffler, Yvonne (2013) 'Lisbeth Salander as Melodramatic Heroine: Emotional Conflicts, Split Focalization, and Changing Roles in Scandinavian Crime Fiction'. In *Rape in Stieg Larsson's Millennium Trilogy and Beyond: Contemporary Scandinavian and Anglophone Crime Fiction*. Ed. Berit Åström, Katarina Gregersdotter and Tanya Horeck. Basingstoke: Palgrave Macmillan, 51–64.
Lehman, Peter (1993) '"Don't Blame This on a Girl." Female Rape-Revenge Films'. *Screening the Male. Exploring Masculinities in Hollywood Cinema*. Ed. Steven Cohan and Ina Rae Hark. London: Routledge, 103–17.
Lentz, Kirsten Marthe (1993) 'The Popular Pleasures of Female Revenge (Or Rage Bursting in a Blaze of Gunfire)'. *Cultural Studies* 7(3): 374–405.
Lerner, Melvin J. and Dale T. Miller (1978) 'Just World Research and the Attribution Process: Looking Back and Ahead'. *Psychological Bulletin* 85(5): 1030–51.
Lerner, Melvin J. and Carolyn H. Simmons (1966) 'Observer's Reaction to the "Innocent Victim": Compassion or Rejection?' *Journal of Personality and Social Psychology* 4(2): 203–10.
Loreck, Janice (2016) *Violent Women in Contemporary Cinema*. Basingstoke: Palgrave Macmillan.
Lorde, Audre (2017) *Your Silence Will Not Protect You*. London: Silver Press.
Lugones, María (2003) *Pilgrimages/Peregrinajes. Theorizing Coalition Against Multiple Oppressions*. London: Rowman and Littlefield.
McBride, Lee A. III (2018) 'Anger and Approbation'. In *The Moral Psychology of Anger*. Ed. Myisha Cherry and Owen Flanagan. London: Rowman and Littlefield, 1–14.
MacDowell, James (2014) *Happy Endings in Hollywood Cinema. Cliché, Convention and the Final Couple*. Edinburgh: Edinburgh University Press.
McEntee, Joy (2022) '*Promising Young Woman* and the cinematic renegotiation of gender in rape-revenge'. *Senses of Cinema*, available at <https://www.sensesofcinema.com/2022/feature-articles/promising-young-woman-and-the-cinematic-renegotiation-of-gender-in-rape-revenge/#fn-43057-45> (last accessed 21 August 2023).
McGinity-Peebles, Adelaide (2020) 'Deconstructing Gendered Norms and Reclaiming Gendered Spaces in Angelina Nikonova's *Twilight Portrait* (*Portret v sumerkakh*, 2011)'. *Film Studies* 22(1): 11–29.
McHugh, Kathleen (2021) 'Prolegomenon: Anger, Aesthetics, and Affective Witness in Contemporary Feminist Cinema'. *Film Quarterly* 75(1): 10–22.
Mackenzie, Scott (2002) '*Baise-moi*, Feminist Cinemas and the Censorship Controversy'. *Screen* 43(3): 315–24.
McRae, Emily (2015) 'Metabolizing Anger: A Tantric Buddhist Solution to the Problem of Moral Anger'. *Philosophy East and West* 65(2): 466–84.
Maguire, David (2018) *I Spit on Your Grave*. London: Wallflower.
Maibom, Heidi L. (2014) 'Introduction: (Almost) Everything You Ever Wanted To Know About Empathy'. In *Empathy and Morality*. Ed. Heidi L. Maibom. New York: Oxford University Press, 1–40.
Man, Glenn (1993) 'Gender, Genre, and Myth In *Thelma and Louise*'. *Film Criticism* 18(1): 36–53.
Mask, Mia (2009) *Divas on Screen: Black Women in American Film*. Urbana: University of Illinois Press.
Maté, Gabor (2019) *When the Body Says No. The Cost of Hidden Stress*. London: Vermillon.
Mayne, Judith (2000) *Framed: Lesbians, Feminists, and Media Culture*. Minneapolis: University of Minnesota Press.
Miller, Chanel (2020) *Know My Name*. London: Penguin.

Miller, William Ian (2006) *Eye for an Eye*. New York: Cambridge University Press.
Modleski, Tania (2007) 'Women's Cinema as Counterphobic Cinema: Doris Wishman as the Last Auteur'. In *Sleaze Artists. Cinema at the Margins of Taste, Style, and Politics*. Ed. Jeffrey Sconce. Durham, NC: Duke University Press, 47–70.
Modleski, Tania (2010) 'Clint Eastwood and Male Weepies'. *American Literary History* 22(1): 136–58.
Modleski, Tania (2016) *The Women Who Knew Too Much. Hitchcock and Feminist Theory*, 3rd edition. New York: Routledge.
Mulvey, Laura (1975) 'Visual Pleasure and Narrative Cinema'. *Screen* 16(3): 6–18.
Murphy, Jeffrie G. (2003) *Getting Even. Forgiveness and Its Limits*. New York: Oxford University Press.
Murray, Jonathan (2015) '*Stella Does Tricks*'. In *Directory of World Cinema: Scotland*. Ed. Bob Nowlan and Zach Finch. Bristol: Intellect, 250–3.
Nannicelli, Ted and Paul Taberham (2014) 'Introduction: Contemporary Cognitive Media Theory'. In *Cognitive Media Theory*. Ed. Ted Nannicelli and Paul Taberham. New York: Routledge, 1–24.
Nisbett, Richard E. and Dov Cohen (1996) *Culture of Honor. The Psychology of Violence in the South*. Boulder, CO: Westview Press.
Nussbaum, Martha C. (2016) *Anger and Forgiveness. Resentment, Generosity, Justice*. New York: Oxford University Press.
O'Day, Marc (2004) 'Beauty in Motion: Gender, Spectacle and Action Babe Cinema'. In *Action and Adventure Cinema*. Ed. Yvonne Tasker. Abingdon: Routledge, 201–18.
O'Donoghue, Heather (2013) 'Old Wine in New Bottles: Tradition and Innovation in Stieg Larsson's *Millennium* Trilogy'. In *Stieg Larsson's Millennium Trilogy: Interdisciplinary Approaches to Nordic Noir on Page and Screen*. Ed. Steven Peacock. Basingstoke: Palgrave Macmillan, 35–57.
Orgad, Shani and Rosalind Gill (2019) 'Safety Valves for Mediated Female Rage in the #MeToo Era'. *Feminist Media Studies* 19(4): 596–603.
Parker-Hay, Katherine (2023) 'Audacity in the age of #MeToo', *Textual Practice*, 37(8): 1328–1334.
Peacock, Steven (2014) *Swedish Crime Fiction: Novel, Film, Television*. Manchester: Manchester University Press.
Peirse, Alison, ed. (2020) *Women Make Horror: Filmmaking, Feminism, Genre*. New Brunswick, NJ: Rutgers University Press.
Pettigrove, Glen (2012) 'Meekness and "Moral" Anger'. *Ethics* 122(2): 341–70.
Pinedo, Isabel Cristina (1997) *Recreational Terror. Women and the Pleasures of Horror Film Viewing*. Albany: State University of New York Press.
Pisters, Patricia (2014) 'The Neurothriller'. *New Review of Film and Television Studies* 12(2): 83–93.
Pisters, Patricia (2020) *New Blood in Contemporary Cinema. Women Directors and the Poetics of Horror*. Edinburgh: Edinburgh University Press.
Plantinga, Carl (1987) 'Defining Documentary. Fiction, Non-fiction, and Projected Worlds'. *Persistence of Vision* 5: 44–54.
Plantinga, Carl (1997) *Rhetoric and Representation in Non-fiction Film*. Cambridge: Cambridge University Press.
Plantinga, Carl (1998) 'Spectacles of Death: Clint Eastwood and Violence in *Unforgiven*'. *Cinema Journal* 37(2): 65–83.
Plantinga, Carl (1999) 'The Scene of Empathy and the Human Face on Film'. In *Passionate Views. Film, Cognition, and Emotion*. Ed. Carl Plantinga and Greg M. Smith. Baltimore: Johns Hopkins University Press, 239–55.

Plantinga, Carl (2009) *Moving Viewers: American Film and the Spectator's Experience*. Berkeley: University of California Press.
Plantinga, Carl (2018) *Screen Stories: Emotion and the Ethics of Engagement*. New York: Oxford University Press.
Povlsen, Karen Klitgaard and Anne Marit Waade (2009) 'The Girl With the Dragon Tattoo: Adapting Embodied Gender from Novel to Movie in Stieg Larsson's Crime Fiction'. *P.O.V.: A Danish Journal of Film Studies* 28: 64–74.
Projansky, Sarah (2001) *Watching Rape. Film and Television in Postfeminist Culture*. New York: New York University Press.
Purse, Lisa (2011) *Contemporary Action Cinema*. Edinburgh: Edinburgh University Press.
Raine, Nancy Venable (1999) *After Silence. Rape and My Journey Back*. London: Virago.
Raney, Arthur A. (2002) 'Moral Judgment as a Predictor of Enjoyment of Crime Drama'. *Media Psychology* 4(4): 305–22.
Raney, Arthur A. (2005) 'Punishing Media Criminals and Moral Judgment: The Impact on Enjoyment'. *Media Psychology* 7(2): 145–63.
Raney, Arthur A. (2011) 'The Role of Morality in Emotional Reactions to and Enjoyment of Media Entertainment'. *Journal of Media Psychology* 23(1): 18–23.
Raney, Arthur A. and Jennings Bryant (2002) 'Moral Judgment and Crime Drama: An Integrated Theory of Enjoyment'. *Journal of Communication* 52(2): 402–15.
Read, Jacinda (2000) *The New Avengers: Feminism, Femininity, and the Rape-Revenge Cycle*. Manchester: Manchester University Press.
Riddle, Karyn (2014) 'A Theory of Vivid Media Violence'. *Communication Theory* 24(3): 291–310.
Roach, Shoniqua (2018) 'Black Pussy Power: Performing Acts of Black Eroticism in Pam Grier's Blaxploitation Films'. *Feminist Theory* 19(1): 7–22.
Robson, Peter (2016) 'Beyond the Courtroom. Vigilantism, Revenge and Rape-Revenge Films in the Cinema of Justice'. In *Framing Law and Crime: An Interdisciplinary Anthology*. Ed. Caroline Joan 'Kay' S. Picart, Michael Hviid Jacobsen and Cecil Greek. Lanham, MD: Rowman and Littlefield, 165–202.
Rodowick, D. N. (2007) 'An Elegy for Theory'. *October* 122: 91–109.
Saddique, Haroon (2020) 'We Are Facing The "Decriminalisation of Rape", Warns Victims' Commissioner'. *The Guardian*, available at <https://www.theguardian.com/society/2020/jul/14/we-are-facing-the-decriminalisation-of-warns-victims-commissioner> (last accessed 27 December 2021).
Schlesinger, Philip, R. Emerson Dobash, Russell P. Dobash and C. Kay Weaver (1992) *Women Viewing Violence*. London: BFI.
Schubart, Rikke (2007) *Super Bitches and Action Babes: The Female Hero in Popular Cinema, 1970–2006*. Jefferson, NC: McFarland.
Schubart, Rikke (2018) *Mastering Fear: Women, Emotions, and Contemporary Horror*. New York: Bloomsbury.
Schwan, Anne (2016) 'Postfeminism Meets the Women in Prison Genre: Privilege and Spectatorship in *Orange Is the New Black*'. *Television and New Media* 17(6): 473–90.
Shoemaker, David (2018) 'You Oughta Know: Defending Angry Blame'. In *The Moral Psychology of Anger*. Ed. Myisha Cherry and Owen Flanagan. London: Rowman and Littlefield, 67–88.
Siddiqi, Ayesha (2021) 'Review: A Promising Young Woman and the End of the Girlboss Era' [blog] available at <https://ayeshaasiddiqi.substack.com/p/id-like-this-to-stop-praise-for-a> (last accessed 27 December 2021).
Siegler, Carol (2007) 'Female Heterosexual Sadism: The Final Feminist Taboo in *Buffy the Vampire Slayer* and the Anita Blake Vampire Hunter Series'. In *Third Wave*

Feminism and Television: Jane Puts It in a Box. Ed. Merri Lisa Johnson. New York: Palgrave Macmillan, 56–90.

Sims, Yvonne D. (2006) *Women of Blaxploitation: How the Black Action Film Heroine Changed American Popular Cinema.* Jefferson, NC: MacFarland.

Smith, Greg M. (2003) *Film Structure and the Emotion System.* Cambridge: Cambridge University Press.

Smith, Murray (1995) *Engaging Characters. Fiction, Emotion, and the Cinema.* Oxford: Clarendon Press.

Smith, Murray (1996) 'The Logic and Legacy of Brechtianism'. In *Post-Theory: Reconstructing Film Studies.* Ed. David Bordwell and Noël Carroll. Madison: University of Wisconsin Press, 130–48.

Smith, Murray (1999) 'Gangsters, Cannibals, Aesthetes, or Apparently Perverse Allegiances'. In *Passionate Views. Film, Cognition, and Emotion.* Ed. Carl Plantinga and Greg M. Smith. Baltimore: Johns Hopkins University Press, 217–38.

Smith, Susan (2000) *Hitchcock: Suspense, Humour and Tone.* London: BFI/Palgrave Macmillan.

Sommers, Tamler (2009) 'The Two Faces of Revenge: Moral Responsibility and the Culture of Honor'. *Biology and Philosophy* 24(1): 35–50.

Sommers, Tamler (2018) *Why Honor Matters.* New York: Basic Books.

Springer, Kimberly (2001) 'Waiting to Set it Off: African American Women and the Sapphire Fixation'. In *Reel Knockouts: Violent Women in the Movies.* Ed. Martha McCaughey and Neal King. Austin: University of Texas Press, 172–99.

Srinivasan, Amia (2018) 'The Aptness of Anger'. *The Journal of Political Philosophy* 26(2): 123–44.

Stacey, Jackie (1993) 'Textual Obsessions: Methodology, History and Researching Female Spectatorship'. *Screen* 34(3): 260–74.

Tasker, Yvonne (1993) *Spectacular Bodies. Gender, Genre and the Action Cinema.* London: Routledge.

Tessman, Lisa (2005) *Burdened Virtues. Virtue Ethics for Liberatory Struggles.* New York: Oxford University Press.

Turvey, Malcolm (2007) 'Theory, Philosophy, and Film Studies: A Response to D. N. Rodowick's "An Elegy for Theory"'. *October* 122: 110–20.

Vaage, Margrethe Bruun (2010) 'Fiction Film and the Varieties of Empathic Engagement'. *Midwest Studies in Philosophy* 34: 158–79.

Vaage, Margrethe Bruun (2013) 'Fictional Reliefs and Reality Checks'. *Screen* 54(2): 218–37.

Vaage, Margrethe Bruun (2015) 'On the Repulsive Rapist and the Difference Between Morality In Fiction and Real Life'. In *The Oxford Handbook of Cognitive Literary Studies.* Ed. Lisa Zunshine. New York: Oxford University Press, 421–39.

Vaage, Margrethe Bruun (2016) *The Antihero in American Television.* New York: Routledge.

Vaage, Margrethe, Bruun (2017) 'From *The Corner* to *The Wire*: On Nonfiction, Fiction, and Truth'. *Journal of Literary Theory* 11(2): 255–70.

Vaage, Margrethe Bruun (2019) 'On Punishment and Why We Enjoy It in Fiction: Lisbeth Salander of the *Millennium* Trilogy and Eli in *Let the Right One In* as Scandinavian Avengers'. *Poetics Today* 40(3): 543–57.

Vaage, Margrethe Bruun (2022) 'Five Theses on the Difficulty of Ending Television Series'. In *Cognition, Emotion, and Aesthetics in Contemporary Serial Television.* Ed. Hector Perez Lopez and Ted Nannicelli. London and New York: Routledge, 160–75.

Vaage, Margrethe Bruun (2023) 'Should We Be Against Empathy? Engagement with Antiheroes in Fiction and the Theoretical Implications for Empathy's Role in Morality'. In *Conversations on Empathy: An Interdisciplinary Encounter*. Ed. Francesca Mezzenzana and Daniela Peluso. New York: Routledge, 116–34.

Vandermassen, Griet (2005) *Who's Afraid of Charles Darwin? Debating Feminism and Evolutionary Theory*. Lanham, MD: Rowman and Littlefield.

Vandermassen, Griet (2011) 'Evolution and Rape: A Feminist Darwinian Perspective'. *Sex Roles* 64: 732–47.

Vares, Tiina (2001) 'Action Heroines and Female Viewers. What Women Have to Say'. In *Reel Knockouts. Violent Women in the Movies*. Ed. Martha McCaughey and Neal King. Austin: University of Texas Press, 219–43.

Walters, Suzanna Danuta (2001) 'Caged Heat: The (R) Evolution of Women-In-Prison Films'. In *Reel Knockouts: Violent Women in the Movies*. Ed. Martha McCaughey and Neal King. Austin: University of Texas Press, 106–23.

Weale, Sally (2023) '"We see misogyny every day": how Andrew Tate's twisted ideology infiltrated British schools'. *The Guardian*, available at <https://www.theguardian.com/society/2023/feb/02/andrew-tate-twisted-ideology-infiltrated-british-schools> (last accessed 8 September 2023).

Williams, Linda (1984) 'When the Woman Looks'. In *Re-Vision: Essays in Feminist Film Criticism*. Ed. Mary Ann Doane, Patricia Mellencamp and Linda Williams. Frederick, MD: University Publications of America, 83–99.

Williams, Linda (2001a) 'When Women Look: A Sequel'. *Senses of Cinema*, available at <https://sensesofcinema.com/2001/freuds-worst-nightmares-psychoanalysis-and-the-horror-film/horror_women/> (last accessed 27 December 2021).

Williams, Linda (2001b) 'Sick Sisters'. *Sight and Sound* 11(7): 28–9.

Williams, Linda (2002) 'Less Rape, More Revenge'. *Sight and Sound* 12(4): 70.

Willis, Sharon (1993) 'Hardware and Hardbodies, What Do Women Want?: A Reading of *Thelma and Louise*'. In *Film Theory Goes to the Movies*. Ed. Jim Collins, Hilary Radner and Ava Preacher Collins. New York: Routledge, 120–8.

Wimmer, Leila (2011) '"Sex and Violence from a Pair of Furies": The Scandal of *Baise-moi*'. In *The New Extremism in Cinema. From France to Europe*. Ed. Tanya Horeck and Tina Kendall. Edinburgh: Edinburgh University Press, 130–41.

Winkler, Cathy (2002) *One Night. Realities of Rape*. Walnut Creek, CA: AltaMira Press.

Wollen, Peter (1982) 'Godard and Counter Cinema: Vent d'Est'. In *Readings and Writings: Semiotic Counter-Strategies*. London: Verso, 79–91.

Wright, Will (1975) *Six Guns and Society: A Structural Study of the Western*. Berkeley: University of California Press.

York, C. A. (2022) 'Fennell's *Promising Young Woman* and Furious Women in Film'. *Film and Philosophy* 26: 1–22.

Young, Alison (2010) *The Scene of Violence. Cinema, Crime, Affect*. Abingdon: Routledge.

Zillmann, Dolf (2000) 'Basal Morality in Drama Appreciation'. In *Moving Images, Culture, and the Mind*. Ed. Ib Bondebjerg. Luton: University of Luton Press, 53–63.

Zillmann, Dolf, and Jennings Bryant (1975) 'Viewer's Moral Sanction of Retribution in the Appreciation of Dramatic Presentations'. *Journal of Experimental Social Psychology* 11(6): 572–82.

Zillmann, Dolf, and Joanne Cantor (1977) 'Affective Responses to the Emotions of a Protagonist'. *Journal of Experimental Social Psychology* 13(2): 155–65.

INDEX

Aaron, Michelle, 43, 151
The Accused, 16, 31, 112, 114–15, 164, 166–8, 169
action film, 5, 12–13, 19, 36, 39–40, 46, 48, 51, 113, 136–7, 138, 140–1, 156–7
Affective Disposition Theory (ADT), 35
agency, 45, 54, 57, 68, 139, 171, 172, 173, 178–9, 180–1
Ahmed, Sara, 83–4
Alias, 19
Aliens, 130, 132, 136
altruism, 34–5
Andrews, David, 67–8, 69
anger, 6, 8, 29, 80–104, 169, 186–7
  action tendency, 91–2
  adverse and positive effects of, 87–8
  anger eliminativists, 89–95
  anger policing, 95
  Black women's anger, 10, 82–3, 114
  as a burdened virtue, 84
  communicative function, 88–9
  definitions, 84
  emotional range, 84–5
  epistemic function, 86–7
  feminists on women's anger, 81–4
  function of, 5, 84–9
  as hard to handle, 141
  male anger, 81
  motivating function, 85–6, 91–2
  neglect of women's anger, 9–10
  and past events, 85
  rape-revenge film as a place of rage, 101–4
  and respect, 81–2, 85, 88
  rogue rage, 88
  as a sign of mental instability, 82, 83
  transition-anger, 85, 93
  unconditional forgiveness in *Twilight Portrait* and *Women Talking*, 95–101
  value of, 5, 10, 11–12
  vindictive anger, 1, 4, 5, 25, 44, 63, 89, 93, 94, 95–6, 105, 120–1, 154
antihero, 28, 154
Appiah, Kwame Anthony, 70, 71, 72–3
Aristotle, 84, 85
Arvas, Paula, 37
Arzner, Dorothy, 172

Bacon, Henry, 35–6
Bad Girls Go to Hell, 2
Baird, Dame Vera, 4
Baise-moi, 2, 6–7, 80, 183

INDEX

Barash, David P., 62–3
Basic Instinct, 49
bell hooks, 112–13
Benson-Allott, Caetlin, 123, 124
Bergman, Ingmar, 1
Bigelow, Kathryn, 132
Birth of a Nation, 110–11
bisexuality, 130
Black Mama, White Mama, 106
Blackmail, 17
blame, 27, 29, 84, 103
   and rape victims, 30–1, 74–6
Blaxploitation film, 10, 12, 105–6, 129, 187–8
   Black rape-revengers, 106–13
   racist stereotypes, 108–9
Blue Steel, 2, 12, 128, 132–5, **135**, 139, 184
Bogle, Donald, 112
Boys Don't Cry, 131
Brecht, Bertolt, 43, 151, 154, 171
Brison, Susan J., 8, 69, 83, 92, 163
Brown, Jeffrey A., 19, 39, 51, 108, 137
Brownmiller, Susan, 110
Bulbbul, 3
Butler, Judith, 129

castration, 18, 106
Charlie's Angels: Full Throttle, 137–8
chastity, 71, 72, 74
Chemaly, Soraya, 81, 83, 91–2
Cherry, Myisha, 82, 84, 87, 88, 95, 140
class, 13, 111–12, 113–14, 118, 182, 184
Clover, Carol, 15–17, 27, 29, 31, 42, 66, 69, 111–12, 162, 187
Coffy, 105, 108, 109, 113
cognitive film theory, 5, 6, 13, 23–5, 30, 41, 111
Cohen, Dov, 70
Colangelo, B. J., 8
comedy, 139, 142, 145
containment strategies, 135–48, 153
contemporary film theory, 5, 10, 14, 150, 151, 184
Cooke, Lucy, 5–6
Cooper, Brenda, 101, 163
counter-cinematic techniques, 171–3
Creed, Barbara, 3, 18, 19, 22, 45, 68, 159, 183, 185, 187, 188
Culture Shock, 3

Daniels, Jessie, 130
Date Movie, 50
Daughter archetype, 39, 51
Daughters of the Dust, 116
Davis, Angela Y., 77, 109, 110, 184
Death Wish, 52, 59, 67, 74
Descent, 117, 131
desirability, 50, 53–4, 55, 140
Despentes, Virginie, 7
Dexter, 2
Dirty Harry, 152, 187
disgust, 73–4, 111, 185–7
Doane, Mary-Anne, 50
Dogville, 2, 142
dominatrix features, 137
Dunn, Stephane, 106, 107, 109, 112–13, 116

Ebert, Robert, 7–8
Ellis, Peter, 164
Elster, Jon, 61, 70, 71
embodied engagement, 138, 141, 170
emotion, 6, 149–81
   argumentative context and the explicit rape sequence, 171–81
   in contemporary film theory, 13, 151–2
   detachment, 155
   didactic argument against revenge, 150–5
   emotional engagement, 5, 10–11, 151–2, 154–5
   function of, 86
   and horror film, 30
   philosophy of, 5, 84–9
   and shock, 165
empathy, 57, 126, 134–5, 141, 162, 174, 180, 183
empowerment/disempowerment, 8, 11, 18, 20–1, 25, 29, 87, 97–9, 132, 133, 135
eroticisation, 49, 55, 68–9
   and female action heroes, 136–7, 140–1
estrangement theory, 10–11, 43, 151, 154, 171
ethical formalism, 171
ethical spectatorship, 10, 43, 151
ethics of watching, 162–71
Everett, Anna, 108
evolutionary psychology, 5–6, 34
executions, 35

201

Exodus, 64
exploitation argument against explicit portrayal of rape, 157–62

fantasy, 41–2
   about revenge, 8–9, 10–11, 28–9, 69, 78–9, 125–7
   and Black women fighters, 113
   blending reality and fantasy, 36–41
   as a place of rage, 101, 102
   realist argument against rape-revenge film, 155–7
female action heroes, 5, 12–13, 19, 45, 105–6, 108, 113, 162
   action babe category, 136–7, 138
   and comedy, 139, 142, 145
   containment of the female avenger on-screen, 135–9, 153
   containment strategies in *Promising Young Woman*, 139–48
   embodied engagement, 138, 141
   gender trouble, 128, 129–35
   non-realist nature of, 137–8
   and realism, 156–7
   sexualisation, 136–7, 140–1
female spectators, 8, 11, 15–23, 30, 146–7
   Black female spectators, 112–13
   and the graphic portrayal of rape, 157–62
   responses, 24
femininity
   and avenger transformation, 46–58
   and feminism, 49
feminism, 4, 5–6
   and femininity, 49
   feminist address, 172
   feminist media theory, 9
   film theory, 6, 11, 15–23, 27, 171–2
   post-feminism, 163
   and women's anger, 81–4
Feminist Media Studies, 9
Feminist New Wave Cinema, 3, 22–3, 159, 183, 187, 188
Femme, 131
Fennell, Emerald, 146
fiction, 182–3
   avenger as a fictional relief, 41–4, 46, 57
   intention-response approach, 41–2
   and punishment, 34–6
film critique, 6–8

Final Girl notion, 16–17, 18, 40, 106
Fine, Cordelia, 5–6
First Blood, 187
Flanagan, Owen, 90, 92
flashbacks, 57, 99, 122, 123, 124, 160, 167, 169, 179
Flesch, William, 34–5
Flory, Dan, 75, 76, 111
foot-binding, 71, 73
forgiveness, 12
   transactional forgiveness, 93–4
   unconditional forgiveness as an alternative to anger, 92–5
   unconditional forgiveness in *Twilight Portrait* and *Women Talking*, 95–101
Foxy Brown, 12, 105, 106, 108, 109, 113, 116–17
Freeland, Cynthia, 23
French, Peter A., 59, 61, 65, 66, 71, 75–6, 78–9
Frenzy, 187
Freudian theory, 18
Frijda, Nico, 28–9, 59–60, 61–2, 63, 64
Frye, Marilyn, 81–2

Game of Thrones, 53
gaslighting, 81, 83
Gates, Philippa, 37
gender
   active male/passive female dichotomy, 18–19
   gender expectations, 25, 131–2, 133, 156–7
   gender roles, 5
   gender trouble, 128, 129–35
   gendered nature of honour, 70–1
Gill, Rosalind, 9–10
Gilpatric, Katy, 138, 139
The Girl Who Kicked the Hornet's Nest, 33
The Girl Who Played with Fire, 33, 38–9
The Girl with the Dragon Tattoo, 1, 11–12, 26, 33, 37–8, 43–4, 151
glasses, taking off, 50
Gledhill, Christine, 172
The Godfather, 59
Grand Theory, 23
Grease, 53, 54
Greene, Joshua, 154
Grier, Pam, 105–6, 107, 108
Guerrero, Ed, 106–7, 110–11, 112, 113

Halberstam, Jack, 101–3, 130
Hannie Caulder, 65, 66, 153
Hansen, Miriam, 19, 20
harmful stereotype test, 152
Heller-Nicholas, Alexandra, 1–3, 128, 142, 187
Henberg, Marvin, 64
Henry, Claire, 3, 5, 10, 21–2, 43–4, 45, 66, 96, 150–1, 159, 162, 185
heterosexuality, 130–1, 131–2, 139
Hill, Annette, 20–1
Hill, Jack, 108
Hills, Elizabeth, 162
Hitchcock, Alfred, 17
Holiday, 2, 13, 173–4, 177–81, 183, 184
homophobia, 131, 176
honour, 11
  cultures, 70–1
  differences between honour cultures and Western culture, 72–3
  gendered nature of, 70–1
  killings, 71, 72–3, 75–6
  as a motivator, 73
  and revenge, 59, 61, 70–8
Horeck, Tanya, 112, 115, 163–4
horror film, 2, 15–16, 18, 19–20, 22–3, 30, 156–7, 187
Huebner, Bryce, 87

I May Destroy You, 2, 12, 105, 183, 185, 187
  critique of conventions, 122–7
  in-betweenness notion, 130
I Spit on Your Grave, 1, 3, 7, 8, 15–16, 18, 22, 31, 42, 45, 68, 80, 106, 116, 187
I Was a Teenage Serial Killer, 3
Irreversible, 2, 13, 131, 168, 173–7, 181

Jacoby, Susan, 59, 60, 63–5, 94
Jeanne Dielman, 23 Quai de Commerce, 1080 Bruxelles, 2
Jeffers McDonald, Tamar, 49–50, 53–5
Johnston, Claire, 172
Just World Theory, 30, 31
justice/injustice, 11, 28, 35, 60, 63–4, 65–6, 97–8, 152
  affective injustice, 82–3, 104
  women and the British justice system, 113–14, 182

Katalin Varga, 150–1
Kauppinen, Antti, 84, 85, 91, 94
Kay, Jilly Boyce, 9
Kennedy, Helena, 113–14
Kent, Jennifer, 159
Kill Bill: Volume 1, 1, 138, 139, 169
Kill Bill: Volume 2, 1–2

La Femme Nikita, 39, 51, 141
landscape, 66–7
Lane, Christine, 132, 133, 171, 172
Larsson, Stieg, 33
The Last House on the Left, 74, 159
Laurentis, Teresa de, 172
Law and Order: SVU, 8
Law of Talion (*lex talionis*), 64, 67, 68, 69
Leboeuf, Céline, 86
Lehman, Peter, 17, 49
Lentz, Kirsten Marthe, 19
Lerner, Gerder, 110
lesbianism, 130–1, 187
Lipton, Judith Eve, 62–3
Little Big Lies, 179
Lorde, Audre, 10, 82–3
Lugones, María, 82, 141
Lupino, Ida, 172
lynching, 77

McBride, Lee A., 86, 94
McGinty-Peebles, Adelaide, 96
McHugh, Kathleen, 3–4
MacKenzie, Scott, 6–7
McRae, Emily, 91
Maguire, David, 3
male spectators, 16–19, 21, 157
Man Bites Dog, 20
Manne, Kate, 143
Marlina the Murderer in Four Acts, 3
masculinity, 39, 74, 107, 119, 122, 130, 132–3, 152, 176–7
Mask, Mia, 106, 107, 108
masochism, 17, 18, 19
The Matrix Revolutions, 139
Medea, 64–5
melodrama, 49–50, 54–5
#MeToo movement, 2, 4, 9, 89
M.F.A., 2, 166, 184
Millennium trilogy, 33–4, 37–41, 42, 43–4
Miller, Chanel, 30–1, 144
misogyny, 87, 119, 120, 122, 143, 182

Modleski, Tania, 17–18, 103, 172–3
Monster, 2, 56–7, 185
monstrous-feminine notion, 18, 22–3
morality, 33, 34, 42, 61, 69, 78
Ms. 45, 3, 16, 50–5, 67, 69, 141
Mulvey, Laura, 18–19, 171–2
Murphy, Jeffrie G., 59, 61

Nannicelli, Ted, 23–4
narrative paradigm scenarios, 102–3
Nestingen, Andrew, 37
New Man notion, 179, 180
The Nightingale, 2, 3, 4, 12, 67, 105, 159, 160, 169, 183, 185
   as post-colonial rape-revenge film, 117–22
Nisbett, Richard, 70
Nussbaum, Martha C., 84, 85, 88, 90, 92–5, 95–6, 98, 101

O'Day, Marc, 136–7
An Old Lady, 3
Orange Is the New Black, 2, 11, 25–7, 91, 92, 106, 130, 183, 185
Orgad, Shani, 9–10
Outrage, 2

payback, 62–3, 84, 85, 93, 94
Peacock, Steven, 36–7
penis envy, 18
Pettigrove, Glen, 86–7
Pinedo, Isabel Cristina, 19–20
Pisters, Patricia, 183, 186
Plantinga, Carl, 10–11, 43, 102, 134, 151–4, 165, 171
Point of No Return, 39
police, 77, 114, 123, 155, 182
power relations, 98–9, 101
Prevenge, 142
Projansky, Sarah, 16, 115–16, 145–6, 163, 164, 179, 180
Promising Young Woman, 2, 3, 12–13, 129, 159, 170, 183, 184
   containment strategies, 139–48
psychoanalytic theory, 23–5
Pulp Fiction, 20
punishment, 5, 11, 25, 28, 33–58, 78
   avenger as a fictional relief, 41–4, 46
   in Exodus, 64
   in fiction, 34–6
   Scandinavian crime fiction and film culture, 36–41
   Scandinavian punishment practices, 33, 36, 42
   third-party punishers, 60, 63–4, 77, 94
   transformed rape-avenger, 44–6
Purse, Lisa, 45, 136, 137–9, 140–2, 153

queerness, 130

race and racism, 12, 75–6, 86, 87, 88, 176
   African Americans in American film, 106–7
   and anger, 82–3
   Black female spectators, 112–13
   Black rape-revengers, 106–13
   critique of conventions in *I May Destroy You*, 122–7
   institutional racism, 77–8
   The Nightingale as post-colonial rape-revenge film, 117–22
   racialised disgust, 111
   racist myths, 108–11
   racist stereotypes, 108–9
   and the rape-revenge film, 105–27
   silencing the Black woman's experience of rape, 113–17
   strong Black female characters, 108–9
   women and the British justice system, 113–14, 182
Raine, Nancy Venable, 8, 9, 69, 163
Raney, Arthur A., 28, 33, 35, 69
rape
   Big Dan's rape case, 115
   Black rapist, myth of, 77, 184
   blaming victims, 30–1
   graphic portrayal of, 149, 157–62, 165–71, 181, 183–4
   and honour, 71–2
   indirect representation, 160
   as a plot device, 160–1
   in real life, 30, 155–6
   response to, 3, 6, 12, 28, 77, 182–3
   and shame, 11, 27, 61, 71–2, 140, 163
   silencing of, 163–4
   silencing the Black woman's experience of rape, 113–17
   and slavery, 109, 110–11
   stranger rape, 155, 173–7, 180, 184
rape-revenge film
   affective structure of, 1–2, 15–31
   anger from critics and spectators, 3–4, 6–7, 80

argumentative context and the explicit rape sequence, 171–81
avenger as a fictional relief, 41–4, 46
avenger transformation as fantasy space and inversion of femininity, 46–58
disrupting powerful rape myths, 74–5, 173, 180, 184
exit doors, 31–2, 145, 162–3, 166, 169
exploitation argument against explicit portrayal of rape, 157–62
in feminist film theory, 15–23
outlining the affective structure, 28–32
as a place of resistance, 7, 101
post-colonial 117–22
realist argument against rape-revenge film, 155–7
revisionist rape-revenge films, 21–2, 25–7, 66, 95–7, 150–1, 185
as a subtype of horror, 15–16, 18, 19–20, 22–3
transformed rape-avenger, 34, 39, 44–6, 69
by women film-makers, 2–3, 183–5
see also revenge
rape-revolt film, 3, 183, 188
Read, Jacinda, 2, 4, 7–8, 17, 49, 140, 153
reality/realism, 41, 56–8, 150
and the fantastic, 36–41
in rape-revenge film, 155–7
tension with the imaginary, 30
Red Road, 185–6
reflexive techniques, 150–2, 154
Reservoir Dogs, 20
Revenge, 2, 3, 47–9, 55, 66–7, 68–9, 73–4, 159–60, 183
revenge/retribution, 5, 10, 25, 29, 35–6, 41, 59–79, 84, 88, 124, 149, 150, 152, 182–3
consequences of, 63
didactic argument against revenge, 150–5
and disreputation, 59–60, 61
erotic aspects, 49, 55, 68–9
fantasies, 8–9, 10–11, 28–9, 69, 78–9, 125–7
gains, levels of, 61–2
historical context, 64
and honour, 11, 59, 61, 70–8
link with justice, 60, 63–4
origin and evolution of, 60–5

and power equalisation, 62
in the rape-revenge film, 65–9, 101–4, 149, 150–5, 182–3, 185
and self-respect, 61, 74
stages of retributive practices, 64
as the victim's responsibility, 43–4
vigilante revenge, 28, 36
violence of, 67–8
as virtuous, 76–7
women's revenge in fiction, 64–5
Riddle, Karyn, 164–5
Rob Roy, 28
Robson, Peter, 65–6
romcoms, 49–50, 54–5, 145

sadism, 19, 137
sadness, 12
as an alternative to anger, 89–92
Scandinavia
crime fiction and film culture, 36–41
punishment practices, 33, 36–7, 42
Schlesinger, Philip, 114–15, 167
Schubart, Rikke, 30, 37, 39, 105–6, 129–30, 137, 172
Screen Theory, 23
The Searchers, 11, 59, 74–6
self-defence, 83, 92
self-esteem, 61–2
self-respect, 61, 74, 81–2, 85, 88, 97–8
sexploitation films, 103, 106
shamefulness/shame, 11, 27, 61, 71–2, 75, 140
She's Gotta Have It, 116
The Shield, 2
Shoemaker, David, 87, 88
Siegler, Carol, 19, 137
Silverado, 59
Sims, Yvonne D., 109
slasher films, 40
slavery, 109, 110–11
social realism, 40, 41–2, 57
Sommers, Tamler, 59, 60, 70, 72
Springer, Kimberly, 108–9
Srinivasan, Amia, 82–3, 86, 88
Stella Does Tricks, 2, 57–8
Straw Dogs, 16
subordination, 62–3, 82, 87
Sudden Impact, 168

Taberham, Paul, 23–4
Tasker, Yvonne, 46–7, 108, 129, 132–3, 135–6, 156, 162

Tate, Andrew, 182
The Terminator, 46
Terminator 2: Judgement Day, 46, 129, 132, 136
Tessman, Lisa, 81, 103–4
Thelma and Louise, 20, 47, 50, 66–7, 69, 101–3, 130, 132, 142, 144, 145–6, 156, 157, 163, 164
Thurman, Uma, 9–10
Tomb Raider, 48
transformation
   avenger transformation as fantasy space and inversion of femininity, 46–58
   transformed rape-avenger, 34, 39, 44–6, 69
transphobia, 131, 176
Traps, 142
True Grit, 152–3
Twilight Portrait, 2, 12, 81, 89, 95–8, 184

Unbelievable, 123

Vandermassen, Griet, 5–6
Vares, Tiina, 20, 25
The Velvet Vampire, 3
victims, 12
   and blame, 30–1, 74–6
vigilantes, 28, 36, 65–6, 77, 152

Violation, 2, 56, 183, 184, 185
violence, 67–8
   and female spectators, 19–21
   in fiction, 35
   graphic violence, 164–5
The Virgin Spring, 1
vulnerability, 83–4, 162

Westerns, 59, 65, 66, 74–6, 152–3
Wiesel, Elie, 90–1
Williams, Linda, 15
Willis, Sharon, 47, 157
Wimmer, Leila, 6, 7
Winkler, Catherine, 8–9
Wishman, Doris, 103
Wollen, Peter, 171–2
women film-makers, 2–3, 6, 56–7, 103, 132, 159–60, 172, 183, 184, 185, 187
   counter-phobic women's cinema, 103, 172–3
women-in-prison films, 2, 11, 25–7, 91, 92, 106, 131, 187
Women Talking, 12, 81, 98–9, 160, 184
Wonder Woman, 134, 137
Wright, Will, 66

York, C. A., 143–4, 182
Young, Alison, 168–70, 184

EU representative:
Easy Access System Europe
Mustamäe tee 50, 10621 Tallinn, Estonia
Gpsr.requests@easproject.com